T0386685

Reef Fishes
of the Indo-Pacific

Reef Fishes of the Indo-Pacific

Matthias Bergbauer
Manuela Kirschner

Consultant:
Lawson Wood

Quick A-Z species finder

Contents

 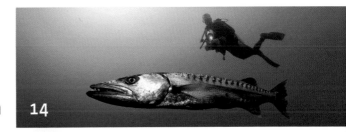

Introduction

Pulsating ecosystem

Tropical coral reefs are among the most species-rich and productive ecosystems on earth. The Indo-Pacific reefs are chiefly celebrated for their overwhelming biodiversity which is far greater than the Atlantic and the Caribbean. In the Indo-Pacific, the biodiversity increases even more compared to the already rich species diversity of the Indian Ocean towards the east. The oceanic area between Indonesia and Malaysia in the west, the Philippines in the north and New Guinea and the Solomons in the east is known as the "coral triangle". With a greater density than anywhere else, the reefs in this region are bursting with life.

Seventy-five percent of all known coral species are represented here. Moreover, they are the habitat, feeding grounds and nursery for more than 40 per cent of all coral reef fishes known worldwide. The extraordinary biodiversity of coral reefs is based on their great structural diversity. Numerous ecosystems and ecological niches share close quarters in this region, offering innumerable animals a livelihood and resulting in a complex reef community with numerous and often surprising relationships. It can be compared to a densely populated metropolis. Such a community also creates the large supply and demand for a broad range of specialities and service providers and the many resulting interactions between them. Some interesting interrelationships in the coral reef are presented on the following pages.

Mimicry – The big bluff

Mimicry is the art of being seen but not recognized, hence pretending to be what one is not. Here is an example of how this works: a fish species is poisonous and therefore protected from various predators. A second fish species now imitates the poisonous fish. The predator which has learned to avoid the poisonous fish will also leave the harmless imitator in peace. This form of imitation is known as Bates Mimicry. It is a "sheep in wolf's clothing" trick.

Like all pufferfish, the Saddled Puffer (*Canthigaster valentini*) contains the highly potent tetrodotoxin in its body tissue, which is why it is avoided by predators. The nontoxic Blacksaddle or Mimic Filefish (*Paraluteres prionurus*) imitates the pufferfish in all details and is therefore likewise avoided by predators. In the case of this Batesian mimicry, it's the somewhat longer back and anal fin of the filefish that distinguish it.

There is also, however, aggressive mimicry. The cleanerfish (Bluestreak Cleaner Wrasse) rids her fish

Saddled Puffer

Blacksaddle or Mimic Filefish

False Cleanerfish

clientele of annoying skin parasites. To this end, her customers are confident of her approach. The False Cleanerfish (*Aspidontus taeniatus*) imitates the Bluestreak Cleaner Wrasse and takes advantage of the trust of potential cleaning customers in order to come near. However, instead of freeing the "customer" from parasites, the swindler bites off parts of the victim's skin, scales or fins on which it feeds itself. The two can be distinguished by a very careful examination of their snouts: the Bluestreak Cleaner Wrasse has a mouth in a terminal position; that of the False Cleanerfish is underslung. Behaviour also allows for certain differentiation: the False Cleanerfish occasionally withdraws into a rock burrow during the day, which the Bluestreak Cleaner Wrasse does not do.

False Cleanerfish

Bluestreak Cleaner Wrasse

Common household

One of the most interesting partnerships is the common household of the Shrimpgoby with the snapping rock-boring shrimp. This is a symbiotic relationship with tangible advantages for both partners. The snapping rock-boring shrimp burrows tunnels in the sandy soil, structures that require constant work for their maintenance, since the sand shifts frequently. The shrimp tirelessly scoops sand out of the burrows throughout the day. For the shrimp, this dredging is also a search for something edible because numerous microoganisms live in the sandy environment. When the shrimp comes to the entrance area of the burrow with its load of sand, it maintains continual contact with a Shrimpgoby through its antennae. The fish lies in front of the burrow entrance, keeping watch and occasionally snapping for small prey in rapid thrusts. When there is a disturbance or a predator approaches, the Shrimpgoby rapidly flees into the burrow. This is simultaneously the signal for the shrimp likewise to flee into the burrow. The advantage of this symbiosis for both partners: for the shrimp, the Shrimpgoby is a sharp-eyed watchman who is instantly alert to approaching predators, and a burrow offers a secure safe retreat for the Shrimpgoby in the featureless sandy ground.

Advantage by cooperation: the symbiosis between the Alpheid snapping rock-boring shrimp and the Shrimpgoby.

This ovulid (*Diminovula culmen*) is excellently adapted to the colour of soft coral.

Two Emperor Shrimps on a nudibranch.

This Wire Coral Crab lives on wire corals.

Commensalism

If the symbiosis is in the form of a close community between two species for their mutual benefit, such as that between the Shrimpgoby and the snapping rock-boring shrimp (see left page), it is designated as mutualism. But if only one partner benefits from the biocoenosis without damage to the other, this is termed commensalism. This relationship is excee- dingly common in the coral reef – especially among small invertebrates. In particular, small crustaceans are exceptionally resourceful in obtaining an advantageous abode. Some hide between the branches of stony corals, others squat astride sea whips or "ride" on nudibranchs. They can be found in the middle of the tentacles of sea anemones, under sea cucumbers, on starfish, sea pens and numerous other creatures.

Cleaning stations

Cleaning wrasse advertise to their customers with a dance-like rocking, while many of the fish customers demonstrate a desire for body care by assuming an inviting position, for example by standing almost upright in the water, lying diagonally on their side, or holding their mouths wide open and spreading their gill lids. Customers visit the cleaning stations from dawn to sunset and often must wait in a queue until they are served. The cleaning activity contributes decisively to the destruction of fish parasites, of which isopods of the gnathia group are the most common. In the sea, these bloodsuckers are similar to what ticks are on land. Only fish isopods are much more common, and fish are almost continually infested with them.

This also makes the cleaning trade ecologically extremely significant for the entire reef community, and cleaning Wrasse are probably the busiest fish in the reef. They hardly take a pause, and at the end of each day their stomachs are jam-packed with the bloodsucking pests that account for more than

Oral hygiene: White-banded Cleaner Shrimp and Tomato Grouper.

95 per cent of their food. A single wrasse can remove about 1,200 parasitic isopods a day from their customers.

The advantage is mutual: the treatment frees their cleaning customers of skin parasites, which in turn serves to feed the cleanerfish.

Cleaning shrimps are active in the same trade and, like the cleanerfish, have a large clientele, among them harmless algae and plankton feeders, but also predators, such as snappers and groupers. The cleaners attend to all, the peaceable as well as the dangerous. Skunk cleaner shrimps swing their antennae as a signal of understanding, while the small urocaridella shrimps perform a characteristic advertising dance, and indeed, the more active they are, the hungrier they are. This conspicuous advertising strategy pays off. Like many other customers, groupers also know how to interpret these signs. If they have a choice, they prefer highly motivated dancing shrimps to the "standard dancers", understanding what awaits them from the passionate dancers: a cleaning session up to eleven times longer and accordingly more thorough body care by hungry shrimps compared to an ordinary session by more or less satiated shrimps.

White-banded Cleaner Shrimp and Moray Eels

Gill care: Cleanerfish and White-belly Damselfish

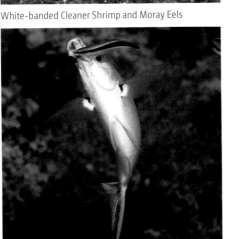

Vertical body position as an invitation to be cleaned: Fusilierfish (left), Yellowhead Wrasse (right).

Fishes

Sharks
Chondrichthyes

Sharks are cartilaginous fish and almost all are predators. The Whale Shark, as the largest species, and the basking shark, however, are plankton filterers. There are about 500 types of shark, of which a relatively small species diversity can be observed by divers in coral reefs. The Blacktip and Whitetip Reef Shark and the Grey Reef Shark are common. They belong to the family of sharks that live on the seabed and are dangerous to humans. To these dexterous and rapid swimmers, the Silver Tip and Oceanic Whitetip Shark also belong, primarily larger, open-sea residents, that can occasionally be seen in the reefs. Apart from these, the Bull Shark and especially the Tiger Shark are dangerous and known for fatal attacks. Some strongly ground-oriented species, such as Nurse and Leopard Sharks, can also be regularly seen in certain territories. The eyes and the nose openings of the Hammerhead Shark typically stand far apart on the hammer-shaped head, a facial geometry that has adapted over millennia to feed on rays from above, the shape probably enhances their spatial visual faculty and ability to locate odour sources.

Oceanic Whitetip Shark
Carcharhinus longimanus

Conspicuously large, rounded back and pectoral fins with white tips.
Size: 350 cm
Biology: Primarily pelagic in the surface water of deep seas, rarely in coastal vicinity, 0–150 m. Frequently accompanied by pilot fish, feeds on bony fish, skate, squid, sea birds, turtles, sea mammals, carrion and rubbish. Potentially dangerous, fatal attacks are known. Fearless and not shy, can circle around divers tenaciously and curiously.
Distribution: circumtropical, in warm water above 18 degrees.

Whale Shark
Rhincodon typus

Spotted pattern on back. Very broad mouth without teeth.
Size: 12–14 m
Biology: Predominantly pelagic, occasionally also approaches reefs. Generally a loner, however gathering places near the reef are known. Harmless plankton filterers, can suck in several tons of water with one "swallow".
Distribution: circumtropical.

Leopard or Zebra Shark
Stegostoma fasciatum or varium

Juvenile black-and-white banded. Adults with leopard-like blotches.
Size: 280 cm
Biology: Inhabits sand, rubble and coral ground of reefs, 5–70 m. Bottom-dwellers, usually dormant on the seabed during the day. At night, predominantly feeds on molluscs, crustaceans and small fish. Harmless, but can bite if harassed.
Distribution: Red Sea, East Africa to S Japan and New Caledonia.

Tawny Nurse Shark
Nebrius ferrugineus

Small mouth with nose barbels. Two dorsal fins of almost equal height.
Size: 320 cm
Biology: Lagoon and external reefs, 1–70 m. Usually lies below overhangs or in cavities during the day. At night it feeds on octopuses, crabs, bottom-dwelling fish, sea snakes and sea-urchins. Quarry is sucked in whole and crushed in the mouth. Generally harmless, but on provocation can bite firmly.
Distribution: Red Sea and East Africa to S Japan, Micronesia and French Polynesia.

Tasselled Wobbegong
Tasselledorrhinus dasypogon

Mouth and side of head with long, tasselled lappets.
Size: 130 cm
Biology: In shallow, protected reefs, 1–40 m. Loner, always swims directly on or close to the seabed. Usually dormant on the seabed during the day. At night feeds on fish such as longfin and soldier fish and probably also invertebrates. Not shy.
Distribution: North Australia, East Indonesia to PNG.

Brown-banded Bamboo Shark
Chiloscyllium punctatum

Juvenile with black and white bands. Older specimens brown to brown-grey, in part with banding still discernible (see photo).
Size: 105 cm
Biology: In coastal reefs, 1–80 m. Nocturnal loner. Hidden in reef crevices during the day. At night also in open areas, swimming directly on the seabed or very close to it. Feeds on invertebrate bottom-dwelling animals.
Distribution: India, Thailand, Indonesia to the Philippines and S Japan.

Indonesian Speckled Carpetshark
Hemiscyllium freycineti

Cream coloured to light brown, numerous brown blotches. A dark spot with an incomplete white border behind the pectoral fin base.
Size: 70 cm
Biology: Often inhabits protected reefs at low depths. Loner, usually hidden during the day. Goes in search of food at night.
Distribution: Raja Ampat and Irian Jaya.

Silvertip Shark
Carcharhinus albimarginatus

Tail, back and pectoral fins with white tips and back edges.
Size: 300 cm
Biology: Lives on deep steep slopes and reefs distant from the coast, sometimes in deep lagoons, two to more than 400 m. Alone or in groups. Feeds on bony fish, eagle rays and octopuses. Generally careful, but can be obtrusive.
Distribution: Red Sea to South Africa, S Japan, Galapagos and French-Polynesia.

Grey Reef Shark
Carcharhinus amblyrhynchos

Dark rear edge of tail fin.
Size: 180 cm
Biology: Deep atoll lagoons, canals, steep outer reef slopes, 1–274 m. Partly in loose groups during the day. Territorial, large home territories. Feeds on fish, cephalopods and crabs. Territorial in the Pacific, known for threatening behaviour. Above the Whitetip and Blacktip Reef Sharks in the hierarchy.
Distribution: Red Sea and East Africa to Taiwan, Hawaii and Easter Islands.

Bull Shark
Carcharhinus leucas

Sturdy body, short snout, small eyes.
Size: 340 cm
Biology: Prefers coastal reefs and brackish water regions, also intrudes into the fresh water of rivers and lakes, 1–152 m. Usually close to the seabed. Very broad feeding spectrum: bony fish, sharks, skates, turtles, invertebrates, mammals, sea birds, whales, also rubbish. Potentially very dangerous.
Distribution: Worldwide in tropical and subtropical seas.

Blacktip Reef Shark
Carcharhinus melanopterus

Both dorsal, anal, pectoral fins and lower caudal fin lobe are black tipped.
Size: 180 cm
Biology: In lagoons and outreefs, 0–75 m. Juveniles often in shallow water on reef roofs. Alone or in groups. Feeds on reef fish and squid. Shy.
Distribution: Red Sea and East Africa to S Japan, Hawaii and Pitcairn. Encroached into the Mediterranean (Tunisia, Israel) by way of the Suez Canal.

Whitetip Reef Shark
Triaenodon obesus

Very slim body. White tips on back and tail fin. Nasal flaps.
Size: 175 cm
Biology: In lagoons and outer reefs, 1–330 m. Frequently rests during the day lying on the seabed, in caves, below overhangs, also alone or in groups on open sand and rubble surfaces. Hunts predominantly at night for reef fish and cuttlefish.
Distribution: Red Sea and East Africa to S Japan, Hawaii, Panama.

Lemon Shark
Negaprion acutidens

Back fins almost equally high, tawny to grey.
Size: 310 cm
Biology: Near-seabed in bays, lagoons and estuaries, also at exposed outer reefs. Often rests on the seabed. Captures bottom-dwelling fish and skates. Do not provoke: this species is usually shy, but can easily be irritated and then potentially dangerous.
Distribution: Red Sea and East Africa to Taiwan, Micronesia and French Polynesia.

Tiger Shark
Galeocerdo cuvier

Broad, blunt head. Upper side of body with dark vertical bands.
Size: 550 cm
Biology: Deep lagoons, bays, external and offshore reefs, 1–300 m. During the day often in deeper water, at night in coastal vicinities in shallower waters. Has large, unconstrained hunting grounds, but sometimes also makes migrations up to more than 3000 km. Very dangerous, but rarely aggressive.
Distribution: All tropical seas, seasonally also in subtropical seas.

Scalloped Hammerhead
Sphyrna lewini

Forehead edge slightly curved with indentation in the middle.
Size: 400 cm
Biology: On continental slopes, underwater ridges and steep reef slopes of offshore islands, 1–275 m. Predominantly feeds on fish, especially stingrays. Usually not aggressive. Can show threat behaviour, attacks on humans are not confirmed.
Distribution: Circumtropical.

Pelagic Thresher Shark
Alopias pelagicus

Typical of the family, extremely long upper tail lobes. Very similar to *A. vulpinus* with white on the upper pectoral fin base.
Size: about 350 cm
Biology: Denizens of the high seas, 1–150 m. Occasionally in the vicinity of the coast, especially at offshore reefs and underwater mounds. Eats bony fish and squid.
Distribution: Red Sea and East Africa to Galapagos and Tahiti.

Rays and Skates
Batoidei

Rays are cartilaginous fish with flattened, disc-shaped bodies. The majority are bottom-dwelling, swimming with undulating movements of the body skirt and can even be seen in shallow water. Many frequently burrow up to their eyes and nostrils. Devil and eagle rays, however, are open-water denizens and swim long distances by flapping their broad, triangular pectoral fin-like wings. Stingrays have one or more long poison barbs on the tail for their defence.

Torpedo Skates
Torpedinidae

Indonesian Electric Ray
Narcine sp.

Reddish brown blotches.
Size: Body plate about 30 cm
Biology: On sand and soft grounds. There are probably still undescribed species or variants of *N. ornata*.
Distribution: Known in the area from Java to Komodo.

Leopard Torpedo Skate
Torpedo panthera

Straight front end. Diffuse white blotches.
Size: 100 cm
Biology: On sand and soft surfaces near the reef, 0.5–55 m. Not shy, when disturbed, swims a short distance away. Numbs its prey with current shocks up to 200 Volt.
Distribution: Red Sea and Arabian Gulf.

Guitarfish
Rhinobatidae

Halavs Guitarfish
Glaucostegus halavi

Dorsal fins almost equal height.
Size: 170 cm
Biology: On sand and seaweed, in bays and coastal reefs, 1–45 m. Feeds on large crustaceans.
Distribution: Red Sea, Gulf of Oman. Migrates into the Mediterranean.

Stingrays
Dasyatidae

Kuhl's stingray
Dasyatis kuhlii

Blue blotches. Tail very long, often with white bands at the back.
Size: body plate 50 cm
Biology: On sand surfaces of lagoons and outreefs, 1–90 m. Common. Often covered with sand. Feeds on invertebrates living in sand.
Distribution: East Africa to S Japan, Micronesia, Samoa and New Caledonia.

Fai's or Pink Stingray
Himantura fai

Rhomboid body, uniformly light grey to brownish. Tail up to three times the length of the body diameter.
Size: body plate 150 cm
Biology: On sandy surfaces in lagoons and outreefs, from shallow water to 200 m. Individual, sometimes also in larger groups.
Distribution: South Africa, the Maldives, India, Thailand to the Mariana Islands, NW Australia and Tuamotus in French Polynesia.

Leopard Stingrays
Himantura uarnak

Numerous and densely placed black blotches on light ground.
Size: body plate 150 cm
Biology: Inhabits sand and mud surfaces of lagoons near reefs, outreefs and estuaries. Frequently buried. Feeds on fish, crustaceans, molluscs and also jellyfish.
Distribution: Red Sea and East Africa to SW Japan, the Philippines and French Polynesia. Migrated through the Suez Canal into the Eastern Mediterranean.

Cowtail Stingray
Pastinachus sephen

Uniformly dark brown, tail underside with broad skin fringe at the back.
Size: body plate 180 cm
Biology: Inhabits sand and muddy surfaces of coral reefs, coastal waters and estuaries, 1–60 m. Occasionally also ventures into fresh water. Feeds on crabs, fish, molluscs and worms.
Distribution: Red Sea, East Africa and Arabian Gulf to Japan, Palau, New Caledonia and SE Australia.

Bluespotted Stingray
Taeniura lymma

Olive-green with large, luminous blue spots.
Size: body plate 90 cm
Biology: On sand and rubble surfaces of coral reefs, 2–30 m. Likes to rest under overhangs or coral tables as well as in small caves. Active day and night. Only slightly timid. Feeds on molluscs, worms and shrimps. Often seeks cleaner stations.
Distribution: Red Sea, Oman, East Africa to the Philippines, Fiji and East Australia.

Round Ribbontail Ray
Taeniura meyeri

Many differently sized irregular black blotches on grey ground.
Size: body plate 164 cm
Biology: On sand and rubble surfaces of coral and rock reefs, 3–500 m. Feeds on bottom-dwelling fish and invertebrates, such as mussels and shrimps. Often blows troughs in the sandy soil in order to expose prey.
Distribution: Red Sea and East Africa to S Japan, Galapagos and Australia.

Porcupine Ray
Urogymnus asperrimus

Light grey with conical sharp thorns. Tail without poison sting.
Size: body plate 100 cm
Biology: Inhabits protected reef areas, on sand, rubble and seaweed. Feeds on crabs, worms and fish. Rather rare. Not shy.
Distribution: Red Sea, Oman and East Africa to Marshall Islands, GBR and Fiji.

Eagle Rays
Myliobatidae

Spotted Eagle Ray
Aetobatis narinari

White spots on back. Head with extended snout.
Size: span width 230 cm
Biology: In open water in front of reefs and in lagoons, 1–80 m. Alone, in groups or large schools. Feeds on molluscs and crustaceans which it excavates from sand and soft ground. Usually shy.
Distribution: Circumtropical.

Thurton's Devil Ray or Smooth-tail Mobula
Mobula thurstoni

Cephalic fins are narrow and stiff. In contrast to mantas, mouth not frontal but rather on underside of head.
Size: span width 180 cm
Biology: Both pelagic as well as in reef vicinity. Swims alone or in groups. Filters plankton from the water. The two very similar species (*M. tarapacana* and *M. ergoodoo-tenkee*) are extremely difficult to distinguish when observing under water.
Distribution: Circumtropical.

Reef Manta Ray
Manta alfredi

Broad mobile cephalic fins. Dark dorsal and light underside, however the distribution of black and white is very variable.

Size: 500 cm

Biology: From the surface to about 40 m. Alone or in groups. Regularly visits cleaner stations. Feeds on plankton that it filters with open mouth while swimming through the water. The reef manta usually swims in coastal vicinity within a few kilometres of land, and can regularly be seen along reefs. The Giant Manta (*Manta birostris*) with a span width of up to more than 700 cm is larger and further distributed, lives further from the coast and possibly makes long migrations. Therefore reef mantas are usually seen around rock and coral reefs. Until a few years ago, it was believed that worldwide there was only one manta species, *Manta birostris*. In 2009 the biologist Andrea Marshall published her investigations showing that actually there are at least two manta species. There is possibly even a third.

Distribution: Circumtropical in land and reef vicinity.

Giant Moray
Gymnothorax javanicus

Brown with small black blotches.
Size: 239 cm
Biology: In lagoons and outreefs, 1–46 m. Inhabits cavities and crevices in reef rock. The largest moray eel species by weight (up to more than 35 kg). Predominantly feeds on fish, among them also juvenile Whitetip Reef Sharks, as well as crustaceans and octopuses. Normally peaceful, even occasionally being fed by divers, however even unprovoked, serious bite injuries have been suffered.
Distribution: Red Sea and East Africa to SW Japan, Hawaii (rarely), Panama and Pitcairn.

Moray Eels
Muraenidae

Moray eels are predominantly dusk- and night-active predators. Holes and reef crevices serve them as shelter during the day. Usually they roam the reef landscape for prey only at night. Principally, they track down fish, crustaceans and octopuses with their fine sense of smell. Some species have short, blunt teeth for cracking crab armour. Many species have sharp, needle-shaped capture teeth which are excellently suited to holding fast even to slippery prey. The regular opening and closing of the mouth is easily mistaken as a threat, however serves only for breathing. But a mouth kept wide open is to be understood as an actual threat. In contrast to snakes, its elongated body is laterally compressed along the length and its skin is without scales. Some species are hermaphrodites, i.e. simultaneously male and female. Many others are sequential hermaphrodites, maturing at first into males and later in their lives changing to females.

Blackcheek Moray
Gymnothorax breedeni

Large dark spot under the eyes.
Size: 120 cm
Biology: Along clear, current-rich outreefs, 425 m. Often in narrow crevices on coral rock, with only its head protruding. Can be aggressive and rapidly bite upon an intrusive approach.
Distribution: East Africa, the Maldives, Seychelles, Christmas Islands to Solomons, Line Islands and French Polynesia.

Yellowmouth Moray
Gymnothorax nudivomer

Inner side of mouth yellow. Gill opening yellowish with dark, diffuse border.
Size: 120 cm
Biology: Prefers outreefs, 1–165 m. Alone or in pairs in rock holes during the day. Hunts fish at night. Upon approach, it often shows the yellow interior of its open mouth as a warning. The skin mucus is poisonous.
Distribution: Red Sea and East Africa to SW Japan, Hawaii and French Polynesia.

Lipspot Moray
Gymnothorax chilospilus

Lower lip frequently has a white spot near to the angle of the mouth. Body with irregular, loosely banded brown blotches.
Size: 50 cm
Biology: Prefers upper slope areas of lagoons and outreefs, also in rock reefs, 0.5–45 m. Can often be seen in a few metres depth.
Distribution: Oman to S Japan and French Polynesia.

Banded Mud Moray
Gymnothorax chlamydatus

Creamy with dark speckles and broad black cross bands.
Size: 70 cm
Biology: Inhabits coastal areas with sandy to muddy surfaces, 8–30 m. Bores a hole for itself in the soft ground by burrowing with the tail foremost.
Distribution: Indonesia to the Philippines, SW Japan and Taiwan.

Honeycomb Moray
Gymnothorax favagineus

White with tightly-spaced black blotches; the white between spaces can be so narrow that they appear as a net pattern.
Size: 220 cm
Biology: Inhabits lagoons and out-reefs, 1–50 m. Not shy, and allows divers to come very close. Active day and night. Even during the day, it can often be observed lying or swimming completely in the open.
Distribution: East Africa, Southern Red Sea and Oman to Taiwan, GBR and Samoa.

Fimbriated Moray
Gymnothorax fimbriatus

Greenish-yellow head, body pale olive colour; speckled with irregular black blotches.
Size: 80 cm
Biology: Inhabits lagoons and outreefs, 1–50 m. Can be observed rather rarely, probably a nocturnal species. Hunts fish and crustaceans.
Distribution: Mauritius and Seychelles to SW Japan, GBR and Society Islands.

Yellow-edged Moray
Gymnothorax flavimarginatus

Speckled yellowish-brown, snout rust brown, amber eyes.
Size: 120 cm
Biology: In lagoons, coral and rock reefs, 0.3–150 m. Frequently looks out of its burrow. Captures small fish and crustaceans. Changes sex from female to male.
Distribution: Red Sea and East Africa to SW Japan, Hawaii, Panama and New Caledonia.

Geometric Moray
Gymnothorax griseus

Whitish with fine dot pattern on the head.
Size: 65 cm
Biology: In coral reefs and along rocky coastal regions, 1–30 m. Often also ranges during the day in the open between seaweed and rubble. Captures small fish and crustaceans. Juveniles especially often share their abodes in groups.
Distribution: Red Sea, East Africa and Oman to the West Indies, Seychelles, Madagascar and Mauritius.

Whitemouth or Turkey Moray
Gymnothorax meleagris

Brown with numerous white spots. mouth has a white interior.
Size: 120 cm
Biology: Inhabits coral-rich, clear lagoons and outreefs, 0.3–36 m. This species is active day and night, and predominantly hunts fish and shrimps. It is often cigu-atoxic. Said to be an imitation of *Calloplesiops altivelis* (see page 77) but this is not proven.
Distribution: East Africa and Southern. Red Sea to SW Japan, Hawaii, Galapagos and SE Australia.

Greyface Moray
Gymnothorax thyrsoideus

Conspicuous white eyes. Blunt snout.
Size: 66 cm
Biology: Inhabits sedimented lagoons and shallow coastal reefs, from tidal zones up to 25 m. Frequently met in tidal basins as well as on sandy to muddy slopes. Lives in pairs or in small groups in burrows, also associated with other moray eel species.
Distribution: Sumatra and Christmas Islands to SW Japan and French Polynesia.

Snowflake Moray
Echidna nebulosa

Whitish with larger brown and smaller yellow blotches.
Size: 75 cm
Biology: In shallow lagoons and outreefs, also on rock and soft surfaces and in tidal areas to 30 m. This predominantly nocturnal species can leave the water abruptly in order to feed on shrimps on rocky beach areas. Juveniles are often seen in low tide pools on the reef roof.
Distribution: Red Sea and East Africa to SW Japan, Hawaii, Panama and French Polynesia.

At night, this species frequently goes hunting in open areas. It feeds on crabs and mantis shrimp, as well as occasionally on small fish and squid.

Barred Moray
Echidna polyzona

Dark cross bands, receding with age. Juveniles have brown-black bands on white background.
Size: 60 cm
Biology: In coastal reefs and lagoons, 1–15 m. Hidden in crevices during the day. Hunts shrimps and crabs at night, then often also easily observed on sandy surfaces. Verifies prey before biting.
Distribution: Red Sea and East Africa to SW Japan, Hawaii, GBR and French Polynesia.

White Ribbon Eel
Pseudechidna brummeri

Cream to light grey with narrow white fin fringe. Head with dark speckles.
Size: 103 cm
Biology: In protected coastal reefs, probably only in shallow areas to 10 m. Very hidden lifestyle, can usually only be observed at night.
Distribution: East Africa to SW Japan, the Mariana Islands, Palau, Cook Islands and Fiji.

Ribbon Eel
Rhinomuraena quaesita

Extremely elongated and compressed laterally, extremely large, pointed, funnel-shaped snout in front.
Size: 120 cm
Biology: Inhabits sand and rubble areas in lagoons and outreefs, 1–57 m. While growing, this exceptionally colourful moray eel passes through two colour changes and one sex change. Juveniles are black with a yellow dorsal fin. Males (to about 65 cm) are luminous blue with a yellow dorsal fin and yellow snout. Females (colour change from about 85 cm) are at first yellowish and finally bright yellow. It is true to its location, has a burrow usually in sand or rubble in the immediate vicinity of rock or coral. Often looks out with head or forward body exposed. Forms very tight body loops while meandering above the seabed. Feeds on small fish.
Distribution: East Africa to SW Japan, Marshall Islands, Australia and Tuamotus in French Polynesia.

Snake Eels
Ophichthidae

Snake eels live on sand and muddy grounds, usually buried with only their head or eyes jutting out. They are most commonly observed on night diving excursions. They are often confused with sea snakes, which however have visible scales, whereas snake eels have smooth skin. Moreover, they have fin seams and pectoral fins which sea snakes lack. The majority of snake eels have a hard, narrow tail point and can rapidly dig into the soft ground backwards.

Crocodile Snake Eel
Brachysomophis crocodilinus

Eyes far forward. Usually cream-coloured to light brown with small dark spots.
Size: 80 cm
Biology: Ambushes passing prey buried in sandy bottom, often only partially visible with their heads.
Distribution: Madagascar, to SW Japan, Australia and French Polynesia.

Reptilian Snake Eel
Brachysomophis henshawi

Often red-coloured, however cream-coloured to whitish specimens are also known.
Size: 106 cm
Biology: Inhabits sand and muddy surfaces, 1–25 m. Ambushes prey buried to their head.
Distribution: Arabian Sea to S Japan, Hawaii and Marquesas.

Saddled Snake Eel
Leiuranus semicinctus

Broad to very broad brown-black saddle bands.
Size: 65 cm
Biology: On sand and seaweed surfaces in lagoons and outreefs, 1–12 m. Feeds on fish and crustaceans.
Distribution: East Africa to S Japan, Micronesia, Hawaii, SE Australia and French Polynesia.

Marbled Snake Eel
Callechelys marmorata

White to cream-coloured, speckled with numerous dark spots.
Size: 87 cm
Biology: In sandy areas of clear outreefs, 3–25 m. Usually buried in sand with only the conical pointed head looking out. Captures small fish and crustaceans.
Distribution: Red Sea and East Africa (to Mozambique) to Marshall Islands and French Polynesia.

Ringed or Harlequin Snake Eel
Myrichthys colubrinus

Black bands, occasionally with spots in the interstices. Is often confused with the Colubrine Sea Krait (see page 342).
Size: 90 cm
Biology: In sand and seaweed zones of bays, lagoons and out-reefs, 0.3–25 m. Predominantly nocturnal, also goes out hunting in open waters. Feeds on fish and crustaceans.
Distribution: Red Sea and East Africa to SW Japan, GBR and French Polynesia.

Spotted or Ocellate Snake Eel
Myrichthys maculosus

Cream-coloured to yellowish with large black spots.
Size: 100 cm
Biology: In bays, lagoons and outreefs, usually 0.3–30 m (one evidence of 262 m). Can be often observed at night, however also during the day in the open, on sandy surfaces and in seaweed patches. Feeds on fish and crustaceans.
Distribution: Red Sea and East Africa to SW Japan, SE-Australia and French Polynesia.

Napoleon Snake Eel
Ophichthus bonaparti

Creamy-whitish colour with dark body banding. Head with variable pattern of light bronze to dark brown spots.
Size: 75 cm
Biology: Inhabits fine and coarse sandy areas on coastal and outreefs, 1–20 m. Usually buried to the head. Ambushes small fish and cuttlefish. Can bite in self-defence.
Distribution: East Africa to S Japan and Society Islands.

Even at night, this species does not usually swim freely while hunting but rather ambushes prey while looking out of the sand with only its head protruding, which is coloured totally differently from the rest of its body.

Highfin Snake Eel
Ophichthus altipennis

Head light to dark brown with several black dots, blue-grey snout. Pale area on the snout in front of the eye is an identification characteristic. Black pectoral fins.
Size: 80 cm
Biology: On soft ground along coasts and in bays, usually 3–10 m. Buried in the ground so that only the head is visible.
Distribution: Malaysia to S Japan, Marshall Islands and French Polynesia.

Many-eyed or Large-spotted Snake Eel
Ophichthys polyphthalmus

Reddish-brown to salmon colour (especially the head), with numerous yellow, dark-edged eyes spots.
Size: 35 cm
Biology: On sand and rubble of lagoons and outreefs, 1–20 m.
Distribution: Mauritius and Réunion to Micronesia, Hawaii and French Polynesia.

Conger and Garden Eels
Congridae

Sea or Big-eyed Conger
Ariosoma anagoides

Large pupils, outlined in silver.
Size: 50 cm
Biology: Inhabits waters and bays with sandy or muddy surfaces to about 20 m. Rarely observed. Digs into soft ground, at night also goes out into the open.
Distribution: Indonesia, the Philippines, Australia.

Barred Conger
Ariosoma fasciatum

Whitish to light brown with large brown irregular spots.
Size: 60 cm
Biology: On sand and rubble surfaces of lagoons and outreefs, 2–32 m. Bores backwards into soft ground with the aid of its firm caudal fin.
Distribution: Madagascar to Indonesia, Marshall Islands, Hawaii and French Polynesia.

Whitespotted Garden Eel
Gorgasia maculata

Light greenish grey. A row of white spots along its lateral line. A few somewhat larger white spots on the head.
Size: 55 cm
Biology: Inhabits sandy surfaces near the reef, 10–45 m. Usually in colonies.
Distribution: Comoro Islands, Seychelles, the Maldives, Andaman Sea to the Philippines, Solomons and Fiji.

Spotted Garden Eel
Heteroconger hassi

Whitish with numerous black spots (with small spots as a variant), a large black spot on the gill opening and another on the back.
Size: 40–70 cm
Biology: Inhabits sandy surfaces in lagoons and out-reefs, 5 to more than 40 m. Usually in large colonies.
Distribution: East Africa, Seychelles, the Maldives to SW Japan, Line Islands and Tonga.

Eeltail Catfish
Plotosidae

Striped Eel Catfish
Plotosus lineatus

Eel-like body. The mouth is surrounded by four pairs of barbels. Two white horizontal stripes along the side.
Size: 33 cm
Biology: In lagoons and coastal reefs, to seaweed patches and sandy surfaces near the reef, 1–60 m, usually above 30 m. Juveniles form dense, spherical schools. The fish move forwards as a compact mass, in which the position of the individual fish continuously changes making a "rolling ball". Feeds on small bottom-dwelling crustaceans and molluscs. The first rays of the dorsal and pectoral fins have developed into poison stings, which, along with the formation of ball-shaped schools, appear to effectively discourage predators. Adults live in groups or alone below overhangs during the day.
Distribution: Red Sea and East Africa to S Korea, Kosrae in Micronesia, SE Australia and Samoa.

Convict Blennies
Pholidichthyidae

Convict Blenny/Goby
Pholidichthys leucotaenia

Juvenile with white horizontal stripes.
Size: 34 cm
Biology: In front of reef crevices and overhangs, 3–25 m. Usually only seen in groups of juveniles to about 5 cm length. These imitate the Striped Eel Catfish. Adults are hidden away and differently coloured.
Distribution: East Indonesia to the Philippines, Solomons and New Caledonia.

Lizardfish
Synodontidae

This small ambushing predator with a cylindrical body, large mouth and numerous sharp teeth is common throughout the region. Alone, and sometimes also in pairs, they lie unmoving on sand and rubble, rock or coral and wait for small fish to swim by. They capture these with a split-second thrust and gobble them up whole. With similar but steeply upward movements they take fish swimming metres above them by surprise. On cautious approach, they let divers come very close, but usually flee at the last moment, only to come to rest a few metres further on.

Variegated Lizardfish
Synodus variegatus

Horizontal stripes of alternating light and dark rectangular spots.
Size: 26 cm
Biology: In lagoons and outreefs, 5–70 m. Lies usually on coral or rock ground, frequently in pairs. Usually switches its position every few minutes.
Distribution: Red Sea and East Africa to SW Japan, Hawaii and French Polynesia.

Two-spot Lizardfish
Synodus binotatus

A few dark points on the snout.
Size: 16 cm
Biology: Inhabits outreefs with rubble and coral, 1–30 m. Usually in shallow depths, lying alone or in pairs on hard surfaces.
Distribution: Gulf of Aden and East Africa to Taiwan, Hawaii, GBR and Tonga.

Sand Lizardfish
Synodus dermatogenys

8–9 dark side spots, often with light centre.
Size: 22 cm
Biology: In lagoons and outreefs, 1–70 m. Alone, in pairs or in small groups on sand and rubble. Often also buried up to the eyes and nostrils.
Distribution: Red Sea and East Africa to SW-Japan, Hawaii, SE-Australia and French Polynesia.

Gracile Lizardfish
Saurida gracilis

Back of body with 2–3 dark spots.
Size: 32 cm
Biology: Prefers turbid, shallow lagoons and protected outreefs, from 1 m depth. Inhabits sand and rubble, lying free on the surface or partially buried.
Distribution: Red Sea and East Africa to SW Japan, Hawaii and French Polynesia.

Snakefish
Trachinocephalus myops

Very short snout, eyes very far forward.
Size: 25 cm
Biology: On sand and other soft ground, 3 to about 400 m. Usually buried, only with the forehead visible. Captures small fish and crustaceans.
Distribution: Worldwide in tropical and warm waters, not in the Eastern Pacific.

Frogfish
Antennariidae

Frogfish can change colour either to perfectly merge with their respective environment or to strongly contrast with it. Such adapta-
tions of an individual animal to its environment usually take place
within a few days. Because of the many possible colour variations,
individual specimens of the same species can very easily be thought
to be different species. The first ray of the dorsal fin, located free
above the upper lip, is reshaped as a fishing rod. The fishing rod
is thin and movable at the base, the end is developed as a fleshy
bait dummy. Fish that approach the putative prey are rapidly sucked
into the mouth that opens instantly. This takes place, in fact, within
six milliseconds: no other vertebrate can grab its prey as rapidly. It
can move slowly over the seabed with its arm-like pectoral fins and
ventral fins. It can swim short stretches according to the propulsion
principle. It sucks water into its mouth and thrusts it out through the
jet-like gill openings.

Giant Frogfish
Antennarius commersoni

The largest species. Very variable in colour, often adapted to its environment (see photo left showing two fish in a sponge). A few knot-like protrusions. Can show crusty blotches (e.g. reddish-brown blotches, photo right).
Size: 36 cm
Biology: In lagoons and outreefs, 1–70 m. Frequently in sponges. Usually alone, occasionally also in pairs.
Distribution: Red Sea and East Africa to SW Japan, Hawaii, Central America.

Scarlet Frogfish
Antennatus coccineus

Back and anal fin extend to the base of the caudal fin.
Size: 12 cm
Biology: In protected lagoons, coastal and outreefs, from shallow water to 70 m, but usually observed in very low depths. Usually on coral rock and rubble, lives hidden.
Distribution: Red Sea and East Africa to SW Japan, Central America and Australia.

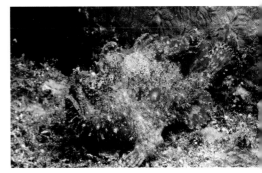

'Eyed' or Ocellated Frogfish
Antennarius sp.

Dark brown to grey-black. Large, orange-coloured ring beneath the rear part of the dorsal fin.
Size: 5 cm
Biology: Inhabits rubble and sandy areas, to about 30 m.
Distribution: known from East Indonesia (Bali, Sulawesi, Alor) and the Philippines.

Hispid or Shaggy Frogfish
Antennarius hispidus

Body often with dark elongated stripes, depending on colour variants, similar to *A. striatus*. Fishing rod about as long as the second fin ray. Great globular bait with fine filaments.
Size: 18 cm
Biology: Inhabits rock and coral reefs, also near reef sandy surfaces, 3–70 m. Often near leaves that have fallen into the water whose colouration it imitates (see photo). Very inconspicuous in such an environment.
Distribution: East Africa to Taiwan, Fiji and Australia.

Warty Frogfish
Antennarius maculatus

Skin with numerous warts and knot-like protrusions. Dark, very irregular blotches. Fishing rod somewhat longer than second ray. Especially wide colour variability.

Size: 8–11 cm

Biology: In protected reefs, 1–15 m. On diverse grounds, observed relatively frequently. On crushed coral rock, corals and sand, also likes to be near sponges.

Distribution: East Africa (possibly also Red Sea) to Mauritius, to SW Japan, the Mariana Islands, Solomons and GBR.

Juvenile (middle photo), typically white with conspicuous orange-red markings. In some specimens, the body is covered with numerous, closely-spaced warts (bottom photo).

Striated Frogfish
Antennarius striatus

Fishing rod usually easily recognised and twice as long as the second spine ray, conspicuous bait with worm-like attachment (see above, the large yellow bushel to the left of the photo). Black-brown stripes and rounded blotches. Closely related to *A. hispidus*.

Size: 22 cm

Biology: Often on or near reef sand or muddy grounds, 3 to more than 200 m. In addition to the very variable colouration, it occurs both as a smooth and as a "hairy" variant with numerous long filaments.

Distribution: Red Sea and East Africa, to SW Japan and Solomons.

Also the white and orange variant (middle photo, with the fishing rod thrust out), this species is usually easy to recognise by the blotches on the base that distinguish it from the Hispid Frogfish.

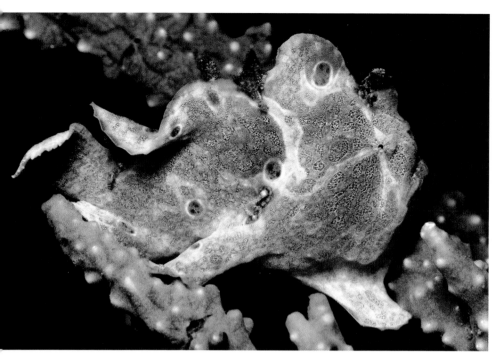

Painted Frogfish
Antennarius pictus

Fishing rod twice as long as second spine ray. The colour is very variable in this species, can adapt to a new environment within days.

Size: 16 cm

Biology: In protected coastal reefs and lagoons, 3–70 m. Also on sand or rubble near the reef, then usually near sponges or other protective objects.

Distribution: Red Sea and East Africa to SW Japan, Hawaii, Australia.

Small juveniles frequently show very striking black colouration with orange spots and blue fin edges (middle photo). Brilliant red (bottom photo), black, yellow, orange and olive-brown specimens are also known. The typical round blotches can usually be observed.

Sabre Squirrelfish
Sargocentron spiniferum
Gill lid with very long spike.
Size: 45 cm
Biology: Inhabits lagoons and outreefs, 1–120 m. Frequently floats immobile below overhangs, in front of cavities, also below table corals during the day. At night it hunts for crabs, shrimps and small fish. Largest species of the family. Not shy.
Distribution: Red Sea, East Africa to S Japan, Micronesia, Hawaii and French Polynesia.

Squirrelfish and Soldierfish
Holocentridae

The colour red dominates in the majority of species of this family which is divided into two subfamilies: soldierfish and squirrelfish. All are nocturnal, have large, light-sensitive eyes and clearly visible scales. Most conspicuous differences: pointed head and a sturdy gill lid spine on squirrelfish; blunt rounded head and no or only very small spines on the soldierfish. Despite their nocturnal activity, they can easily be observed up close during the day, since then they rest quietly in the protection of caves, overhangs or below table corals. Some species are seen individually, others in small groups and some form dense shoals. They leave their shelters in the night. Soldierfish then hunt zooplankton in open water. Squirrelfish feed on bottom-dwelling prey, such as crustaceans, worms and small fish.

Silverspot Squirrelfish
Sargocentron caudimaculatum

Red with white scale edges and white tail root (at night this becomes red).
Size: 25 cm
Biology: In deep lagoons and out-reefs with rich coral growth, 2–50 m. Alone or in loose groups. Usually in protected locations, such as overhangs and caves. Hunts small fish and crabs at night.
Distribution: Red Sea, S Oman and East Africa to S Japan, Micronesia, GBR and French Polynesia.

Crowned Squirrelfish
Sargocentron diadema

Red with white stripes. First dorsal fin black-red.
Size: 17 cm
Biology: In lagoons and outreefs, 2–60 m. During the day, often found alone or in small groups below overhangs or in front of cavities. Captures snails, worms and small crabs at night on sandy surfaces.
Distribution: Red Sea, Oman, East Africa to SW Japan, Hawaii, SE Australia and French Polynesia. Migrated into the eastern Mediterranean.

Shadowfin Soldierfish
Myripristis adusta

Basic colouration light to pale salmon colour with dark scale edges. Rear dorsal, anal and caudal fins with black edge and tips.
Size: 32 cm
Biology: Prefers coral-rich outreefs, 3–25 m. During the day, inactive below overhangs or in caves alone or in loose groups.
Distribution: East Africa to SW Japan, Micronesia, Line Islands, New Caledonia and French Polynesia.

Pinecone Soldierfish
Myripristis murdjan

All fins except pectoral fins with narrow white edge fringe.
Size: 25 cm
Biology: Inhabits lagoons and outreefs, 2–50 m. Inactive during the day, usually below overhangs or in caves, alone or in groups. Disperses at night in search of food. Captures worms, shrimp larvae and small crabs in open water.
Distribution: Red Sea and East Africa to SW Japan, Micronesia, GBR and Samoa.

Lattice or Violet Soldierfish
Myripristis violacea

Silvery with dark scale edges. Unpaired fin with red tips. Red stripes along the gill lid edge.
Size: 20 cm
Biology: Inhabits coral-rich lagoons and outreefs, 3–25 m. Floats immobile like other soldierfish during the day in protected places and hunts at night.
Distribution: East Africa to SW Japan, Micronesia, Line Islands, New Caledonia and French Polynesia.

Whitetip Soldierfish
Myripristis vittata

Orange-red. First dorsal fin with white tips.
Size: 20 cm
Biology: Prefers outer reef slopes, 3–80 m. Floats immobile in groups, sometimes in larger shoals, in caves or below overhangs during the day, usually below 10 m depth.
Distribution: Seychelles, Madagascar, the Mascarenes to SW Japan, Hawaii, Micronesia, New Caledonia and French Polynesia.

Spotfin Squirrelfish
Neoniphon sammara

Silvery with narrow auburn stripes. A red-black spot is located in front of the first dorsal fin.
Size: 32 cm
Biology: In various reef habitations, from steep outer reef slopes to small coral formations in seagrass fields, 3–45 m. Frequently alone, however also in small loose groups. Often with branch coral.
Distribution: Red Sea, S Oman and East Africa to SW Japan, Micronesia, Hawaii, GBR and French Polynesia.

Trumpetfish and Cornetfish
Aulostomidae and Fistulariidae

Trumpetfish
Aulostomus chinensis

Elongated thin body. Often brownish with several whitish horizontal stripes. Can rapidly change colour pattern and show dark cross markings. A yellow variant regularly occurs depending on territory.
Size: 70 cm
Biology: In rock and coral reefs, 2–122 m. Usually alone, sometimes also in loose pairs. For camouflage, occasionally stands vertically between horn coral or swims "piggyback" over larger fish in order to approach prey undetected.
Distribution: East Africa to S Japan, Northern New Zealand and East Pacific.

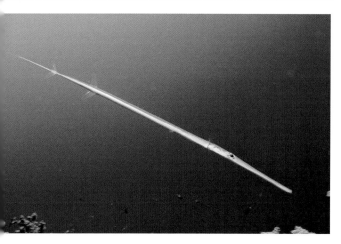

Cornetfish or Smooth Flutemouth
Fistularia commersonii

Extremely elongated, needle-thin tail. Can change colouration in a matter of seconds to very pale or dark grey brown.
Size: 150 cm
Biology: In almost all reef habitations, 1–128 m. Slowly ranges alone or in loose groups over reef or floats lurking at one spot. Captures small fish and crustaceans.
Distribution: Red Sea, East Africa to SW Japan, Hawaii, Panama, New Zealand and French Polynesia.

Needlefish
Belonidae

Crocodile Houndfish
Tylosurus crocodilus

Long pointed snout with needle-like teeth. Silvery with a blueish shimmer.
Size: 150 cm
Biology: Usually near the surface in coastal waters. Often on the reef top or at the reef edge, Also visits cleaner stations there. Predatory feeder on fish.
Distribution: Circumtropical.

Seamoths
Pegasidae

Little Dragonfish
Eurypegasus draconis

Hard body armour formed from bone plates. Long snout. Basic colouration adapted to the particular background.
Size: 8 cm
Biology: Inhabits protected areas in lagoons and quiet bays, 1–90 m. Alone or in pairs on sand, mud and rubble. Feeds on tiny invertebrates. Seamoths creep over the seabed with their finger-like ventral fins. Their name comes from the wing-like pectoral fins (spread out, upper photo). Because of their body armour, you can only see the tail move, but cannot see the body bend.
Distribution: Red Sea and East Africa to SW Japan, Micronesia, Marquesas and Society Islands.

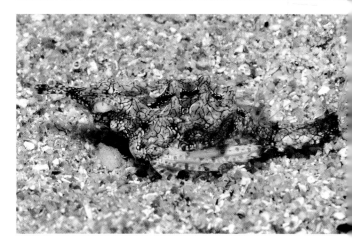

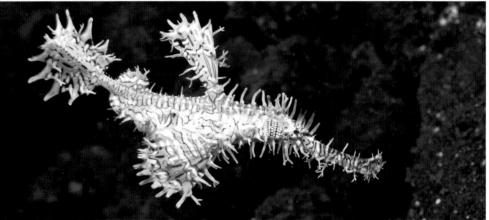

Ghost Pipefish
Solenostomidae

Small family with only a few species. Some are highly variable in colour as well as in form. Some species are therefore still not reliably described. The female is probably larger than the male, and unlike the related sea needles and seahorses, bears the brood. For this purpose, they have a breeding pocket formed from the ventral fin, which can hold about a hundred eggs. After ten to twenty days the transparent larvae hatch. Primarily, tiny shrimps and amphipods serve as nutriment for the false pipefish, which it sucks in with its tube mouth.

Ornate Ghost Pipefish
Solenostomus paradoxus

"Prickly" skin appendages. Colouration depending on environment, e.g. white, red, pink, black. Always with white, red or yellow markings.
Size: 11 cm
Biology: In rock and coral reefs, 3–30 m. Often protected by feather stars, also on horn coral, Soft Coral and Black Coral. Usually in pairs, less often in small groups.
Distribution: Red Sea (rarely) and East Africa to S Japan, Marshall Islands, SE Australia and Fiji.

Robust Ghost Pipefish
Solenostomus cyanopterus

Colouration variable, often brown or green, but also pale cream-coloured, rarely red. The size especially of tail and pectoral fins is likewise variable.
Size: 16 cm
Biology: In lagoons and protected coastal reefs, 1–20 m. Usually above sandy bottom and between algae and seagrass. Often in pairs, swims around slowly. Can sway back and forth like torn-off seagrass leaves in a heavy sea.
Distribution: Red Sea and East Africa (to Mauritius) to S Japan, Australia and Fiji.

The brown couple (lower photo) swim in an environment of dead brown seagrass leaves. With their irregular light speckles, the fish even closely imitate the typical crusty upgrowth of the leaves.

Halimeda Ghost Pipefish
Solenostomus halimeda

Head about equally as long as body. Variable in colour, green to whitish-grey, reddish brown.
Size: 6.5 cm
Biology: In lagoons and protected coastal reefs, 3–20 m, described in 2002. In halimeda green algae, coraline algae or in sand rubble areas. Alone or in pairs.
Distribution: the Maldives to NW Australia, Marshall Islands, Indonesia, PNG, Fiji.

Hairy Ghost Pipefish
Solenostomus paegnius

Brownish to pale greyish. The number of hairy filaments is variable.
Size: 11 cm
Biology: Usually on protected sand and rubble areas, 5–20 m.
Distribution: East Africa to S Japan, PNG, Solomons and Fiji.

Seahorses and Sea Needles
Syngnathidae

The members of this family have an armoured body without scales, with osseous skin rings, an individual dorsal fin and a tubal snout. It uses its snout to suck in tiny, bottom-dwelling invertebrates and plankton and swallows them whole. With its long grappling tail, which it can roll up into a spiral, seahorses clasp onto seagrasses, horn coral and other growths. It can also glide through water using slight movements of the dorsal fin. The male is responsible for the incubation of the eggs in this family. Propagation for seahorses begins with a long and complex mating ritual that can take up to three days. Finally, the female lays her eggs in the brood pocket on the male's abdomen. There it is fertilized by the male and incubated for several weeks. When the young finally slip from the eggs, the male, with strong pumping movements, presses them out of a small opening of the abdomen pocket into the open. The sea needle males carry the eggs easily visible along the side of the abdomen (see page 57, middle photo).

Tiger Tail Seahorse
Hippocampus comes
Yellow, black or grey with about 15 cross bands primarily on the tail which are distinctive in places and less so in others. Yellow specimens with dark to black bands. Male often black with yellow bands.
Size: 19 cm
Biology: In protected reef areas and bays, 2–20 m. Usually above 10 m, Frequently between coral, branched sponges or larger seagrass. Alone or in pairs. Probably predominantly nocturnal, feeds on zooplankton.
Distribution: Thailand and Malaysia to Indonesia, the Philippines and Vietnam.

Spiny Seahorse
Hippocampus histrix

Long snout. Conspicuously large, pointed barbs. Colouration variable: yellow, red, brown, greenish.
Size: 17 cm
Biology: In protected coastal reefs, 6–20 m. In seagrass fields, on soft and hard grounds with growths of soft coral, hydrozoa, sea whips, sponges or algae.
Distribution: East Africa (Tanzania, Mauritius) to India, the Philippines, S Japan, Micronesia, PNG, Samoa and Tonga.

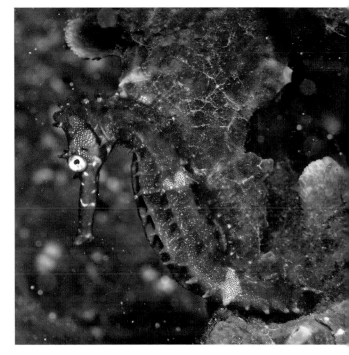

Jayakar's Seahorse
Hippocampus jayakari

Colouration usually beige to light brown, also intensive yellow. The plate edges often with dark thorny points.
Size: 14 cm
Biology: Inhabits protected bays and shallow coastal reefs, 1–20 m. Often on rubble-algae mixed zones and seagrass (frequently Halophila seagrasses), where it holds fast to plants with its grappling tail.
Distribution: Red Sea to Oman, Arabian Sea and Pakistan.

Pygmy Seahorse
Hippocampus bargibanti

Large, bulbous tubercles strewn over the body. General colouration is usually red. Yellow and very pale versions also occur (see photos where colour adapted to their horn coral host).

Size: 2 cm

Biology: On horn coral, 10–40 m. Colouration adapted to the environment and the skin structure, especially the wart-like tubercles, finely adapted to exactly match the horn coral on which it lives (especially *Muricella* species). Alone or in small groups and true to their location on the respective host coral. Because of its small size, it is also not easily discovered.

Distribution: Indonesia to S Japan, North Australia and New Caledonia.

Denise's Pygmy Seahorse
Hippocampus denise

Salmon colour to orange. Without raised crown on the head.
Size: 2 cm
Biology: 10–90 m. lives on horn coral (*Annella reticulata, Muricella sp.* and *Echinogorgia sp.*), probably reproduces over the entire year. This species was only described in 2003.
Distribution: Malaysia and Indonesia to the Philippines, Palau, PNG, Solomons and Vanuatu.

Pontohi Pigmy Seahorse
Hippocampus pontohi

Greenish to yellow-orange. Mostly solid colour throughout. Frequently whitish on the head, back, neck and abdomen. Small, fleshy-reddish appendages on the back.
Size: to 1.7 cm
Biology: Often in protected micro-locations in current-exposed regions, also at steep slopes, 5–25 m. Frequently on hydrozoa (*Aglaophenia sp.*), between algae and small sea squirts. Often in pairs.
Distribution: Eastern Indonesia.

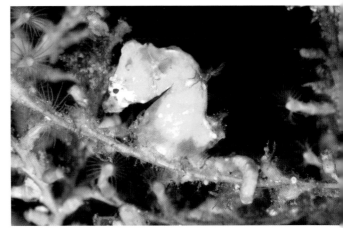

Common Seahorse
Hippocampus kuda

Brown to brown-black with numerous tiny black and white spots. Crown on the head sloped slightly backwards.
Size: 20 cm
Biology: On sand, seagrass, between mangroves, 1–12 m, occasionally also in deep water (to 55 m).
Distribution: the Maldives, Andaman Sea, Indonesia to Australia, Solomons.

Network Pipefish
Corythoichthys flavofasicatus
Cream-coloured to pale yellowish with dark markings.
Size: 15 cm
Biology: In coral reefs on rock, rubble, grit and living coral, 1–25 m. Alone, in pairs or in small groups.
Distribution: Red Sea to Mauritius and the Maldives.

Broad-banded Pipefish
Dunckerocampus boyleri

Banding alternately red to reddish-brown and cream-coloured stripes. Caudal fin red with white border. Very similar to *D. dactyliophorus*, but lacks the white spot in the centre of the tail.
Size: 16 cm
Biology: Usually on outreefs, 15 to more than 35 m. Typically in crevices, caves and below overhangs. Alone or in pairs.
Distribution: Red Sea, East Africa, Mauritius to Bali.

Banded Pipefish
Dunckerocampus dactyliophorus

Banding of alternate red to reddish brown and cream-coloured stripes. Caudal fin red with white border and a white spot in the centre.
Size: 18 cm
Biology: In lagoons and outreefs, 3 to more than 30 m. Usually floats in crevices, caves and below over-hangs. Often in pairs or in groups. Was earlier confused with *D. boyleri* (Indian Ocean).
Distribution: West Pacific species, East Indonesia to SW Japan and French Polynesia.

Many-banded Pipefish
Dunckerocampus multiannulatus

Reddish brown with about 60 fine white rings.
Size: 16 cm
Biology: In lagoons and outreefs, 1–75 m. Usually floats a short distance above seabed in protected places, such as crevices or over-hangs, usually head first below cave cover. Often in pairs. Territorial male, defends his territory from competitors.
Distribution: Red Sea, East Africa, Mauritius to the Maldives and Sumatra.

Orange-banded Pipefish
Dunckerocampus pessuliferus

Alternate red and orange-yellow bands. Red caudal fin with white upper edge and yellow spot.
Size: 16 cm
Biology: Inhabits coastal reefs, 10–35 m. Usually in protected areas of small coral heads on soft ground. Alone or in pairs. The animal in the photo carries red eggs on its abdomen.
Distribution: Bali to NW Australia, the Philippines and Sulawesi.

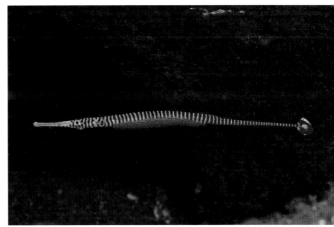

Double-ended or Bent Stick Pipefish
Trachyrhamphus bicoarctatus

Conspicuously large species, diffe-rent colouration: white, greenish, yellow, brown.
Size: 40 cm
Biology: Inhabits sand, mud and rubble in protected coastal reefs, 3–25 m. Usually lies on the seabed with only the hindmost body area up and the front of its body and head raised.
Distribution: Red Sea and East Africa to S Japan, Australia and New Caledonia.

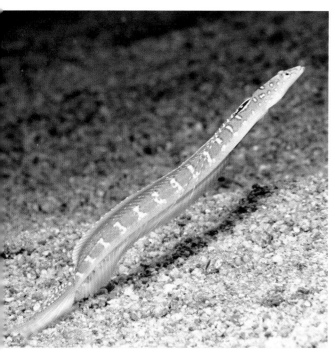

Sand-divers
Trichonotidae

Nikii Sand-diver
Triochonotus nikei

For the male, the first two spine rays of the dorsal fin are developed as long filaments.
Size: 12 cm
Biology: On protected sandy slopes, e.g. in reef crevices, 2–90 m. Usually glide in groups 0.5–3 m above the sandy soil and feed on zooplankton. When disturbed, they dive rapidly into the sand. They also sleep there at night. The males are territorial, have a harem and, as part of the mating ritual, frequently spread their dorsal and ventral fins.
Distribution: Red Sea.

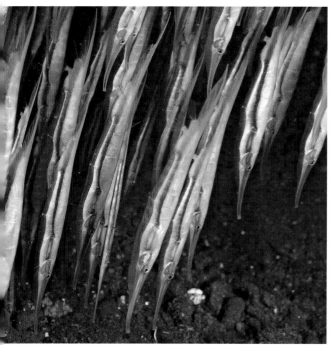

Snipefish
Centriscidae

Grooved Razorfish
Centriscus scutatus

Silvery with brown-red horizontal stripe. Body end with an immobile dorsal fin spine. On the similar *Aeoliscus strigatus* this is bendable.
Size: 14 cm
Biology: In protected reefs, 1–30 m. In small to large, dense groups. Often in front of sea whips, black coral and branch coral. It also moves freely over the seabed especially in larger groups. Swims vertically with head downwards, flees on danger into a horizontal position. With its pipette mouth it sucks plankton from the water.
Distribution: Aldabra Atoll and Seychelles to SW Japan, GBR and New Caledonia.

Clingfish
Gobiesocidae

Crinoid Clingfish
Discotrema crinophilum

Bright horizontal stripe from the eye to the tail, bonded at the brow by a same colour area. Colouration varies depending on the colouration of the relevant feather stars.
Size: 3 cm
Biology: Inhabits feather stars, about 8–20 m. It is difficult to discover because of its colour camouflage and its very hidden lifestyle.
Distribution: Christmas Islands to SW Japan, Fiji and GBR.

The blue variant in particular shows how excellently this species is camouflaged by the feather star.

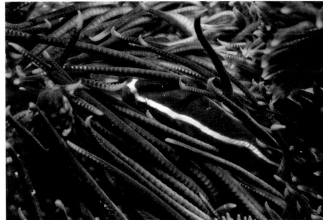

Longsnout Clingfish
Diademichthys lineatus

Red to dark reddish-brown with two white to pale yellowish horizontal stripes from the snout to the tail. Caudal fin with yellow spot.
Size: 6 cm
Biology: Frequently in the protection of the barbs of diadem sea urchins, 2–25 m. Also between branched coral or freely swimming in reef crevices and cavities.
Distribution: Oman to SW Japan, North Australia and New Caledonia.

Scorpionfish
Scorpaenidae

Various groups belong to the scorpionfish family, such as lionfish and fire fish. Have poisonous barbs on the dorsal, anal and ventral fins. Lionfish are conspicuously splendid fish that move slowly over the reef and frequently glide unperturbed around one spot. Their typical hunting technique is to drive smaller fish into a tight corner, using their large pectoral fins like blocking nets. Scorpionfish are typically bottom-dwelling and are poor swimmers who lie motionless on the bottom most of the time. They are predominantly well camouflaged and ambush passing prey.

Stonefish
Synanceidae

Reef Stonefish
Synanceia verrucosa

Lump-shaped form, vertical mouth opening, large fleshy pectoral fins.
Size: 38 cm
Biology: In lagoons and outreefs, 0.3 – 45 m. On sand and rubble, often dormant partly buried or protected on coral rock. Can occupy its regular place for months. Sometimes two or three animals lie together. Feeds on small fish and crustaceans.
Distribution: Red Sea and East Africa to S Japan, Micronesia and French Polynesia.

Even at close range, this stonefish, partially buried in sand, deceptively resembles a piece of coral rock overgrown with a red algae crust. Actually there were exactly such rocks strewn about in its immediate environment. With some practice, one can also discover such camouflaged stonefish by the striking line of their vertical mouth opening.

Estuarine Stonefish
Synanceia horrida

Eyes high up with bony lumps. A deep large cavity beneath each eye.
Size: 30 cm
Biology: On sand, mud and rubble, in estuaries and coastal reefs, 1–40 m. Frequently mostly buried. Lifestyle similar to *S. verrucosa*, however more commonly seen in murky waters.
Distribution: India to SW Japan, the Philippines, S Queensland and New Caledonia.

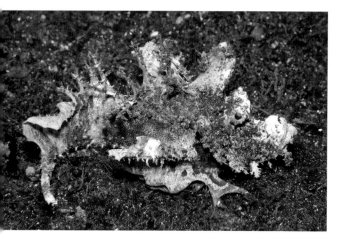

Devilfish
Choridactylinae

Spiny Stinger or Devilfish
Inimicus didactylus

Inner side of the pectoral fins varies from white to yellow, orange or pink.
Size: 19 cm
Biology: Inhabits protected reefs with free sand, mud and seagrass, 1–80 m. It frequently lies buried up to eyes and mouth, waiting for prey to swim by. The most common and wide-spread devilfish species.
Distribution: Andaman Sea to S Japan, Palau, NW Australia, Vanuatu and New Caledonia.

If they feel threatened, devilfish spread their pectoral fins to show their conspicuous warning colours on the underneath.

Filament-finned Stinger
Inimicus filamentosus

The upper one to two rays of the pectoral fins are extended as filaments. The inner sides of the pectoral fins have a luminous pattern of yellow-orange and black.
Size: 25 cm
Biology: Lives on sand, mud and rubble of lagoons, protected bays and outreefs, 3–55 m. Sits on the bottom or is partially buried. Uncommon.
Distribution: Red Sea to Mauritius and the Maldives. Only *Inimicus* species in the West Indian Ocean.

Stingfish

Minoinae

Painted Stinger
Minous pictus

Cheek and base of the pectoral fin is red.
Size: 10 cm
Biology: In coastal waters with fine sand or mud, 5-160 m. Uses the lower open pectoral fins ray to aid movement. Predominantly nocturnal predator, often buried during the day.
Distribution: Indonesia and the Philippines.

Waspfish

Tetrarogidae

Cockatoo Waspfish
Ablabys taenianotus

Dorsal fin is like a sail, beginning above the eyes and extending to the tail stalk. The colouration is variable, yellow to dark brown, the face sometimes contrasting.
Size: 15 cm
Biology: Inhabits protected sand, mud and rubble, 1–80 m. Alone or in pairs. Sways sideways in order to imitate a dead leaf.
Distribution: Andaman Sea to SW Japan, Palau, SE Australia and Fiji.

Brown specimens usually do not sit on high-contrast ground, but rather on dark sand or fine rubble. They are well camouflaged on such ground and from some distance they are easily mistaken for withered leaves.

Whiteface Waspfish
Richardsonichthys leucogaster

Dorsal fin deeply gashed between the barbs, especially in the anterior area. In contrast to other waspfish, the head is not laterally flattened, but rather is reminiscent of the scorpionfish.
Size: 8 cm
Biology: On sand and mud of coastal reefs, 3–90 m. Occasionally partially buried.
Distribution: East Africa to S China and New Caledonia.

Lionfish
Pteroinae

Red Lionfish
Pterois volitans

Red to almost black bands and pairs of white stripes.
Size: 43 cm
Biology: In lagoons, coastal and outer reefs, 1–50 m. Common species. Often suspended below overhangs during the day, occasionally also active in search of food. Hunts predominantly at night, feeds on small fish, shrimps and crabs. Not shy, often even approaches divers.
Distribution: Gulf of Thailand to Western Australia, SW Japan, Micronesia, Marquesas Islands, Pitcairn Islands and now the Caribbean as an alien invader.

Common Lionfish
Pterois miles

Red to almost black bands and pairs of white stripes.
Size: 38 cm
Biology: Inhabits lagoons, bays and outer reefs, 1–60 m. Often in overhangs, cavities and in wrecks. Hunts fish, crabs and shrimps at sunset and at night. Will not be scared away, can even sting divers at such attempts.
Distribution: Red Sea and East Africa to Andaman Sea, Sumatra, Lombok and Sumbawa. Further to the east, it is replaced by *P. volitans*. Migrated through the Suez Canal into the Mediterranean, and now the Caribbean as an alien invader.

Mombassa Lionfish
Pterois mombasae

Membranes of the pectoral fins have dark blotches. Similar to: *P. antennata* with longer pectoral fin spines and a few blotches.

Size: 19 cm

Biology: Prefers outer reefs, 10–60 m. Usually on hard ground, often in areas with soft coral and sponges.

Distribution: East Africa (rarely also in the Red Sea) to Sri Lanka, NW Australia and PNG.

Spotfin Lionfish
Pterois antennata

Long pectoral fin spines, bonded at the base with a membrane with a few dark spots.

Size: 20 cm

Biology: Inhabits lagoons and outer reefs, 1–50 m. Usually inactive during the day below overhangs and in cavities. Alone or in small groups. Hunts shrimps and crabs in the late afternoon and at night. Common species.

Distribution: East Africa to SW Japan, Micronesia, S Australia and French Polynesia.

Clearfin Lionfish
Pterois radiata

Long white pectoral fin spines, largely free-standing. White horizontal line on the tail base.
Size: 24 cm
Biology: In lagoons and outreefs, 1–25 m. Alone or in small groups, Usually inactive during the day and protected in caves and overhangs, occasionally along with *P. antennata*. Predominantly hunts shrimps and crabs at night.
Distribution: Red Sea and East Africa to SW Japan, Micronesia, New Caledonia and Society Islands.

Zebra Lionfish
Dendrochirus zebra

Fan-shaped pectoral fins, inner side with dark radial stripes.
Size: 20 cm
Biology: Found in protected inner reefs, 1–70 m. Often at individual coral heads or overgrown rocks. Hunts crabs, shrimps and small fish from the late afternoon (up to 3 hours before sunset) and at night. Then are often observed on sandy ground. Male aggressively defends his territory with several harem females.
Distribution: from central Red Sea and East Africa to SW Japan, Marshall Islands, SE Australia and Samoa.

Shortfin Lionfish
Dendrochirus brachypterus

Pectoral fins are fan-shaped with up to 10 concentric dark bands on the inner side.

Size: 15 cm

Biology: Inhabits coastal reefs and lagoons, 2–80 m. Alone or in small harems. Frequently in sediment-rich areas at individual coral heads or overgrown rocks. Hunts at night for small crustaceans close to the seabed.

Distribution: Red Sea and East Africa to SW Japan, the Mariana Islands, Australia and Samoa.

Twinspot Lionfish
Dendrochirus biocellatus

Two, occasionally also three conspicuous eye spots at the back in the dorsal fin. Inner side of the pectoral fins with three dark, concentric bands.

Size: 10 cm

Biology: Inhabits coral-rich reefs with clear water, 1–40 m. Shy. Keeps hidden in caves and below overhangs during the day. Can usually only be observed on its nocturnal hunt.

Distribution: Mauritius to NW Australia, SW Japan, Micronesia and Society Islands.

Scorpionfish
Scorpaeniformes

Leaf Scorpionfish
Taenianotus triacanthus

Greatly flattened laterally, high-backed body. Highly variable in colour: cream, yellow, greenish, brown, also white, red or pink.

Size: 12 cm

Biology: On coral, rock or rubble of protected and exposed reefs, 1–134 m. If required, it imitates a swaying leaf by lateral waving in the current. Regularly replaces its external skin layer.

Distribution: East Africa to SW Japan, Galapagos, Hawaii, Australia and Fiji.

Leaf scorpionfish are usually adapted to the colour of the environment (upper and middle photos), and only rarely contrasted to it, as is shown in the lower photo.

Eschmeyer's or Paddleflap Scorpionfish
Rhinopias eschmeyeri

Large paddle-shaped tentacle above the eye. Dorsal fin not gashed. Only a few and typically unbranched skin tassels. Variable colouration, often pale red to purple or orange to brownish.
Size: 21 cm
Biology: Inhabits sand and rubble on outreefs, 3–55 m.
Distribution: Mauritius to the Philippines and East Indonesia.

Different coloured specimens can also occur in small areas. Lurking for prey, it sits motionless in one spot and waits for passing prey.

Weedy Scorpionfish
Rhinopias frondosa

Branching skin tassels. Dorsal fin gashed by spines. Variable colouration, yellow, orange-brown, violet, partly with roundish markings.
Size: 23 cm
Biology: On rock or coral heads and sand spots of outreefs, 2–90 m. Creeps over the seabed with its pectoral and pelvic fins. Can sway from one side to the other. Replaces skin about every 13 days.
Distribution: East Africa to S Japan, Caroline Islands and New Caledonia.

Ambon Scorpionfish
Pteroidichthys amboinensis

Eyes lying high on the head, each with an enormous skin tentacle above. Colouration usually yellowish to dark brown. Also red and pink-coloured versions are known.
Size: 12 cm
Biology: On sand and mud, also in algae areas, 3–50 m. Creeps over the seabed with pectoral and pelvic fins.
Distribution: West Indonesia to SW Japan, North Australia and Fiji.

Apart from the variable colouration, it can also have skin tassels of different number and length.

Devil Scorpionfish
Scorpaenopsis diabolus

High dorsal hump. Inside pectoral fins with orange and yellow bands.
Size: 30 cm
Biology: On rubble, sand or coral in lagoons and outer reefs, 1–70 m. Feeds on small fish. When harassed, it shows the luminous coloured inner surface of the pectoral fins. Divers often confuse it with the stonefish, but these have a vertical mouth opening.
Distribution: Red Sea and East Africa to SW Japan, Micronesia, Hawaii and French Polynesia.

Tasselled Scorpionfish
Scorpaenopsis oxycephala

Numerous skin tassels on the head and chin. Relatively long snout.
Size: 36 cm
Biology: Inhabits lagoons, bays and outer reefs, 1–43 m. Usually rests on a hard bottom surface of living coral, rubble, rock and on sponges. Usually in coral-rich reefs with clear water. Common species.
Distribution: Red Sea and East Africa to Taiwan, Palau and Indonesia.

Poss's Scorpionfish
Scorpaenopsis possi

Numerous skin tassels on the head. Similar to *S. oxacephala* and *S. papuensis*, however with a shorter snout.
Size: 25 cm
Biology: Inhabits rock and prefers coral areas of outreefs, 1–40 m. Feeds predominantly on fish.
Distribution: Red Sea and East Africa to SW Japan and Pitcairn. Replaced by *S. eschmeyeri* between GBR and Fiji.

Bearded Scorpionfish
Scorpaenopsis barbata

Short snout, about as wide as the eye diameter.
Size: 25 cm
Biology: Lives on rock and coral reefs, 3–42 m. In regions with mixed sand and coral areas. Captures fish and shrimps.
Distribution: Red Sea to Arabian Gulf and Somalia.

Flatheads
Platycephalidae

Giant Flathead or Crocodilefish
Cymbacephalus beauforti

Camouflage colour, usually with dark band on the cheek (not a definitive characteristic). Black variant known.
Size: 50 cm
Biology: On sand, rubble and rock, 2–12 m.
Distribution: Singapore, Borneo to the Philippines, Palau, Yap and New Caledonia.

Tentacled Flathead
Papilloculiceps longiceps

Usually pale with diffuse greenish grey "camouflage markings".
Size: 100 cm
Biology: In bays and coastal reefs, 1–40 m. Usually on sand or rubble, often more or less covered with sand.
Distribution: Red Sea to Oman.

Welander's Flathead
Rogadius welanderi

Usually with whitish area at the back of the head. Dark pectoral fins with light blotches.
Size: 12 cm
Biology: On or near reef sand, rubble and mud, 3–50 m. Often partially buried during the day.
Distribution: Indonesia to Marshall Islands and Samoa.

Jawfish
Opistognathidae

Gold-specs or Black-cap Jawfish
Opistognathus randalli

Upper eye border luminous yellow. Black spot in front of the dorsal fin.
Size: 12 cm
Biology: On sand and rubble near reef, 5–30 m. Inhabits sand pipe that it has built, fortifying the entrance with rubble. Feeds on zooplankton and invertebrate bottom-dwellers. It occasionally protrudes prominently from its burrow or even leaves it for a moment, but then immediately slips back in again.
Distribution: Borneo and Bali to the Philippines and East Indonesia.

All jawfish are mouth breeders. After pairing, the male takes the fertilized eggs into his mouth. The clutch (see middle photo) of up to hundreds of eggs is well protected there and is provided with oxygen-rich fresh water. The young hatch after about 5 days.

Solor Jawfish
Opistognathus solorensis

Lips light-dark striped.
Size: 5 cm
Biology: Little-known species and like other jawfish inhabits burrows in sand and rubble that it builds itself near the reef.
Distribution: West Pacific, Indonesia.

Flying Gurnards
Dactylopteridae

Oriental Flying Gurnard
Dactylopterus orientalis

Elongated body. Very large, wing-like pectoral fins.
Size: 38 cm
Biology: On protected sand surfaces near the reef, 1–100 m. Loner. Creeps over the seabed with its modifed ventral fins. If threatened, splays its enormous, fan-shaped pectoral fins. Can then also rapidly move short distances forwards and immediately "sails off" a short distance over the seabed with its extended rigid pectoral fins. Predominantly feeds on invertebrate bottom-dwellers.
Distribution: Red Sea and East Africa to S Japan, Mariana Islands and Pohnpei in Micronesia, Hawaii, Northern New Zealand and French Polynesia.

Stargazers
Uranoscopidae

Whitemargin Stargazer
Uranoscopus sulphureus

Club-shaped body, very large head. Large black spot in the dorsal fin.
Size: 38 cm
Biology: On sand and muddy grounds of coastal waters, 5–150 m. Usually largely buried in sand. What look like teeth in the mouth are actually skin tassels on the lips. They help to keep the sand away. Lurking for prey with worm-shaped lappets on the lower jaw (can be folded in or protruding). The bait entices small fish which it swallows up with a split-second opening of its mouth.
Distribution: Red Sea, Réunion to the Mariana Islands; Samoa and Tonga.

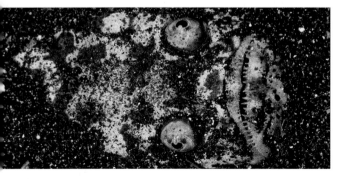

Flagtail Tilefish
Malacanthus brevirostris

Neck yellowish green. Two black stripes on the caudal fin.
Size: 30 cm
Biology: On sand and rubble of outreefs, 5–61 m. Alone or, especially for juveniles, in loosely formed groups. Frequently territorial, but shy. Flees on disturbance into holes in the seabed which are often underneath larger stones. Feeds on invertebrate bottom-dwellers.
Distribution: Red Sea and East Africa to SW Japan, Hawaii, Panama and SE Australia.

Tilefish
Malacanthidae

These elongated fish live near the bottom over sand and rubble regions on reefs. They live in pairs or harems, often in colonies, and feed on invertebrate bottom-dwellers or zooplankton that drift by.

Blue Blanquillo
Malacanthus latovittatus

Blue head. Black side stripe.
Size: 50 cm
Biology: On sand and rubble of lagoons, patch reefs and outreefs, 5–70 m. Usually a short distance above the bottom. Very shy, keeps its distance from divers. Adults in monogamous pairs.
Distribution: Red Sea, East Africa to SW Japan, Micronesia and Cook Islands.

Stark's Tilefish
Hoplolatilus starcki

Blue head, body whitish with pale yellow back.
Size: 15 cm
Biology: On outer reef slopes with rubble or sand patches, 15–100 m. Hovers usually in pairs a short distance above the seabed, rapidly flees on danger into its burrow in the ground.
Distribution: Bali to the Philippines, Micronesia, North Australia, Fiji.

Remoras
Echenidae

The small family of the remoras consists of about eight species. For all members, the first dorsal fin is reshaped to a unique suction plate. With its crosswise furrowed surface, it looks like the sole of a shoe. It acts like a suction cup and can produce an under pressure that allows it to hold tight to larger fish and be pulled along. Often they attach to various sharks, among them especially whale sharks, mantas and mobulas, turtles, large bony fish and dugongs. Remoras feed on small fish, possibly also on the prey of their hosts, and also feed on parasites from the skin of the host. They live in the open ocean, usually between 1 and 60 metres, also are often in reefs with their respective host.

Sharksucker
Echeneis naucrates

Black side strip, each seamed above and below with a white stripe. There is a variant in pale grey.
Size: 100 cm
Biology: The adult in the photo shows typical colouration and has attached itself to the shell of a Green Sea Turtle.
Distribution: All warm seas.

Common Remora
Remora remora

Grey to almost black, usually with fine white speckles. Body somewhat higher than *E. naucrates*.
Size: 50 cm
Biology: See above.
Distribution: All warm seas.

Juveniles and sub-adults show typical black and white patterning. May be seen swimming freely in the reef in search of a host to attach to. There are even instances of this species trying to attach to a diver.

Cobias
Rachycentridae

Cobia
Rachycentron canadum

Sub-adults with black horizontal stripe (similar to remora). Adults are monochrome brown-grey.
Size: 200 cm
Biology: Pelagic, only rarely in coral reefs, 0–50 m. Occasionally accompanying whale sharks (see photo), other sharks and large skates. Fully grown adults are larger and often taken to be sharks. Only species of the family.
Distribution: Circumtropical.

Longfins
Plesiopidae

Comet
Calloplesiops altivelis

Numerous white spots, more numerous with age. Eyespot below the dorsal fin.
Size: 20 cm
Biology: In lagoons and outreefs, 3–45 m. Hidden in crevices and caves during the day. When disturbed, withdraws even deeper.
Distribution: Red Sea, East Africa to SW Japan, Line Islands and French Polynesia.

Soapfish
Grammistinae

Sixline Soapfish
Grammistes sexlineatus

White horizontal stripe. Upon ageing, this breaks up into short dashes.
Size: 27 cm
Biology: In lagoons, bays and outreefs, also in brackish water, 1–40 m. Juveniles are common, but usually hidden in shelters. Adults move into deeper zones.
Distribution: Red Sea and East Africa to SW Japan, Micronesia, GBR and French Polynesia.

Arrowhead Soapfish
Belonoperca chabanaudi

Yellow spot above on the tail base. Black, blue-bordered eyespot in front on the dorsal fin.
Size: 15 cm
Biology: Inhabits outer reef slopes, 3–45 m. Hidden in caves and deep overhangs during the day, 3–45 m. Very shy. On approach, withdraws deeper into its covered shelter. Goes into the open only with onset of darkness.
Distribution: East Africa to SW Japan, Micronesia, Samoa and New Caledonia.

Barred Soapfish
Diploprion bifasciatum

A narrow crossband above the eye, a very broad one on the body rear.
Size: 25 cm
Biology: Prefers coastal reefs, also with brackish water and easily disturbed sediment, 1–40 m. Alone or in small, loose groups. Feeds predominantly on fish.
Distribution: India and the Maledives to SW Japan, Australia and New Caledonia.

Red Sea or Yellowfin Soapfish
Diploprion drachi

Grey-blue with black dorsal fin base and yellow marking on the eye.
Size: 14 cm
Biology: On coral-rich slopes where it stays in the protection of cavities, overhangs and crevices during the day, 3–40 m. At dusk, it moves along the reef hunting for small fish and crustaceans.
Distribution: Red Sea.

Dottybacks
Pseudichromidae

Splendid Dottyback
Manonichthys splendens

Yellow tail, black eye stripes, black
ventral fin with blue outer edge.
Size: 13 cm
Biology: On steep reef slopes,
always close to the seabed, 5–40
m. Alone, always near niches,
frequently near tube sponges into
whose tubes it can withdraw.
Distribution: East Indonesia and
NW Australia.

Magenta Dottyback
Pictichromis porphyrea

All magenta-coloured, which
makes it easy to identify.
Size: 6 cm
Biology: In steep outer reef slopes
and channels, 5–50 m. Alone or in
small loose groups. In front of small
cavities in the reef wall, above coral
or rubble, always hovers very close
to the seabed.
Distribution: the Philippines to
SW Japan, Palau, the Moluccas,
Marshall Islands and Samoa.

Sunrise Dottyback
Pseudochromis flavivertex

Male blue, broad, yellow back
stripe extends to the chin. Female
yellowish.
Size: 7 cm
Biology: Usually at the foot of patch
and fringe reefs, above sand and
rubble, 2–30 m. Has a regular place
in a small territory. The female lives
more in hiding, and is even more
shy than the male and can therefore only very rarely be observed.
Distribution: Red Sea and Gulf of
Aden.

Anthias
Anthiinae

These diurnal, agile fish feed on zooplankton floating by. They always remain close to the reef or near coral blocks where they seek protection when disturbed. They spend the night hidden in the reef crevices or between branch coral. Anthias typically occur in groups with many females, still more juveniles and few males, because an anthias group, the basic unit of larger congregations, is a harem. Depending on the species, there are from several to over 30 females for one male. The males are somewhat larger and develop from a high-ranking female by sex conversion. A new colouration is associated with this sex change.

Scalefin Anthias
Pseudanthias squamipinnis

Male (above): orange with yellow spots on body scales, crimson spot on pectoral fin. Extended dorsal fin ray. Female (below): orange with violet edged red-orange-coloured cheeks stripes.

Size: 15 cm

Biology: In clear lagoons and outer reef slopes, 1–35 m. Especially in front of reef crowns and at coral heads, forms small or large, sometimes colossal groups. A male usually guards a harem of 5–10 females.

Distribution: Red Sea and East Africa to SW Japan, Palau, Solomons, SE Australia and Fiji.

Stocky Anthias
Pseudanthias hypselosoma

Male (both photos): red spot on dorsal fin, rounded caudal fins with a thin, blue fringe at the back edge. Female: slightly indented caudal fin with red tips.
Size: 19 cm
Biology: In lagoons and protected outreefs, 10–35 m. Readily stays at coral heads and protrusions. Forms smaller groups or larger congregations.
Distribution: the Maldives to SW Japan, Palau, GBR, New Caledonia and Samoa.

The male can also be very differently coloured within a group, from vivid orange-red to predominantly whitish pale-pink.

Red Sea Anthias
Pseudanthias taeniatus

Male: whitish with two broad dark red horizontal stripes. Female: orange with light abdomen.
Size: 13 cm
Biology: In coral-rich, clear lagoons and outreefs, 12–50 m. Harem groups with up to 15 females. Frequently at deep patch reefs and prominent coral formations. Female fairly near seabed, male often metres above.
Distribution: Red Sea; the Gulf of Aden to Arabian Gulf replaced by the very similar Townsend anthias (*P. townsendi*).

Peach Fairy Basslet
Pseudanthias dispar

Male: luminous red dorsal fin with blue fringe. Female: orange, whitish chin.
Size: 9,5 cm
Biology: Prefers steep outer reef slopes, 2–15 m. In groups to about three metres above the reef.
Distribution: Christmas Islands to S Japan, Line Islands (Central Pacific), Micronesia and GBR.

Yellowstriped Fairy Basslet
Pseudanthias tuka

Male (upper photo): crimson spot at the back of the dorsal fin.
Size: 12 cm
Biology: At outer reef slopes, 2–40 m. In schools to about 3 m above the reef feeding on plankton. Also feeds on fish eggs.
Distribution: Indonesia to SW Japan, Palau, Vanuatu and GBR.

Female (lower photo): orange-yellow back stripe to upper end of the caudal fin. Lower tail lobe edge is similarly coloured.

Evan's Anthias
Pseudanthias evansi

Purple (appears blue below water without artificial light) with broad yellow stripes from the neck to the tail root and in the two tail lobes.
Size: 10 cm
Biology: Usually at reef slopes near or hardly more than two metres above the seabed, 3–40 m. Usually in small groups, less often in larger schools.
Distribution: East Africa to Mauritius, Andaman Sea and Christmas Islands

Squarespot Anthias
Pseudanthias pleurotaenia

Male (above): magenta-coloured with large, bright rect-angle on the side.
Size: 20 cm
Biology: Prefers steep outer reef slopes, 10 to more than 100 m, usually below 20 m. In loose groups, male with harem of up to about eight females.
Distribution: Bali to NW Australia, SW Japan, Microne-sia, Samoa and New Caledonia.

Female: orange, with a few violet stripes from the eye to the lower tail base. Similar to the females of scalefin anthias, whose stripes extend only to the pectoral fin base.

Red-cheeked Fairy Basslet
Pseudanthias huchti

Male: body is lilac coloured, red stripes from the eye to the pectoral fin base. Female: pale yellow green, yellow caudal fin edges.
Size: 12 cm
Biology: In clear, coral-rich lagoons and outreefs, 3–20 m. Alone or in small groups, snaps at zooplankton at the reef edge or in protrusions.
Distribution: Indonesia to the Philippines, Palau, Solo-mons, GBR and Vanuatu.

Hawkfish or Fathead Anthias
Serranocirrhitus latus

Unusually high-backed for an anthias. Yellow spot at the gill lid and two broken yellow cheek stripes.
Size: 13 cm
Biology: Prefers outreefs, 15–70 m. Usually keeps very near overhangs and cavities of reef slopes, Alone or in small groups.
Distribution: Indonesia to SW Japan, the Philippines, Palau, GBR and New Caledonia.

Groupers
Serranidae

Groupers are loners, some larger ones however make seasonal migrations to spawning grounds where they congregate. The majority of this vigorous bottom-dwelling fish inhabits coral reefs and rock grounds which offer perfect cover. They are territorial and have protected shelters such as crevices and overhangs in their territory in which they usually spend a large part of the day. Some however also roam more or less openly through the reef during the day. Groupers belong to the most common and most important predatory fish in the reef. Their staple food consists of crustaceans, fish and cuttlefish. They can thrust forward surprisingly rapidly and take even faster fish by surprise. Large species can become several decades old.

Yellow-edged Lyretail
Variola louti

Caudal fin is sickle shaped with yellow back edge. Photos: above adult, below sub-adult fish.
Size: 80 cm
Biology: In lagoons, channels and outreefs, 1–150 m. Also ranges through the reef during the day as a stealth hunter. Feeds on fish and crustaceans. Not shy. Juvenile possibly imitate goatfish which they often accompany in search of food.
Distribution: Red Sea, East Africa to SW Japan and French Polynesia.

Slender Grouper
Anyperodon leucogrammicus

Slim, usually greenish body with red spots. Often some pale horizontal stripes.
Size: 52 cm
Biology: In lagoons and outreefs with rich coral growth, 2–50 m. Usually remains in shelters. Feeds on fish. Juveniles imitate horizontal striped Halichoeres wrasse in order to approach closer to their prey.
Distribution: Red Sea and East Africa to SW Japan, Micronesia, Samoa and GBR.

Peacock Grouper
Cephalopholis argus

Olive-brown to greenish with numerous blue spots. Body rear often with more or fewer light cross bands.
Size: 55 cm
Biology: Prefers clear, coral-rich lagoons and outreefs, 1–40 m. Often rests in protected places on hard ground. Adults are also in pairs or small groups. Can rapidly brighten or darken its colouration.
Distribution: Red Sea and East Africa to S Japan and French Polynesia

Leopard Grouper
Cephalopholis leopardus

Reddish-brown with cream-coloured patches and speckles. A dark brown, lightly bordered spot above the tail root.
Size: 22 cm
Biology: In lagoons, coastal and outreefs with good coral growth, 3–35 m. Frequently hidden, e.g. below overhangs and usually shy.
Distribution: East Africa to SW Japan, Micronesia, GBR and French Polynesia.

Bluespotted Grouper
Cephalopholis cyanostigma

Reddish-brown, slightly mottled, with numerous pale blue, dark-edged spots.
Size: 35 cm
Biology: Inhabits lagoons and outreefs, 1–50 m. Can be found in zones with seagrass as well as those with good coral growth. Feeds on fish and crustaceans.
Distribution: Andaman Islands and Malaysia to the Philippines, Palau, Solomons and GBR.

Bluelined Hind or Grouper
Cephalopholis formosa

Olive-brownish with blue horizontal stripes. Fins frequently clearly contrasting with predominant blue areas. Similar to *C. polleni* with more yellow-green basic colouration, fins not predominantly dark to blue.
Size: 34 cm
Biology: Prefers protected, shallow, partly-silted reefs with moderate to low coral growth.
Distribution: The Maldives, India, Andaman Sea to SW Japan, the Philippines and N Australia.

Yellowfin Hind
Cephalopholis hemistiktos

Pale brown-red to red. Small blue points at the head area.
Size: 35 cm
Biology: In coral-rich bays and outreefs, 5–50 m. At coral heads with cavities and crevices as shelters. Captures fish and crustaceans.
Distribution: Red Sea to Arabian Gulf, Pakistan and Somalia..

Saddle Grouper
Cephalopholis sexmaculata

6-7 saddle patches, turning into bright bands.
Size: 50 cm
Biology: In cavities at outer reef slopes, 5–150 m. Shy. Almost always in their shelters, hard to observe in the open. Abdomen always faces the seabed, also at caves, roofs and walls.
Distribution: Red Sea, East Africa to SW Japan and French Polynesia

Coral Grouper
Cephalopholis miniata

Entire body with blue, dark-edged spots. Can show pale vertical stripes.
Size: 40 cm
Biology: In lagoons and outreefs, 3–150 m. Prefers clear, coral-rich regions. Common and not shy, lets divers get close.
Distribution: Red Sea and East Africa to SW Japan, Line Islands Australia and French Polynesia.

Juveniles show a yellow to orange basic colouration and a few intensively coloured spots. The fish shown is about 10 cm long.

Tomato Grouper
Cephalopholis sonnerati

Orange-red to reddish-brown, numerous small red dots on the head. Body occasionally with white spots or a spotted pattern.
Size: 57 cm
Biology: Inhabits rock and coral reefs, lagoons and outreefs, 10–60 m. Can usually be met only below 20 m, frequently at free-standing coral blocks with cleaner shrimp stations.
Distribution: Gulf of Aden and East Africa to SW Japan, Line Islands and New Caledonia.

Flagtail Grouper
Cephalopholis urodeta

Light to brown-red, dark at the back. Caudal fin with two white diagonal edge stripes (only in the West Pacific). Reddish brown spot above the pectoral fin (only in the Indian Ocean).
Size: 28 cm
Biology: Clear lagoons and out-reefs, 3–50 m. Prefers low depths to about 15 m. Feeds on fish and crustaceans.
Distribution: East Africa to SW Japan, Micronesia and French Polynesia.

Strawberry Grouper
Cephapholis spiloparaea

Uniformly red, only a pale band at the tail end.
Size: 22 cm
Biology: In clear, coral-rich and mostly outer reef slopes. Usually only below 20 m to more than 100 m.
Distribution: East Africa to SW Japan, Micronesia and Polynesia.

Baramundi or Humpback Grouper
Cromileptis altivelis

Unmistakeable with its small head, inwardly arched (concave) brow and black spots.
Size: 70 cm
Biology: In lagoons and outreefs, predominantly in silted or decayed areas, 2–30 m. Alone and usually encountered in or in front of its shelter.
Distribution: Andaman Sea and Indonesia to SW Japan, Guam and New Caledonia.

Blacktip Grouper
Epinephelus fasciatus

Dark "beret" over snout and brow. Spines of the dorsal fin usually with black tips.
Size: 40 cm
Biology: In bays, lagoons and outreefs, 1–160 m. On coral, rubble ground and on small coral heads in seagrass fields. Rarely shy, common in some territories.
Distribution: Red Sea to SW Japan, Marquesas Islands and Pitcairn.

For a grouper, this species is exceptionally variable in colour. The range extends from almost white to pale cream and bright red to deep reddish-brown and olive-brown. There are frequently 4–5 strong or pale orange-brown vertical stripes on the body.

Whitespotted Grouper
Epinephelus caeruleopunctatus

Black tail and anal fin. Back edge of the caudal fin is rounded (convex).
Size: 60 cm
Biology: In lagoons and outreefs, 4–65 m. Usually in or near its shelter.
Distribution: East Africa and Arabian Gulf to SW Japan, Marshall Islands, Kiribati, Tonga and East Australia.

Brown-marbled Grouper
Epinephelus fuscoguttatus

Brow slightly deformed (concave). Small black saddle spot on the tail stalk.
Size: 90 cm
Biology: In lagoons and outreefs, 3–60 m. Shy loner, difficult to approach. Uncommon in the majority of regions. Feeds on fish, cuttlefish and crustaceans.
Distribution: Red Sea, East Africa Southern to Mauritius, SW Japan, Samoa and New Caledonia.

Highfin Grouper (juv)
Epinephelus maculatus

Brownish, entire body and fins speckled with dark spots. Two white patches on the back.
Size: 60 cm
Biology: In bays, lagoons and outreefs, 3–100 m. Juveniles also especially common on rubble, between stones and in sandy, muddy areas in shallow water. Adults often rest on open sand surfaces. It captures fish and crustaceans as well as octopuses.
Distribution: Cocos Keeling to SW Japan, Micronesia and Samoa.

Camouflage Grouper
Epinephelus polyphekadion

Black saddle spot on the tail stalk. Some irregular light patches and numerous small dots. The latter are often missing on the head upper side.
Size: 75 cm
Biology: Inhabits coral-rich lagoons and outreefs, 1–45 m. Often in the vicinity of shelters such as cavities. Not shy. Predominantly feeds on small fish and crustaceans.
Distribution: Red Sea, East Africa to Mauritius, SW Japan and French Polynesia.

White-streaked Grouper
Epinephelus ongus

Brown with several large light patches and numerous small light patches lying approximately in a row.
Size: 35 cm
Biology: Prefers protected, shallow coastal reefs and lagoons, 5–25 m. Somewhat more shy and usually observed in the vicinity of cavities or crevices.
Distribution: East Africa to SW Japan, Marshall Islands, GBR and Tonga.

Juveniles (specimen shown about 10 cm) are dark brown with numerous small white to pale yellow spots.

Greasy Grouper
Epinephelus tauvina

Body and fins covered with rust-brown spots. Sides often with diffuse cross bands.
Size: 70 cm
Biology: Prefers clear, coral-rich lagoons and outreefs, 1–40 m. Usually encountered lying on the seabed. Not shy. Feeds predominantly on fish.
Distribution: Red Sea and East Africa to SW Japan, Micronesia and French Polynesia.

Potato grouper
Epinephelus tukula

Pale grey with large grey-black patches.
Size: 200 cm
Biology: In deep lagoons, deep patch reefs and out-reefs, 3–150 m. Prefers clear, coral-rich regions. Usually a loner, only at some sites in loose groups. Not shy. Feeds on fish, crustaceans and squid.
Distribution: Red Sea (rarely) and East Africa to S Japan and GBR. It only occurs in certain areas in its entire range.

Blacksaddled Coral Grouper
Plectropomus laevis

Two colour variants: grey variant with olive-coloured to grey head and 3–5 saddle spots of same colour.
Size: 125 cm
Biology: Coral-rich lagoons and outreefs, frequently in reef channels, 5–90 m. Shy. Feeds predominantly on fish, also relatively large ones, among them parrot fish and groupers.
Distribution: East Africa to SW Japan, Marshall Islands and French Polynesia.

The black-yellow variant shows very high-contrast black saddle spots on white ground. Snout, fins and tail stalk with more or less yellow.

Roving Coral Grouper
Plectropomus pessuliferus

Variable in colour: light beige to reddish-brown with red to reddish-brown vertical stripes and numerous blue, round and vertically, slightly elongated patches. Conspicuous fangs.
Size: 110 cm
Biology: In lagoons and outreefs, 3–50 m. Also during the day often patrolling slowly along the reef. Predominantly feeds on fish.
Distribution: Red Sea (only the subspecies *marisrubi*). The subspecies *pessuliferus* in the Indian Ocean.

Redmouth Grouper
Aethaloperca rogaa

Relatively high body, brown to black. Red mouth inside.
Size: 60 cm
Biology: In coral-rich bays and protected outreefs, 3–50 m. Usually encountered in shelters, usually rests in cavities, also in wrecks. Shy species. Feeds on fish and crustaceans.
Distribution: Red Sea and East Africa to SW Japan, Fiji and GBR.

White-edged Lyretail
Variola albimarginata

Caudal fin is sickle-shaped with white back edge.
Size: 55 cm
Biology: Inhabits lagoons, coastal and outreefs, 5–90 m. Less common than the Coral Grouper. Likewise swims openly just above the reef during the day.
Distribution: East Africa to SW Japan, Mariana Islands, GBR and Samoa.

Juveniles are pale red with bright backs. The caudal fin is not yet sickle-shaped and is half transparent at the rear.

Masked Grouper
Gracilia albomarginata

Usually easily recognised by the white rectangle on the side. Also by black spot at the tail stalk and lines on the head.
Size: 45 cm
Biology: Prefers steep outer reef slopes and canals, 5–120 m. Usually alone. But sporadically several fish can be observed in a small reef section. Usually swims or hovers a short distance above the reef.
Distribution: East Africa to SW Japan, Micronesia and French Polynesia.

This species can rapidly change its colour intensity, whereby the white rectangle can totally disappear.

Bigeyes
Priacanthidae

Crescent-tail Bigeye
Priacanthus hamrur

Usually dark to bright red
Size: 40 cm
Biology: Inhabits clear, coral-rich lagoons and outreefs, 10–100 m. It hovers immobile at coral formations, below overhangs or in the vicinity of caves during the day. Occasionally also rests in larger congregations just above the reef, also floats in a current. Nocturnal, feeds on zooplankton.
Distribution: Red Sea, Oman and East Africa to SW Japan, Micronesia, SE Australia and French Polynesia.

This species can change its colouration from red to red-silvery striped or almost completely silvery-white in a matter of seconds. Such differently coloured specimens can often be observed together in congregations.

Glass Bigeye or Glasseye
Heteropriacanthus cruentatus

Can very rapidly change colouration from red to silvery. Fins with speckles or mottled.
Size: 32 cm
Biology: In lagoons and outreefs, 2–20 m. Usually hovers motionless in the vicinity of coral formations during the day. Catches zooplankton at night.
Distribution: Circumtropical.

Freckled Hawkfish
Paracirrhites forsteri

Several colour variants, however all with black to red spots on the head.
Size: 22 cm
Biology: In clear lagoons and out-reefs, 1–40 m. Not shy. Usually lurks exposed on small branch coral species, also on other stony corals, fire corals and rock protrusions. Feeds on small fish as well as shrimps.
Distribution: Red Sea and East Africa to S Japan, Hawaii and Ducie Island off Pitcairn.

Hawkfish
Cirrhitidae

The tiny thread bushels at the tips of the anterior ten spines of the dorsal fin identify this family. The name, hawkfish refers to its hunting behaviour. It typically squats on a raised observation post of coral, rock or large sponge and surveys the surrounding area in order to capture juvenile fish or shrimps which it accomplishes with a short rapid thrust. The exception of the family in this respect is the Swallowtail Hawkfish, which feeds on zooplankton and for this purpose ascends up to several metres into open water. Hawkfish are protogynic hermaphrodites: they sexually mature first as females and can later in life change to males if required.

Arc-eye Hawkfish
Paracirrhites arcatus

An arching, blue-red-orange line
("monocle") behind the eye. Usually
a broad white horizontal stripe on
the body rear.
Size: 14 cm
Biology: Lives in clear lagoons and
outreefs, 1–35 m. Prefers to squat
on the outer edge of small branched corals, such as the *Acropora*,
Pocillipora and *Stylophora* species.
Feeds on small crustaceans.
Distribution: East Africa to S Japan,
Hawaii and French Polynesia

Longnose Hawkfish
Oxycirrhites typus

Long snout. Unmistakable red
"tartan" markings.
Size: 13 cm
Biology: On steep, current-rich outreefs, 5-100, usually only below 20
m. Usually in large venus sea fans
and black coral bushes. Snaps for
zooplankton at its exposed station,
also feeds on small bottom-dwelling crabs.
Distribution: Red Sea to Mauritius,
S Japan, Hawaii, Panama and New
Caledonia.

Giant or Marbled Hawkfish
Cirrhitus pinnulatus

Olive-brown with large white and
small black patches.
Size: 30 cm
Biology: At rock and coral reefs,
0.3–5 m. Inhabits surf-exposed
external reef tops and reef edges.
Usually common in specific areas,
however well camouflaged and
shy. Feeds on crustaceans, also
sea-urchins, brittle starfish and
small fish.
Distribution: Red Sea and E Africa
to SW Japan, Micronesia and French
Polynesia.

Swallowtail or Lyretail Hawkfish
Cyprinocirrhites polyactis

Only hawkfish with sickle tail. It is often confused with anthias.
Size: 15 cm
Biology: At steep slopes and current-exposed coral heads, 10–132 m. While other hawkfish squat on the bottom and capture bottom-dwellers, this species usually swims some metres above the seabed and snaps at zooplankton, crustaceans and larvae floating by.
Distribution: East Africa to S Japan, Palau, New Caledonia and Tonga.

At night, this species also squats on the seabed in the manner typical of its family.

Dwarf Hawkfish
Cirrhitichthys falco

Two reddish diagonal stripes below the eye.
Size: 7 cm
Biology: Reefs with medium-sized and rich coral growth, often at outreefs, however also in protected bays, 3–46 m. Squats on hard grounds on quite diverse growths, typically at the base of small coral or rock formations, also on small sand patches in front of such formations.
Distribution: The Maldives to S Japan, Caroline Islands/Micronesia, Fiji and Samoa.

Threadfin Hawkfish
Cirrhitichthys aprinus

Brown, light-bordered spot on the gill lid.
Size: 12 cm
Biology: In rock and coral reefs, 5–40 m. Squats on coral and overgrown hard grounds, also has preference for sponges.
Distribution: The Maldives and Andaman Sea, to S Japan, Micronesia, Cocos Keeling, PNG and GBR.

Coral or Pixy Hawkfish
Cirrhitichthys oxycephalus

Whitish with reddish-brown, differently large patches. Colour variants known for specimens from somewhat larger depths with pale pink basic colouration and densely-spaced, predominantly red patches.
Size: 9 cm
Biology: In lagoons, bays and out-reefs, 1–40 m. Not shy. Squats on various coral and on coral rock, less frequently also amongst seagrass.
Distribution: Red Sea and East Africa to S Japan, Panama and New Caledonia.

The colouration of this species appears to depend on depth and also on region. Specimens in the lower range of the depth distribution are predominantly red, and are also almost entirely missing the dark patches on the head.

Ringtailed Cardinalfish
Apogon aureus

Orange, fading to the back. A pair of blue stripes is drawn through the eyes and above the snout. Blue stripes in the angle of the mouth, black tail band.
Size: 12 cm
Biology: Inhabits protected lagoons and coastal reefs, 2–40 m. Often in larger groups.
Distribution: East Africa to SW Japan, GBR and Tonga.

Cardinalfish
Apogonidae

Cardinal perch are predominantly small fish that are rarely larger than 12 centimetres. The majority of species are active at dusk and night. They are slow swimmers, live near the seabed and are confined to a small territorial area. During the day, they prefer to glide quietly in crevices, between branched coral, partly also in the open, but then remain close to a coral block or rock. They leave their shelters at dusk. The majority then hunt for zooplankton, small fish and bottom-dwelling crustaceans. The Tiger Cardinal Fish, with its large fangs, predominantly feeds on fish. Cardinalfish are known for their special brood care. After spawning, the fertilized eggs are collected by the male and incubated in his elasticated oral cavity for about one week. The eggs are protected from predators and bathed in the oxygen-rich respiratory water. This is an exceptionally effective brood care, during which time the male consumes no nourishment.

Split-banded Cardinalfish
Apogon compressus

Dotted back line. A bright side stripe beginning above the eye is cut short beneath the forward edge of the first dorsal fin. Blue, usually incomplete eye-ring.
Size: 12 cm
Biology: In lagoons and protected outreefs. Usually in shoals in front of cavities or branch coral.
Distribution: Malaysia to SW Japan, GBR and Solomons.

Yellowstriped Cardinalfish
Ostorhinchus cyanosoma

An orange-yellow side stripe beginning above the eye and cut off beneath the back edge of the first dorsal fin.
Size: 8 cm
Biology: In lagoons and protected outreefs, 1–50 m. Floats during the day in small or larger groups in front of coral or coral rock. Hunts zooplankton alone at night.
Distribution: Red Sea, Arabian Gulf and East Africa to SW Japan and Marshall Islands, GBR and Fiji

Spotgill Cardinalfish
Apogon crysopomus

Orange-yellow markings on the gill lid. Dark spot on the tail root.
Size: 9 cm
Biology: Inhabits protected reef areas, 1–20 m. Frequently rests during the day in small groups in front of coral branches.
Distribution: Java to the Philippines and Solomons.

Narrowstripe Cardinalfish
Apogon exostigma

Dark horizontal stripe narrowing towards the back. A black spot on the tail root somewhat above the midline.
Size: 11 cm
Biology: In lagoons and outreefs, 2–20 m. Inactive at coral heads, overhangs or crevices during the day. At night usually hunts zoo-plankton over sandy soil.
Distribution: Red Sea and East Africa to SW Japan, Line Islands, Samoa and French Polynesia.

Hartzfeld's Cardinalfish
Apogon hartzfeldii

Pale tail with black spot on tail root. Fine white eye and back stripes.
Size: 11 cm
Biology: In protected coastal reefs and lagoons, 2–20 m. Active at night, usually in small groups near the seabed in front of living coral, coral rubble or rock during the day. Also seeks protection around long spiny sea urchins.
Distribution: Bali and Borneo to the Philippines, Palau and Solomons.

Frostfin Cardinalfish
Apogon hoevenii

Back edge of the first dorsal fin with conspicuous white fringe. Some small white dots strewn along the back.
Size: 5 cm
Biology: In protected bays and reefs, also on soft ground, 1–30 m. During the day it floats in groups in front of coral, algae or other protected places, such as near long spiny sea urchins.
Distribution: Bali and Borneo to SW Japan, PNG and GBR.

Many-lined Cardinalfish
Apogon multilineatus

Light cream-coloured with numerous dark horizontal stripes of different widths. Head dark brownish with several white stripes.
Size: 10 cm
Biology: In lagoons and coastal reefs, 2–25 m. Alone or in small groups.
Distribution: Sumatra and Malaysia to the Philippines and Solomons.

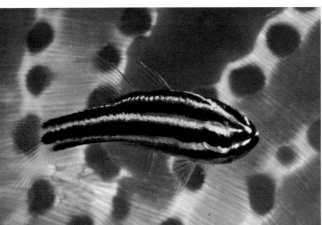

Blackstripe Cardinalfish
Apogon nigrofasciatus

Brown to black background with four whitish to yellow stripes.
Size: 9 cm
Biology: In lagoons and outer reef slopes, 3–50 m. Alone or in pairs, often at the base of coral formations, below overhangs or in front of cavities and crevices. Feeds on invertebrate bottom-dwellers.
Distribution: Red Sea, East Africa to SW Japan, Micronesia and French Polynesia.

Orange-lined or Silty Cardinalfish
Apogon properuptu

Orange-yellow with silvery light grey horizontal stripes. The lowest is very short and extends only to or shortly behind the back edge of the gill lid.
Size: 8 cm
Biology: In lagoons and outreefs, 2–20 m.
Distribution: Andaman Sea to PNG and E Australia and New Caledonia.

Broadbanded Cardinalfish
Apogon quadrifasciatus

A brown stripe extending from the eye to the caudal fin is bordered above and below by a whitish-silvery line.
Size: 10 cm
Biology: Inhabits coastal reefs and coastal areas with sandy to muddy grounds.
Distribution: Red Sea, Arabian Gulf and East Africa to N Australia and the Philippines.

Half-barred Cardinal
Apogon thermalis

Front edge of the first dorsal fin has black seam. Black eye stripes, extending over upper snout.
Size: 8 cm
Biology: In protected coastal reefs, 2–15 m. During the day in small groups in front of coral formations, often in front of such in areas with sandy patches.
Distribution: East Africa to SW Japan, Solomons and Vanuatu.

Three-spot Cardinalfish
Pristicon trimaculatus

Three short, irregular saddle spots on the back. Dark spot on the gill lid, which can also fade. The specimen shown lacks this dark spot. It is very similar to *P. rhodopterus*, which, however, has dark rear scale edges and no dark spot between the dorsal fins.
Size: 15 cm
Biology: In lagoons and outreefs, 2–15 m, alone or in pairs.
Distribution: Malaysia to SW Japan, GBR and Samoa.

Twinspot Cardinalfish
Archamia biguttata

One black spot each on the tail root and at the "temple".
Size: 10 cm
Biology: Inhabits lagoons and protected outreefs, 2–18 m. Usually in groups in front of shelters, such as crevices and caves.
Distribution: Sumatra to SW Japan, Palau, the Mariana Islands and Samoa.

Orangelined Cardinalfish
Archamia fucata

Black spot on tail base. A pair of blue stripes drawn through the eyes over the snout.
Size: 8 cm
Biology: Inhabits protected lagoons and outreefs, 2–60 m. Usually in relatively dense groups at places offering shelter, such as cavities or branch coral. Feeds at night on zooplankton.
Distribution: Red Sea and East Africa to SW Japan and Samoa.

Dusky-tailed Cardinalfish
Archamia macroptera

Numerous fine, orange-bronze-coloured vertical stripes that are ranged at a slight diagonal. Tail root is diffuse dark or with a clear black delimited band.
Size: 9 cm
Biology: Inhabits lagoons and outreefs, 2–15 m. In small, very dense groups in front of coral or rock during the day.
Distribution: Andaman Sea and Sumatra to Taiwan and Samoa.

Wolf Cardinalfish
Cheilodipterus artus

Eight horizontal stripes, yellow tail spot with black dot. Specimens also commonly have darker basic colouration and black or sooty tail stalk. Adults are probably capable of rapid colour changes.
Size: 12 cm
Biology: Inhabits protected bays, patch reefs and lagoons, 3–20 m. Usually in small loose groups in front of cavities and coral outcrops, frequently in front of branch coral. Feeds on small fish.
Distribution: East Africa to SW Japan and French Polynesia.

Dog-toothed Cardinalfish
Cheilodipterus isostigmus

Five black horizontal stripes Yellow patch with black dot at base of tail, slightly above the central stripe.
Size: 10 cm
Biology: In lagoons and protected outreefs, 3–40 m. Close to protection such as in front of caves, crevices and coral branches. Usually in groups.
Distribution: Borneo and South China Sea to the Philippines, Marshall Islands, Solomons and Vanuatu.

Tiger Cardinalfish
Cheilodipterus macrodon

Brown horizontal stripes. Pale white tail root for juveniles with a diffuse dark band.
Size: 25 cm
Biology: Inhabits protected, coral-rich lagoons and outreefs, 0.5–40 m. Alone, sometimes also in small groups, usually in caves or below overhangs, less often outside. Stays in same territory. Feeds predominantly on small fish.
Distribution: Red Sea, Arabian Gulf and East Africa to SW Japan and French Polynesia.

Five-lined Cardinalfish
Cheilodipterus quinquelineatus

Five black horizontal stripes. Yellow patch with black dot at base of tail, at same height as the central stripe.
Size: 12 cm
Biology: In lagoons and outreefs, 1–40 m. Usually in congregations in front of coral and rocks during the day. Also seeks protection between coral branches and the long barbs of Diadem sea urchins. Active during the day, feeds on crustaceans and small fish.
Distribution: Red Sea and East Africa to SW Japan, Micronesia, SE Australia and French Polynesia.

Sharpsnout Cardinalfish
Foa hyalina

Rose-opaque, with reddish brown stripes: on the head, radial around the eye, on the front of its body as vertical stripes.
Size: 5 cm
Biology: In lagoons and coastal reefs, 2–15 m. Frequently seeks protection between soft coral (see photo).
Distribution: Eastern Indonesia and PNG to the Philippines and Palau.

Banggai Cardinalfish
Pterapogon kauderni

Unmistakable with extended fins, black stripe pattern and white dots.
Size: 6 cm
Biology: Inhabits protected areas with sand, mud or rubble, occasionally also in algae growth, 1–15 m. In groups of a few to several dozen fish, always close to the seabed. Seeks protection between sea urchin barbs and anemones.
Distribution: Known from Bali, Banggai Island and North Sulawesi.

Pyjama Cardinalfish
Sphaeramia nematoptera

Red iris. Ochre head, dark band beneath the first dorsal fin, body rear is whitish with reddish-brown spots.
Size: 8 cm
Biology: In protected bays, lagoons and coastal reefs, 1–14 m. In groups during the day, often between branch coral (e.g. *Porites cylindrica* see photo). At night scavenges the seabed for food.
Distribution: Java and Bali to SW Japan, Palau and Pohnpei in Micronesia, GBR and Fiji.

Orbiculate Cardinalfish
Sphaeramia orbicularis

Silvery light grey. Narrow dark vertical stripe. Dark dots on the body rear.
Size: 10 cm
Biology: Inhabits protected bays and coastal reefs, 0.5–5 m. Close to shore in congregations at mangroves, rock, civilization waste and at wharves.
Distribution: East Africa to SW Japan, the Mariana Islands and Kirabati, south to New Caledonia.

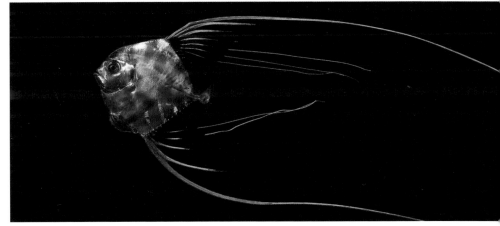

African Pompano
Alectis ciliaris

High-backed, with a laterally greatly compressed body. Steep head profile. Juveniles bear very long filaments on back and anal fin, which on sub-adults become shorter and absent on large adults.
Size: 110 cm
Biology: Pelagic lifestyle, adults sometimes in front of steep drops to 100 m depth. Juveniles more likely in surface water, appear to imitate jellyfish with their thread-like filaments.
Distribution: Circumtropical.

Jacks
Carangidae

Jacks are active day and night and continually in movement since their swim bladder is rudimentary or even totally absent. Their narrow tail stalk with a strongly forked caudal fin makes them tenacious, high-speed hunters. Primarily hunting fish in small groups, their impressive speed on the hunt can frequently be experienced along reefs. In large, semi-stationary schools, the bigeye mackerel assemble at some reefs, when the individual fish move slowly in a tight circular orbit. Jacks are often confused with genuine mackerels (*Scombridae*), to which the tuna belongs. Keeled scale plates are conspicuous for many species. Bony side keels strengthen the tail root and often also extend over the rear end of the lateral line.

Orange-spotted Trevally
Carangoides bajad

Silver grey to pale blueish, always with yellow-orange spots. Can very rapidly change basic colouration brighter or darker.
Size: 55 cm
Biology: Common denizens of lagoons and outreefs, 2–70 m. Alone or in small groups. Always in the vicinity, often in fact directly at the reef.
Distribution: Red Sea, Arabian Gulf, Seychelles to SW Japan, Palau and Solomons.

A bright yellow variant is common depending on the area. They can be seen moving through the reef both individually as well as in small groups.

Shrimp Scad
Alepes djedaba

Prominent black "ear spot" at upper edge of gill cover.
Size: 40 cm
Biology: Adults close to reefs, often forming large schools. Eats shrimps and other small and planktonic crustaceans, also crustacean larvae and small fish.
Distribution: Red Sea and East Africa to Japan and New Caledonia. Has colonised the Mediterranean via the Suez Canal.

Rainbow Runner
Elegatis bipinnulatus

A pair of pale blue horizontal stripes along the side.
Size: 120 cm
Biology: Pelagic species, however occasionally comes in schools or small groups to outer reef slopes, less often also into deep lagoons, 1–150 m. Agile and fast, but relatively shy. Feeds on small fish, in addition to larger plankton crustaceans.
Distribution: Circumtropical.

Giant Trevally
Caranx ignobilis

Steep brow, small black spot at the pectoral fin base. Often with several short light back stripes.
Size: 170 cm
Biology: Usually along outer reef slopes, also in lagoons, 5-80 m. Usually alone, occasionally also in small groups. Shy and a relatively rare species in the majority of regions. Feeds on fish and crustaceans.
Distribution: Red Sea, East Africa to SW Japan, Panama and French Polynesia.

Bluefin Trevally
Caranx melampygus

Greenish-blueish. Numerous speckles. Blue fins.
Size: 100 cm
Biology: In lagoons and outreefs, 1–190 m. Usually patrols in small groups at outer reef slopes, occasionally also in larger groups. Hunts reef fish predominantly. Accompanied occasionally by other fish, e.g. goatfish, in order to approach close to their prey.
Distribution: Red Sea, East Africa to SW Japan, Panama and French Polynesia.

Bigeye Trevally
Caranx sexfasciatus

Black spot above on the gill lid. White tips on back side and anal fin.
Size: 90 cm
Biology: At clear outreefs, 2–90 m. Often swimming in spirals in large, semi-stationary schools during the day. Hunts fish at night alone. During the mating ritual, it swims in pairs close together in open water, when the male becomes almost black.
Distribution: Red Sea, East Africa to SW Japan and Central America.

Golden Trevally
Gnathonodon speciosus

Sub-adult silvery with dark vertical stripes. Adults silvery with a few black patches.
Size: 120 cm
Biology: In deep lagoons and outreefs, 1–50 m. They feed on invertebrates such as crustaceans, which they grub from sandy grounds, they also feed on fish.
Distribution: Red Sea and East Africa to SW Japan and Panama.

Juveniles are metallic-yellow with black vertical stripes. For their own protection against predators in open water, sub-adults sometimes also accompany large fish, such as sharks and groupers, also turtles and dugongs. Very small juveniles also often make use of jellyfish.

Pilotfish
Naucrates ductor

Silvery-white with broad black vertical stripes.
Size: 70 cm
Biology: Pelagic lifestyle, accompanies high seas sharks, skates, occasionally also turtles. Occasionally in large numbers of several dozen fish when accompanying sharks. Juvenile sometimes in the protection of jellyfish or flotsam.
Distribution: Circumtropical.

Yellowstripe Scad
Selaroides leptolepis

Silvery with a pale or vivid yellow horizontal stripe from head to tail. Dark spot at the back edge of the gill lid. Narrow, strip-like row of bone keels from the middle of the body to the tail.
Size: 20 cm
Biology: At reef edges, coastal reefs and bays, frequently to be seen near pier jettys, 3–20 m. Usually forms large, dense schools.
Distribution: Arabian Gulf to SW Japan, and North Australia.

Doublespotted Queenfish
Scomberoides lysan

Silvery with 6–8 dark, horizontal patches in a double row (not always completely discernible).
Size: 70 cm
Biology: In lagoons, bays and outreefs, 1–100 m. Adults usually alone, often near the surface along coastal and reefs, they feed on small fish and crustaceans. Juveniles bite scales from the skin of other swarming fish.
Distribution: Red Sea, Arabian Gulf, East Africa to SW Japan, SE Australia and Samoa.

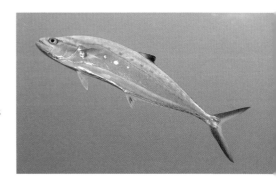

Greater Amberjack
Seriola dumerili

Dark stripes from the upper lip over eye to the back.
Size: 190 cm
Biology: In open water, often coastal vicinity, to more than 300 m. Rapid, untiring swimmers. Hunts small fish alone or in groups, also feeds on invertebrates. Juveniles are often in small schools, below flotsam or under the protection of jellyfish.
Distribution: Worldwide in tropical and temperate seas.

Black spotted Pompano (Small-spotted Dart)
Trachinotus bailloni

Usually with 2–5 dark patches on the lateral line.
Size: 54 cm
Biology: In coastal waters, near surface in lagoons and outreefs, often also in surf regions of sandy beaches. Alone or in small, loose groups. Feeds on small fish.
Distribution: Red Sea to S Japan, Marshall Islands, Line Islands and French Polynesia.

Snubnose Pompano
Trachinotus blochi

High-backed, relatively short body, blunt, rounded snout. Juvenile with extended anal and dorsal fin.
Size: 65 cm
Biology: In rock and coral reefs, deep bays and outreefs, 5–50 m. Swims alone or in schools. Juveniles often along the shore, shallow sand and muddy grounds. Feeds on snails and crustaceans.
Distribution: Red Sea, Arabian Gulf and East Africa to SW Japan, SE Australia and Samoa.

Snappers
Lutjanidae

Snappers are reef-dwelling fish that remain close to the seabed; usually inactive during the day. They typically float either alone or in small groups at protected places such as below overhangs, often also can be found out in the open in sizeable shoals close to the seabed. In many reefs, colossal stationary snapper shoals are some of the most impressive encounters. Fully grown specimens of some large species are confirmed loners. Snappers are nocturnal predators and feed predominantly on bottom-dwelling invertebrates, especially crustaceans, as well as cuttlefish, small fish and plankton. Large fish-eating species are often easily recognised by their fangs. Snappers form a large family with more than 100 species. They are distributed worldwide in the tropics and subtropics. Many are important and valuable edible fish. However some species in various regions can cause ciguatera fish poisoning and must not be eaten there.

Bluestripe Snapper
Lutjanus kasmira

Yellow with four pale blue horizontal stripes. Pale underside, dark shadow around eye.
Size: 35 cm
Biology: In lagoons and outreefs, 3–265 m. Alone, in groups and in large shoals (see photo left). Hunts alone at night for small fish and bottom-dwelling crustaceans.
Distribution: Red Sea and East Africa to SW Japan, Micronesia, SE Australia and French Polynesia.

Spanish Flag Snapper
Lutjanus carponotatus

Silvery with up to nine yellow or gold-brown horizontal stripes. Black spot at the pectoral fin base.
Size: 40 cm
Biology: Inhabits lagoons and outreefs, also in somewhat murky water, 3–35 m. Alone or sometimes in larger groups.
Distribution: India to S China, Solomons and GBR.

Yellow or Golden-lined Snapper
Lutjanus rufolineatus

Usually with a reddish shimmer, especially at the front of its body and snout. Often with black spot at the upper rear dorsal area.
Size: 25 cm
Biology: At outer reef slopes, 6–50 m. Usually in groups, somewhat higher above the seabed.
Distribution: The Maldives to SW Japan, N Australia, Samoa and Tonga.

Two-spot Red Snapper
Lutjanus bohar

Yellow eye. Dark leading edge of the pectoral fin, sometimes also black.

Size: 80 cm

Biology: In lagoons and outreefs, 3–70 m. Alone, in groups, occasionally also in large shoals (photo above), usually in open water in front of the reef. Hunts small fish. Regularly ciguatoxic in certain regions.

Distribution: Red Sea, S Oman and East Africa to SW Japan, Micronesia, GBR and French Polynesia.

Juveniles have two conspicuous white patches on their rear back. They remain close to the seabed and usually keep close to coral.

Twospot Snapper
Lutjanus biguttatus

Broad white horizontal band, bordered above and below by a brown-red horizontal stripe. Back brownish-grey with two or three white patches.
Size: 20 cm
Biology: In coral-rich lagoons and outreefs, 3–30 m. Nocturnal species. During the day usually in small to large congregations in the vicinity of coral formations.
Distribution: The Maldives to the Philippines, Solomons, Fiji and GBR.

Checkered Snapper
Lutjanus decussatus

Whitish with bronze-brown horizontal stripe, same colour short vertical stripes additionally across the back. Black spot on the tail root.
Size: 30 cm
Biology: In lagoons, coastal and outreefs, 2–35 m. Alone or in loose groups. Often also to be encountered above small sand-rubble areas between coral blocks.
Distribution: India and Andaman Sea to SW Japan and PNG.

Ehrenberg's Snapper
Lutjanus ehrenbergii

Five yellow, narrow, low-contrast horizontal stripes. Large black spot on the horizontal line in the rear body area.
Size: 35 cm
Biology: Prefers bays and coastal reefs, 3–20 m. Usually in schools, not shy. Also in rock reefs, and juveniles especially in estuaries and mangrove regions.
Distribution: Red Sea, Oman and East Africa to SW Japan, Caroline Islands, the Moluccas and GBR.

Blacktail Snapper
Lutjanus fulvus

Pale yellow. Blackish back and caudal fin. Ventral, anal and pectoral fins are yellow.
Size: 40 cm
Biology: Inhabits rock and coral reefs, in lagoons and semi-protected outreefs 1–75 m. Alone or in small loose groups. At night, feeds on fish and invertebrate bottom-dwellers.
Distribution: Red Sea and East Africa to SW Japan, Micronesia.

Humpback Snapper
Lutjanus gibbus

Reddish-grey with dark dorsal and caudal fins. High-backed in the neck area.

Size: 50 cm

Biology: In deep lagoons and protected outreefs, 1–150 m. Alone, but also frequently in large, semi-stationary and inactive schools. At night it hunts alone for crustaceans.

Distribution: Red Sea and East Africa to SW Japan, Micronesia, SE Australia and French Polynesia.

Humpback snappers regularly form very large, dense shoals in certain regions.

Bigeye Snapper
Lutjanus lutjanus

A relatively large eye. Yellow to tawny stripes behind eye along to the tail.

Size: 30 cm

Biology: In bays and semi-protected outer reef slopes, 5–90 m. During the day usually in large, dense shoals. Goes alone in search of food at night.

Distribution: Red Sea and East Africa to SW Japan, GBR and Solomons.

Russell's Snapper
Lutjanus russelli

Five bronze-coloured stripes, which slope upwards near the top of the back. Usually with a large black spot at the rear of the body.

Size: 35 cm

Biology: Inhabits rock and coral reefs, 3–80 m. Alone or in groups. Juveniles in mangroves and estuaries.

Distribution: Red Sea and East Africa to SW Japan, SE Australia and Fiji.

One-spot Snapper
Lutjanus monostigma

Red eye. All fins yellow. Sometimes with a black spot on the side at the rear.
Size: 55 cm
Biology: Prefers outreefs, also in lagoons, 5–60 m. Alone or in small loose groups. Often around wrecks and reef edges with caves and overhangs. Hunts fish, predominantly at night.
Distribution: Red Sea and East Africa to SW Japan, Micronesia, Line Islands and French Polynesia.

The eponymous spot on the back is not always as distinctive as it is in this specimen.

Black-banded Snapper
Lutjanus semicinctus

Dark vertical stripes along the upper body. Large black spot at the tail stalk, extends to the caudal fin.
Size: 35 cm
Biology: In lagoons and outreefs, 5–35 m.
Distribution: the Philippines to Caroline Islands, the Moluccas, GBR and Fiji.

Small-toothed Jobfish
Aphareus furca

Silvery with greenish or blueish shimmer. Large mouth, swallowtail, yellowish-brown stripes on the gill lid.
Size: 40 cm
Biology: In lagoons and outreefs, 2–120 m. Alone or in small groups. Feeds on fish and crustaceans.
Distribution: Red Sea and East Africa to SW Japan, Panama and Australia.

Midnight snapper
Macolour macularis

Colouration changes in the course of development. Adults with yellow-golden iris.

Size: 60 cm

Biology: Prefers the steep slopes of lagoons and out-reefs, 5–50 m. Alone or in small loose groups.

Distribution: The Maldives to SW Japan, Palau, Southern Mariana Islands, Solomons and New Caledonia.

Juveniles (below) have a high-contrast, characteristic black-white pattern and very long ventral fins. For sub-adults (middle), the black parts are brown and the white portion is narrower.

Black and White Snapper
Macolor niger

Adults are grey with dark fin.
Size: 65 cm
Biology: Prefers deep lagoons and steep outer reef slopes, 3–90 m. Juveniles alone, adults often in large inactive groups in front of steep drops. At night they feed alone on zooplankton.
Distribution: Red Sea and East Africa to SW Japan, Micronesia, Samoa and New Caledonia.

Juvenile (below) solid white and very high-contrast with black fin and black eye spot. Sub-adult (middle) with characteristic grey-white pattern.

Fusiliers
Caesionidae

Fusiliers are closely related to snappers, but live more in open water and feed on zooplankton. They therefore have a small mouth and a streamlined body with a deep forked caudal fin as an adaptation to the open water. In many regions, fusilier fish with their large schools form a large proportion of the sea's abundance. During the day, these skilled, untiring swimmers usually keep to the open water in large numbers. They live along steep outer reef slopes as well as in lagoons. At night, they hide in reef crevices, when they often take on a reddish colouration. They seek the reef during the day in order to be attended to at cleaner stations. Fusilier fish are protogynic sequential hermaphrodites and a valued edible fish.

Yellowtail Fusilier
Caesio cuning

Unusually high-backed for its genus. Greenish-blue with blue face markings. Yellow swallowtail.
Size: 35 cm
Biology: Prefers steep outreefs and patch reefs, 3–30 m. In schools in open water, sometimes immediately above the reef. Also in murky water. Can often be observed at cleaner stations. Not shy.
Distribution: Sri Lanka, Andaman Sea to SW Japan, Palau, GBR and Vanuatu.

Blue and Yellow Fusilier
Caesio teres

Yellow tail. The yellow covers about the rear two-thirds of the back. Remaining body is blue.
Size: 35 cm
Biology: Along steep outer reef slopes and patch reefs, 5–35 m. In open water in groups for feeding on plankton.
Distribution: East Africa to SW Japan, Micronesia, Line Islands, GBR and Samoa.

Scissortail Fusilier
Caesio caerulaurea

A yellow horizontal stripe from the head to the tail. Tail is forked, with a black stripe on both fins.
Size: 35 cm
Biology: At outer reef slopes and patch reefs, 3–30 m. In schools in open water for feeding on plankton.
Distribution: Red Sea (rarely) and East Africa to SW Japan, Micronesia, GBR and Samoa.

Lunar Fusilier
Caesio lunaris

Blue to greenish. Black tail tips. Juveniles have yellow tail with black tip.
Size: 35 cm
Biology: Usually in large schools along steep slopes, in front of patch reefs and drop-offs, 2–40 m. Frequently territorial, not shy. Also mixes with schools of other fusiliers.
Distribution: Red Sea and Arabian Gulf to Seychelles, SW Japan, Palau, GBR, Solomons and Fiji.

Red Sea Fusilier
Caesio suevica

Pale blue. White-black tail tips.
Size: 25 cm
Biology: Prefers outreefs, 1–25 m. In large schools in open water over reefs, feeds on zooplankton. Comes regularly to cleaner stations, whereby it frequently has its mouth extensively cleaned. Not shy.
Distribution: Red Sea.

Variable-lined Fusilier
Caesio varilineata

Yellow horizontal stripe. Black tail tips.
Size: 25 cm
Biology: In lagoons and outreefs, 1–25 m. Sometimes in very large schools in open water feeding on zooplankton above the reef. Often with other fusilier fish species. Not shy.
Distribution: Red Sea, Arabian Gulf, Seychelles to Sumatra.

Yellowback Fusilier
Caesio xanthonota

Yellow tail. The yellow on the back extends to the neck or even to the brow.
Size: 35 cm
Biology: At outer reef slopes and patch reefs, 3–35 m. In schools, feeds on zooplankton in the open water.
Distribution: East Africa to the Maldives, Andaman Sea and the Moluccas in Indonesia.

Marr's or Twinstripe Fusilier
Pterocaesio marri

Narrow yellow horizontal stripe along the lateral line and a second stripe higher on the back.
Size: 35 cm
Biology: In lagoons and outreefs, 5–30 m. Forms large shoals along reef slopes during the day.
Distribution: East Africa to SW Japan, Micronesia and French Polynesia.

Dark-banded or Bluestreak Fusilier
Pterocasio tile

Silvery-blue with dark scale stripes on the back and a dark horizontal stripe.
Size: 25 cm
Biology: In clear lagoons and outreefs, 5–40 m. Feeds on zooplankton. The colouration of the lower body half switches to reddish-brown whenever it comes into the reef, e.g. in order to seek protection or let itself be cleaned.
Distribution: East Africa to S Japan, New Caledonia, Rapa and French Polynesia.

During the day, Dark-banded Fusiliers often form huge schools over or near a reef.

Sea Chub
Kyphosidae

Blue Sea Chub or Topsail Drummer
Kyphosus cinerascens

Second dorsal and anal fin high.
Size: 45 cm
Biology: At outreefs, 1–25 m. Alone or in small groups, often below landing stages, at exposed surf-swept coastal reefs. Feeds on drifting and sprouting algae.
Distribution: Red Sea, East Africa to SW Japan, Hawaii, SE Australia and French Polynesia.

Brassy Chub or Lowfin Drummer
Kyphosus vaigensis

Second dorsal and anal fin low. Brass-coloured stripes. Can rapidly switch colouration to a pattern with white patches.
Size: 60 cm
Biology: In lagoons and outreefs, also at rocky coasts, 1-25 m. Usually in small groups along current-rich reef slopes. Predominantly feeds on drifting and sprouting algae.
Distribution: Red Sea, Oman and East Africa to SW Japan, Hawaii and French Polynesia.

Moonfish
Monodactylidae

Silver Moonfish or Diamondfish
Monodactylus argenteus

Back, tail, often also parts of the anal fin yellowish.
Size: 22 cm
Biology: Prefers lagoons, river deltas and protected, turbid coastal reefs, 0–15 m. Not shy. Usually in schools. Most common species of the family sighted by divers.
Distribution: Red Sea, Oman and East Africa to SW Japan, Samoa and New Caledonia.

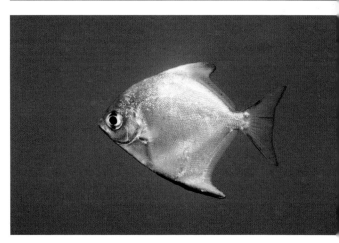

Sweetlips
Haemulidae

During the day, sweetlips rest quietly in the water, alone, in small groups, sometimes also in large shoals. They are usually not shy and some species are attractively coloured. Some like to be in open, also exposed places, some, such as the Oriental Sweetlips, often stand at cleaner stations, others prefer somewhat protected areas below table corals or overhangs. Juveniles of the *Plectorhinchus* species in particular often show markedly deviating colouration, and in contrast to the quiet way of adults, some swim alone and in an agitated manner. At night, sweetlips go alone in search of food. They feed on invertebrate bottom-dwellers, also worms and small fish, and some feed on zooplankton in open water.

Oriental Sweetlips
Plectorhinchus vittatus

Dark horizontal stripes, fin yellow. Back, anal and caudal fin with dark patches.
Size: 75 cm
Biology: Prefers clear, coral-rich lagoons and outreefs, 2–25 m. Alone, they also often rest in groups at reef protrusions and large coral heads.
Distribution: East Africa to SW Japan, Mariana Islands and Caroline Islands in Micronesia, Australia and Samoa.

Yellow-banded Sweetlips
Plectorhinchus lineatus

Back with diagonal black stripes. Lips and fin yellow, back and caudal fin with black patches.
Size: 50 cm
Biology: Inhabits coral-rich regions of lagoons and outreefs, 2–35 m. Alone or in small groups. Goes alone at night in search of food.
Distribution: Indonesia roughly from Bali to SW Japan, the Philippines, Guam, GBR and New Caledonia.

Lemonfish or Gold-spotted Sweetlips
Plectorhinchus flavomaculatus

Adults are grey. Body with numerous orange-yellow spots. Head with yellow patches and stripes.
Size: 60 cm
Biology: Inhabits deep lagoons, protected coastal reefs and bays, 3–35 m. Usually alone, occasionally in small groups. Uncommon. Feeds on small fish and crustaceans.
Distribution: Red Sea (not in the northern part), East Africa and Oman to SW Japan, PNG and SE Australia.

Two sub-adult specimens: cream-coloured with large orange spots, also on the head (below) and grey-blue with gradually smaller spots and the beginnings of stripes on the head (middle).

Many-spotted Sweetlips
Plectorhinchus chaetodonoides

Adults creamy-coloured with numerous dark spots.
Size: 70 cm
Biology: Inhabits coral-rich lagoons and outreefs, 1–35 m. Usually alone, during the day frequently at protected locations, can be seen in front of coral blocks or below overhangs. Juveniles always swim close to a seabed with plenty of hiding places.
Distribution: the Maldives to SW Japan, Fiji and New Caledonia.

Juvenile (below): Bright reddish brown with a few large white, dark-edged patches. Conspicuous by their extremely restless and lurching mode of swimming. Older juveniles (middle) are grey-brown with large white patches and are already developing the dark dots of the adults.

Giant Sweetlips
Plectorhinchus albovittatus

Ventral fins are black, sometimes also anal and pectoral fins. Back and caudal fin with black edges.
Size: 100 cm
Biology: Inhabits deep lagoons and outreefs, 2–50 m. Largest species among the sweetlips. Can usually be seen during the day above rocky areas or rubble-sand ground, swimming leisurely or floating quietly suspended at one spot.
Distribution: Red Sea and East Africa to SW Japan, Fiji and New Caledonia.

Goldlined Sweetlips
Plectorhinchus chrysotaenia

Thin yellow horizontal stripes. All fins are luminous yellow.
Size: 50 cm
Biology: Inhabits coral-rich regions in lagoons and protected outreefs, 5–60 m. Alone, during the day often in larger groups which disperse in the nocturnal search for food.
Distribution: Bali to SW Japan, GBR and New Caledonia.

Blackspotted Sweetlips
Plectorhinchus gaterinus

Fins and upper lip yellow. Numerous black spots, also on the back and caudal fin.
Size: 45 cm
Biology: Inhabits lagoons, bays and protected outreefs, 3–35 m. Frequently rests during the day in groups at protected places or exposed at protrusions.
Distribution: Red Sea, East Africa, Mauritius and Arabian Gulf.

Largespot Sweetlips
Plectorhinchus macrospilus

Whitish with large black patches, usually merged to vertical stripes on the snout. Tail, anal and rear part of the dorsal fins are pale yellow.
Size: 30 cm
Biology: A little-known species that was only scientifically described in 2000. Quite shy and uncommon, evidently keeps to the vicinity of crevices or overhangs.
Distribution: Probably endemic in Thailand, Andaman Sea.

Ribbon Sweetlips
Plectorhinchus polytaenia

Pale blue, black-edged horizontal stripes on yellow basic colouration, all fins are yellow.
Size: 40 cm
Biology: Inhabits lagoons and outreefs, 3–40 m. Often seen in coral-rich regions, readily rests in front of coral blocks or other semi-protected places during the day. Feeds at night on invertebrate bottom-dwellers.
Distribution: Indonesia about from Bali to NW Australia, the Philippines and PNG.

Sub-adults still have a darker basic colouration and fewer stripes. Also the tail is still striped. This specimen is just beginning to change its colour. The light stripes are already blueish. They are totally white on juveniles, on an almost totally black basic colour.

Painted or Silver Sweetlips
Diagramma pictum

Adults silvery light grey. Sub-adult with yellowish brown stripes and patches, juveniles with black-white stripe pattern.

Size: 90 cm

Biology: In lagoons and outreefs, usually above mixed zones with hard rubble and soft ground, e.g. at patch reefs with sandy areas, 3–40 m. During the day alone or in small groups, goes in search of food at night alone, feeds on invertebrate bottom-dwellers.

Distribution: Red Sea and East Africa to SW Japan, PNG and New Caledonia. Occurs in several regional subspecies.

Juvenile (below): With black-white horizontal stripe pattern. Sub-adult (middle) cream-yellow, the stripes beginning to dissolve in patches.

Emperor Fish
Lethrinidae

Many species of this family are silver-grey, with no obvious pattern. Emperor fish also have widely varying body shapes. Some, for example, have a steep brow, others a pointed head. Smaller species often live in groups, larger ones are usually loners. For many, the juveniles and adults bear different colouration. Emperor fish predominantly feed on bottom-dwelling invertebrates such as crustaceans and worms, also small fish and sometimes plankton. The majority feed at night, some also during the day, many are even active both day and night. All species are sequential hermaphrodites: they sexually mature first as females and later in life turn into males.

Striped Large-eye Bream
Gnathodentex aureolineatus

Silver-grey with a luminous yellow spot at the rear base of the dorsal fin.
Size: 30 cm
Biology: Inhabits lagoons and outer reef slopes, 2–20 m. Often floats during the day in stationary congregations in the vicinity of coral formations. Disperses at night in search of food.
Distribution: East Africa to SW Japan, Micronesia, Line Islands, SE Australia and French Polynesia.

Snubnose Emperor
Lethrinus borbonicus

Continuously silvery-green.
Size: 40 cm
Biology: Often above small sand surfaces in lagoons and protected outreefs, 1–40 m. Not shy. Feeds on hard-shelled invertebrates which it seeks at night in the reef at low depth.
Distribution: Red Sea and Arabian Gulf to Mozambique and Mauritius.

Yellowfin Emperor
Lethrinus erytracanthus

Blueish head, fins yellow to dingy yellowish.
Size: 70 cm
Biology: In deep lagoons and outer reef slopes, 10– 120 m. One of the largest species of its genus. Loner. Shy and uncommon. It feeds on sea urchins, starfish, mussels and shelled snails.
Distribution: East Africa to SW Japan, Micronesia, GBR and French Polynesia.

Sky Emperor
Lethrinus mahsena

Pale grey-blue head without markings. several verical bands across the back.
Size: 65 cm
Biology: In bays and outreefs, 3–100 m. Loner, feeds on echinoderms, among them also long-spiked sea urchins, and fish and crustaceans.
Distribution: Red Sea and Gulf of Oman to Mauritius and Sri Lanka.

Yellowlip Emperor
Lethrinus xanthochilus

Pale colouration. Yellow upper lip, yellow to red spot on the base of pectoral fins.
Size: 60 cm
Biology: In lagoons and outreefs. 3–50 m. Usually above mixed sand, rubble and coral zones near a reef. Alone or in small groups. Feeds on hard-shelled invertebrates and fish.
Distribution: Red Sea and East Africa to SW Japan, Micronesia and French Polynesia.

Humpnose Big-eye Bream
Montaxis grandoculis

Silvery light-grey. Often with metallic yellowish spots on the head.
Size: 60 cm
Biology: In lagoons and outreefs, 1–100 m. Often rests during the day alone or in loose groups along the reef edge. Goes alone in search of food at night, feeds on hard-shelled invertebrates.
Distribution: Red Sea and East Africa to SW Japan, Micronesia, Hawaii and French Polynesia.

Juvenile with three blackish saddle spots and bright lower body half. Middle: older juvenile.

Two-lined or Bridled Monocle Bream
Scolopsis bilineatus

Adult (top): White, curved band from the snout to the rear back. Juvenile (above): Upper body half striped black-yellow.
Size: 25 cm
Biology: In lagoons and protected outreefs, at sand and rubble ground of the reef, 1–25 m. Feeds on small invertebrates and fish.
Distribution: Laccadive Islands and the Maldives to SW Japan, West Micronesia, New Caledonia and Fiji.

False Snappers
Nemipteridae

False snappers are interval swimmers: they swim a short distance, then glide motionlessly above the seabed and make a grab for small bottom-dwelling invertebrates, sometimes also fish, then once again swim a short distance searching the seabed for nutriment, once again remaining still for a time. In some places they are a valued edible fish.

Bald-spot or Rainbow Monocle Bream
Scolopsis temporalis

Two blue horizontal stripes on the snout. Black spot above the rear eye rim. Very similar to S. *monogramma* (from Andaman Sea eastwards).
Size: 40 cm
Biology: Above sand surfaces of lagoons and coastal reefs, 5–35 m. Usually swims alone, also in small groups.
Distribution: Sulawesi and the Moluccas, to PNG, Solomons and Fiji.

Peters' or Pale Monocle Bream
Scolopsis affinis

Beige to pale brown-grey. Yellowish tail. Juvenile with dark brown horizontal stripe.
Size: 30 cm
Biology: Above sand and rubble in lagoons and coastal reefs, 3–35 m. Swims alone or in small loose groups.
Distribution: Andaman Sea to SW Japan, Palau, Solomons and GBR.

Saw-jawed or Whitestreak Monocle Bream
Scolopsis ciliatus

White horizontal stripe beneath the base of dorsal fin. Some scale rows on the side with yellow spots.
Size: 20 cm
Biology: Above sand and mud beds of lagoons and protected coastal reefs, 2–20 m. Swims alone or in small loose groups.
Distribution: Andaman Sea to SW Japan, Palau, Yap, Solomons and Vanuatu.

Pearly Monocle Bream
Scolopsis margaritifer

Back with dark-edged scales. Half of lower side with rows of yellow dots.
Size: 25 cm
Biology: Inhabits sand and rubble beds of lagoons and coastal reefs, 2–25 m. Feeds on invertebrates bottom-dwellers, such as bristle-worms, molluscs, also small fish.
Distribution: Sumatra to Taiwan, Palau, Vanuatu and North Australia.

Small Toothed or Double Whiptail (Juv.)
Pentapodus emeryii

Blue with two yellow horizontal stripes, the upper narrower than the lower. Adults with two long caudal fin filaments.
Size: 30 cm
Biology: Inhabits coastal reefs, 3–35 m. Alone or in small groups. Shy species.
Distribution: NW Australia to East Indonesia to the Philippines.

Arabian Monocle Bream
Scolopsis ghanam (pale grey Var.)

Whitish with dark back stripe.
Size: 18 cm
Biology: Usually above sandy areas of bays and protected outreefs, 1–20 m. Common species, not shy. Feeds on invertebrate bottom-dwellers. Often swims next to goat-fish in order to grab exposed prey.
Distribution: Red Sea, East Africa to Madagascar, Arabian Gulf to Andaman Sea.

Oblique Barred or Pearl-streaked Monocle Bream
Scolopsis xenochrous

Short blue, dark-edged diagonal stripes above the pectoral fin. Blue slash at edge of the upper eye.
Size: 25 cm
Biology: Inhabits lagoons, coastal reefs and outreefs far from the coast, 5–50 m. Alone or in loose groups above sand and rubble. Feeds on invertebrate bottom-dwellers.
Distribution: The Maldives and Andaman Sea to Taiwan, Australia and Solomons.

Whitecheek Monocle Bream
Scolopsis vosmeri

Reddish-brown with white band at the back of the head. Tail yellow or whitish.
Size: 25 cm
Biology: Inhabits sand, rubble and mudflats of coastal reefs, 2–40 m. Swims alone or in pairs. Feeds on invertebrate bottom-dwellers.
Distribution: Red Sea, Arabian Gulf and East Africa to SW Japan, GBR and PNG.

Three-striped Whiptail
Pentapodus trivittatus

Grey with white abdomen and chin. A dark stripe is drawn from the rear lower eye to the rear gill lid edge. Variant is uniformly pale grey with yellow spot at the body rear.
Size: 25 cm
Biology: Inhabits lagoons and protected coastal reefs, 3–30 m.
Distribution: Malaysia to the Philippines, Caroline Islands and Solomons.

Seabream
Sparidae

Seabream are represented in the Indo-Pacific by only a few species and are relatively shy, so that approaching them is difficult. Much richer in species and individuals in the Atlantic, Caribbean and Mediterranean Seas, where they also play an important ecological role..

Three-striped Whiptail
Acanthopagrus bifasciatus

Two black vertical stripes on the head, the back, tail and pectoral fins are yellow.
Size: 50 cm
Biology: Inhabits reef slopes, deep lagoons, bays and outreefs, 1–20 m. Watchful and shy species, but in some places they are regularly seen. At high tide at reef tops, also prefers being at and in front of outreefs with heavy seas and surf. Swims alone or in small groups.
Distribution: Red Sea, Arabian Gulf, East Africa and Mauritius.

Mullets
Mugilidae

This family is represented worldwide in tropical and subtropical seas, some also in brackish and fresh water. Travels in loose groups, grazes on fine algae and detritus from the seabed. Only a few species can be observed on coral reefs, and these only rarely.

Fringelip Mullet
Crenimugil crenilabis

Black spot on base of the pectoral fins.
Size: 55 cm
Biology: In lagoons, estuaries, harbours, 0.5–15 m. Migrates close to shore along the coast in small schools, often also at coral reef slopes. Grazes on algae and also feeds on various small invertebrates.
Distribution: Red Sea and East Africa to SW Japan, Line Islands, SE Australia and French Polynesia.

Hatchetfish
Pempheridae

Hatchetfish are generally nocturnal and hunt zooplankton in the open water. They usually spend the day at protected locations, especially in caves, crevices, below overhangs, in the protection of large coral blocks and also in wrecks. The brownish hatchetfish are laterally greatly compressed, high-backed and have the typical "hatchet belly". The sweepers, however, have an elongated body.

Glassy or Golden Sweeper
Parapriacanthus ransonneti

Head yellowish green. Body translucent, light brown grey.
Size: 10 cm
Biology: In lagoons, bays and protected areas of outreefs, 0.5–40 m. Not shy. During the day in dense, stationary shoals, usually below overhangs, in cavities or crevices. At night alone, feeds on zooplankton above the reef.
Distribution: Red Sea to South Africa, Gulf of Oman, SW Japan, Marshall-Islands, New Caledonia, Fiji.

Copper Sweeper
Pempheris oualensis

Front edge and tip of the dorsal fin is black. Base of the pectoral fins with black spot.
Size: 22 cm
Biology: In clear lagoons and at outreefs, 2–35 m. In schools at protected places such as overhangs and caves during the day. Disperses for nocturnal search for food in the form of plankton and small bottom-dwelling animals.
Distribution: Red Sea to SW Japan, Micronesia and French Polynesia.

Silver sweeper
Pempheris schwenkii

Front edge of the dorsal fin is dark. Body is silvery to copper colour. Especially with the latter colouration, it is difficult to distinguish from several very similar species, with which it is additionally often associated.
Size: 15 cm
Biology: In rock and coral reefs, lagoons and outreefs, 1–40 m. During the day in groups in protected areas.
Distribution: Red Sea and East Africa to Indonesia, Fiji and GBR.

Vanikoro Sweeper
Pempheris vanicolensis

Tip of the dorsal fin is dark. Tail and anal fins with black fringe.
Size: 20 cm
Biology: In lagoons, bays and protected outreefs, 2–40 m. During the day, in groups usually below overhangs and in caves. At night, goes alone in search of food, feeds on plankton and small fish.
Distribution: Red Sea and Gulf of Oman to Mozambique, the Philippines and Samoa.

Goatfish
Mullidae

Typically, goatfish bear two long barbels on the chin. These can be retracted into a throat pit below the chin, for instance when swimming, and are then barely visible. The barbels are organs of touch, especially rich in taste buds and help the fish to detect food. In sandy soil, goatfish rummage with their chin barbels thrust out, looking for crustaceans, molluscs, worms, brittle starfish and fish, and often also grub their prey deep out of the seabed. Often accompanied by other fish such as snappers or wrasse, that hope to capture animals startled by the digging activity. Goatfish can be active day and night. They sometimes move alone, frequently however gregariously in small groups.

Goldsaddle Goatfish
Parupeneus cyclostomus

Purple blue, greenish and blue-grey. Tail stalk often with yellowish saddle. A monochrome yellow variant is not uncommon.
Size: 50 cm
Biology: In lagoons and outreefs, Above coral, sand and rubble, 2–95 m. Moves alone or in small groups. Feeds primarily on small fish, can drive these from their hiding-place with its barbels.
Distribution: Red Sea, East Africa to SW Japan and Pitcairn.

Red Sea Goatfish
Parupeneus forsskali

Black horizontal stripe and black spot on the tail stalk.
Size: 28 cm
Biology: In lagoons and protected outreefs, 1–30 m.
Common. Not shy. Searches in sand and rubble for
small invertebrates during the day. Is often accompa-
nied by other fish.
Distribution: Red Sea and Gulf of Aden.

Manybar Goatfish
Parupeneus multifasciatus

Colouration highly variable from light grey-brownish to
dark scarlet. Short, dark stripe at the rear of the eye and
two dark patches at the body rear.
Size: 30 cm
Biology: In lagoons and outreefs, above coral, sand and
rubble, 3–140 m. Searches for food alone or in small
loose groups during the day.
Distribution: Cocos Keeling and Christmas Islands to S
Japan, Hawaii and Pitcairn.

Sidespot Goatfish
Parupeneus pleurostigma

Light grey with purple shimmer to yellowish or light
reddish. A large black spot at the side, backed by a white
area. Photo: Night colouration. Tail stalk usually with
row of blueish dots.
Size: 33 cm
Biology: Above sand and rubble near reefs, 3–40 m.
Also above rock and seagrass fields. Usually alone.
Distribution: East Africa to SW Japan, Hawaii and
French Polynesia.

Long-barbel Goatfish
Parupeneus macronema

Base of the second dorsal fin with black stripes. Black
stripe from the eye to rear of body, black spot on tail stalk.
Size: 30 cm
Biology: Inhabits lagoons, bays and outreefs, 3–35
m. Common and not shy. In vicinity of coral. It ranges
alone or in small groups above sand and rubble areas in
search of invertebrate bottom-dwellers.
Distribution: Red Sea and East Africa to the Philippines
and New Guinea.

Yellowfin Goatfish
Mulloidichthys vanicolensis

Yellow back, yellow horizontal stripe from the eye to tail base, yellow fin.
Size: 38 cm
Biology: In lagoons and outreefs, 1–50 m. Common and not shy. Often floats during the day in large congregations at reef slopes and large coral formations. At night goes alone in search of food, feeds on invertebrate bottom-dwellers.
Distribution: Red Sea and East Africa to S Japan, Hawaii and Easter Islands.

Thicklip or Doublebar Goatfish
Parupeneus crassilabris

Two dark saddle spots, the first extends downwards not beyond the pectoral fin. Small dark spot at the eye. Purple variant is less high-contrast.
Size: 35 cm
Biology: In lagoons and outreefs, 2–80 m. Alone, not shy. Rests motionlessly on coral or stony ground. Feeds on invertebrate bottom-dwellers.
Distribution: Eastern Indian Ocean to SW Japan, the Philippines, New Caledonia and Tonga.

Freckled Goatfish
Upeneus tragula

Reddish-brown, often has broken horizontal stripe. Caudal fins with dark stripes.
Size: 30 cm
Biology: On sandy to muddy grounds, often in turbid lagoons, bays and protected outreefs, 1–20 m. Ranges alone or in small groups in search of bottom-dwelling invertebrates.
Distribution: Red Sea and East Africa to S Japan, Vanuatu and New Caledonia.

Freckled goatfish can rapidly change their colouration from pale beige (above) to vivid red (bottom).

Melon Butterflyfish
Chaetodon trifasciatus

Base of the caudal fin is orange. On the very similar *C. lunulatus,* it is pale blueish.
Size: 15 cm
Biology: In coral-rich lagoons and protected outreefs, 2–20 m. Roams a home territory in pairs which it aggressively defends. Feeds exclusively on coral polyps, especially the Pocillopora coral.
Distribution: East Africa to Gulf of Bengal and Bali.

Butterflyfish
Chaetodontidae

Butterflyfish (worldwide there are about 120 species) are uniformly active during the day. Their high, greatly compressed laterally, almost disc-shaped body is ideal for skilful manoeuvering between the coral. Their night is spent hidden between coral branches and crevices of the reef. Many live in pairs, some for life, other less permanently; they often also swim alone. Some species form large congregations or shoals, probably as protection from predators, where they feed on zooplankton in open water in front of the reef. The majority however feed on bottom-dwelling reef inhabitants. Some are specialists and predominantly pluck polyps from stone or soft coral, others with a larger prey spectrum feed on small crabs, worms, fish eggs and blanket-weed algae. Their social behaviour includes the occupation of territories and their defence against fellow species. This can be agressive, however is usually limited to ritualized behavioural patterns. Many juveniles, also some adults, have eye spots in the rear body area. The genuine eye is also frequently camouflaged by dark stripes. Both are probably to confuse predators.

Oval or Redfin Butterflyfish
Chaetodon lunulatus

Orange-red anal fin, the base of the caudal fin is whitish to light blueish. Very similar: *C. trifasciatus* with an orange caudal fin base.
Size: 15 cm
Biology: Prefers coral-rich coastal reefs and lagoons, 2–20 m. Swims in pairs through a home territory, feeds exclusively on coral polyps.
Distribution: NW Australia to S Japan, Hawaii and French Polynesia.

Philippine or Panda Butterflyfish
Chaetodon adiergastos

Dark grey diagonal stripes, oval, black "Panda" spot around eye, small black brow spot.
Size: 16 cm
Biology: Apart from coral-rich out-reefs, in some places it also inhabits somewhat turbid, coral-poor coastal reefs, 3–25 m. Usually in pairs, occasionally also in groups.
Distribution: Malaysia and Java to the Philippines, SW Japan and NW Australia.

Vagabond Butterflyfish
Chaetodon vagabundus

Black vertical stripes at the rear body edge stopping short of the rear dorsal fin.
Size: 23 cm
Biology: In coastal and outreefs, also in turbid water with silted areas, 1–30 m. Frequently in pairs. Feeds on bristleworms, anemone, coral polyps and algae.
Distribution: East Africa to SW Japan, Micronesia and French Polynesia.

Indian Vagabond Butterflyfish
Chaetodon decussatus

Black stripe covers rear dorsal fin.
Size: 20 cm
Biology: In coral-rich reefs as well as in silted, turbid areas with rubble and rock, 1–30 m. Juveniles alone, adults usually in pairs and with a home territory. Predominantly feeds on coral polyps and algae.
Distribution: Oman, the Maldives, Sri Lanka and Andaman Sea to Bali, Timor and NW Australia.

Melon or Chevroned Butterflyfish
Chaetodon trifacialis

Angular stripes. Tail black with yellow edge.
Size: 18 cm
Biology: In coral-rich reefs, 2–30 m. Alone or in pairs. Very territorial, defends territory from members of the same species and other coral-feeding butterfly fish. Often at horn or table corals, feeds on their polyps and mucus.
Distribution: Red Sea to South Africa, S Japan, Hawaii and French Polynesia.

Threadfin Butterflyfish
Chaetodon auriga

Body rear is yellow, dorsal fin with filaments. In Red Sea without black spot on the dorsal fin.
Size: 23 cm
Biology: Above coral, rubble or algae grounds in coral reefs, 1–40 m. Common, not shy. Alone, in pairs or in small groups. Plucks off small pieces from anemone, coral polyps, bristleworms and algae.
Distribution: Red Sea, East Africa to S Japan, Hawaii and French Polynesia.

Blackback Butterflyfish
Chaetodon melannotus

Back and tail root are black. Similar:
C. ocellicaudus, with isolated tail
base spot.
Size: 15 cm
Biology: In coral-rich reefs,
lagoons, bays and outreefs, 1–20 m.
Swims alone or in pairs through a
large home territory. Feeds on
polyps of stony and soft coral.
Distribution: Red Sea and East
Africa to S Japan, Micronesia and
Samoa.

Spot-tail Butterflyfish
Chaetodon ocellicaudus

Distinct singular black spot on the
tail stalk. Similar: *C. melannotus*,
black spot however merges with
black back area.
Size: 14 cm
Biology: In coral-rich lagoons, more
frequently, however, at outer reef
slopes and in channels, 3–50 m.
Usually ranges in pairs, feeds on
stony and soft coral polyps.
Distribution: Malaysia to the Philippines, Palau, New Guinea and GBR.

Peppered or Spotted Butterflyfish
Chaetodon guttatissimus

Pale cream coloured with numerous dark spots, dorsal fin with
yellow edge.
Size: 12 cm
Biology: Inhabits lagoons and
outreefs, 3–30 m. Alone or in pairs,
feeds predominantly on coral
polyps, bristleworms and algae.
Distribution: East Africa to the
Maldives, Christmas Islands, Bali
and Andaman Sea.

Speckled Butterflyfish
Chaetodon citrinellus

Anal fin with black edge fringe.
Size: 13 cm
Biology: In coastal and outreefs, often in low depths and in open areas with scattered coral growth, 1–30 m. Usually in pairs, feeds on coral polyps, small invertebrates and algae.
Distribution: East Africa to S Japan, Hawaii, Marquesa Islands/French Polynesia.

Crochet or Yellow-rimmed Butterflyfish
Chaetodon guentheri

Numerous dark dots arranged in rows. Yellow area at the rear of body to top of the back.
Size: 14 cm
Biology: Prefers coral-rich outer reef slopes, also in rock reefs, 3 to more than 40 m.
Distribution: Bali to SW Japan, New Guinea and GBR.

Spotband Butterflyfish
Chaetodon punctatofasciatus

Dark vertical stripes on upper body half, numerous dark dots in the area of the tail base.
Size: 12 cm
Biology: Prefers clear, coral-rich lagoons and outreefs, 1–40 m. Usually in pairs. Feeds on blanket-weed algae, coral polyps and bottom-dwelling invertebrates.
Distribution: Christmas Islands and Rowley Shoals to SW Japan, Line Islands and GBR.

White collar Butterflyfish
Chaetodon collare

Dark grey-olive-green, white "collar", adults with red tail base.
Size: 16 cm
Biology: At coastal and coral-rich outreefs, 2–20 m. In pairs or in small groups. Not shy. Feeds on coral polyps and bristleworms, occasionally also algae.
Distribution: Gulf of Aden, Gulf of Oman and the Maldives to East Indonesia and the Philippines.

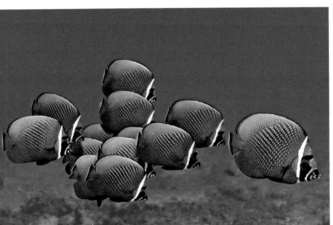

During the day, collar butterflyfish frequently float in highly conspicuous small to larger stationary groups in front of coral heads.

Scrawled or Meyer's Butterflyfish
Chaetodon meyersi

Blueish-white with black arched stripes.
Size: 18 cm
Biology: Inhabits coral-rich lagoons and outreefs, 2–25 m. Adults usually swim in pairs through their home territory. Juveniles are usually alone and in horn corals. They feed exclusively on coral polyps.
Distribution: East Africa, the Maldives, Gulf of Bengal to the Philippines, SW Japan, Line Islands and GBR.

Ornate Butterflyfish
Chaetodon ornatissimus

Usually six orange diagonal stripes, black stripes in caudal fin.
Size: 20 cm
Biology: Frequently at outer reef slopes, less often also in lagoons, 1–40 m. Juveniles can be seen alone and usually between branch coral. Adults patrol in pairs through their home territory. Feeds on coral polyps and mucus.
Distribution: the Maldives to SW Japan, Hawaii and French Polynesia.

Andaman Butterflyfish
Chaetodon andamanensis

Yellow with black eye stripes, black spot on the tail root.
Size: 15 cm
Biology: Inhabits coastal and outreefs, 8–40 m. This species was previously listed as a local variant of the Blueblotch Butterflyfish (*C. plebeius*) in the Andaman Sea, where the blue spot is absent. However, it is a separate species.
Distribution: the Maldives, Sri Lanka and Andaman Sea to Sumatra.

Yellowhead Butterflyfish
Chaetodon xanthocephalus

Snout, throat, back and anal fins are yellow-orange.
Size: 20 cm
Biology: In shallow, coral-rich reefs, likewise in rocky areas with algae growth, 2–25 m. Not shy. Often roams the reef alone, sometimes also in pairs.
Distribution: East Africa to Mauritius, Chagos Islands, the Maldives and Sri Lanka.

Dotted Butterflyfish
Chaetodon semeion

Blue brow. Dorsal fin with filaments.
Size: 24 cm
Biology: In lagoons and outreefs with rich coral growth, 2–50 m. Uncommon. Shy. Usually swims in pairs through the reef, occasionally also in small groups. Feeds on small, bottom-dwelling invertebrates.
Distribution: the Maldives to SW Japan, Micronesia and French Polynesia.

Bennett's or Eclipse Butterflyfish
Chaetodon bennetti

Blue-ringed black spot. Two blue diagonal stripes.
Size: 18 cm
Biology: Prefers coral-rich lagoons and outreefs, 3–30 m. Alone or in pairs. Feeds on coral polyps and other invertebrate bottom-dwellers. Juveniles often between the branches of acropora horn corals.
Distribution: East Africa, the Maldives to S Japan, New Guinea and Pitcairn.

Pacific Double-saddle Butterflyfish
Chaetodon ulietensis

Back is yellow with black tail root spot. Two dark, diffuse saddle spots.
Size: 15 cm
Biology: Inhabits coral-rich lagoons and outreefs, 2–30 m. Lives alone, in pairs or small groups. Feeds on various small animals and plant matter.
Distribution: Cocos Keeling and Malaysia to S Japan, Micronesia and French Polynesia.

Lined Butterflyfish
Chaetodon lineolatus

Curved black band from middle of the back to the base of the anal fin.
Size: 30 cm
Biology: Largest butterfly fish. In coral-rich lagoons and outreefs, 2 to more than 50 m (170 m). Alone or in pairs, claims large home territories. Predominantly feeds on coral polyps, anemone, small invertebrates and algae.
Distribution: Red Sea and East Africa to S Japan, Micronesia and French Polynesia.

Teardrop Butterflyfish
Chaetodon unimaculatus

White with yellow back sde and black, tear-shaped spot, caudal fin whitish to transparent.
Size: 20 cm
Biology: In clear lagoons and outreefs, 5–60 m. Alone or in small, loose groups. Feeds on polyps from stony and soft coral, bristleworms, small crabs and blanket-weed algae.
Distribution: Indonesia and the Philippines to SW Japan, Hawaii and French Polynesia.

Yellow or Indian Teardrop Butterflyfish
Chaetodon interruptus

Yellow with black, tear-shaped spot, caudal fin whitish to transparent.
Size: 20 cm
Biology: Coral-rich lagoons and outreefs, 10–40 m. Alone, in pairs or in small groups. Feeds on stony and soft coral, also bristleworms, small crustaceans and blanket-weed algae.
Distribution: East Africa to Andaman Sea and Sumatra.

Mirror or Ovalspot Butterflyfish
Chaetodon speculum

Yellow with black blindfold and large black spot on the middle back. Yellow caudal fin with transparent end fringe.

Size: 18 cm

Biology: In clear lagoons and outreefs with rich coral growth, 3–30 m. Less common species, ranges usually alone through the reef. Feeds on coral polyps and invertebrate bottom-dwellers.

Distribution: Malaysia and Christmas Islands to SW Japan, New Guinea and Tonga.

Blackwedged or Saddleback Butterflyfish
Chaetodon falcula

Two large, wedge-shaped black saddle spots. Tail base with black stripes.

Size: 20 cm

Biology: In coral-rich lagoons and outreefs, often in the reef edge area and upper reef slope, 1–15 m. Usually in pairs, sometimes also in small groups. Not shy. Predominantly feeds on small invertebrates.

Distribution: East Africa to Mauritius, Chagos Islands, the Maldives, Sri Lanka and Andaman Sea.

Blueblotch or Bluespot Butterflyfish
Chaetodon plebeius

Elongated blue side spot. Eyespot on tail root.

Size: 15 cm

Biology: Shallow lagoons, coastal and outreefs, 2–15 m. Predominantly feeds on polyps of Acropora coral, occasionally also picks parasites from the skin of other fish. Usually in pairs. Juveniles between branched coral.

Distribution: Andaman Sea to SW Japan, Palau, New Guinea, Fiji and Tonga.

Blacklip Butterflyfish
Chaetodon kleinii

Black lips, yellow caudal fin with transparent back edge.
Size: 14 cm
Biology: In rock and coral reefs, 3–60 m. Alone, in pairs or in loose groups to more than two dozen fish. Feeds on polyps of soft coral (especially *Sarcophyton* and *Litophyton*), algae, zooplankton and small bottom-dwelling invertebrates.
Distribution: East Africa and the Maldives to SW Japan, Hawaii and Samoa.

Triangle Butterflyfish
Chaetodon triangulum

Black triangle on the caudal fin. Similar: *C. baronessa* with yellowish grey tail.
Size: 15 cm
Biology: In lagoons and outreefs, 3–25 m. Territorial, usually at Acropora table corals, feeds predominantly on their polyps. Juveniles alone. Adults in pairs and not shy.
Distribution: Madagascar to the Maldives, Gulf of Bengal, Andaman Sea and Java.

Raccoon Butterflyfish
Chaetodon lunula

Black eye mask, white headband, black spot on the tail base.
Size: 20 cm
Biology: In lagoons and outreefs, frequently at exposed reef slopes, 1–30 m. usually in pairs, also in larger, static formations during the day. Feeds on coral polyps, algae, small invertebrates, and also plucks tentacles from tube worms.
Distribution: East Africa to SW Japan, Hawaii, Galapagos and Ducie Islands.

Latticed Butterflyfish
Chaetodon rafflesi

Yellow with net pattern of grey lines, blue brow.
Size: 15 cm
Biology: Predominantly in coral-rich regions of lagoons, protected interiors and outreefs, 2–15 m. Un-common, ranges sometimes alone, often in pairs through the reef and feeds in part on bristleworms and anemones, also the polyps of stony and soft coral.
Distribution: Sri Lanka to S Japan, New Guinea and French Polynesia.

Saddle Butterflyfish
Chaetodon ephippium

Large black spot, set off by a white stripe, at the rear of upper body.
Size: 23 cm
Biology: In coral-rich lagoons and outreefs, to 30 m. Ranges alone, in pairs or small groups through the reef. Its nutritional sources include small invertebrates, sponges, coral polyps, fish eggs and blanket-weed algae.
Distribution: Sri Lanka and Cocos Keeling to SW Japan, Hawaii and French Polynesia.

Seychelles Butterflyfish
Chaetodon madagaskariensis

Angle pattern. Black, white-bordered brow spot.
Size: 14 cm
Biology: Prefers coral-rich outreefs and lagoons, 3–35 m. Usually in pairs. Feeds on invertebrate bottom-dwellers and algae.
Distribution: East Africa, Mada-gascar, the Mascarenes to Chagos Islands, the Maldives, Seychelles, Sri Lanka, Andaman Sea and Christmas Islands

Eight-banded Butterflyfish
Chaetodon octofasciatus

Black vertical stripes. Variant with a whitish basic colouration.
Size: 12 cm
Biology: In coral-rich lagoons and protected coastal reefs, also in murky water, 3–20 m. Juveniles in groups between branched acropora coral, adults usually in pairs. Feeds exclusively on coral polyps.
Distribution: the Maldives, Andaman Sea to SW Japan, Palau and the Solomons.

Pyramid Butterflyfish
Hemitaurichthys polylepis

White pyramid-shaped area and two yellow saddle spots on the back.
Size: 18 cm
Biology: Prefers outer reef slopes exposed to current, 3–50 m. Usually in large formations and often several metres away from the reef, in order to feed on zooplankton in the open water.
Distribution: Cocos Keeling and Christmas Islands to SW Japan, Hawaii and Pitcairn.

Brown-and-white or Black Pyramid Butterflyfish
Hemitaurichthys zoster

Broad white middle band, front and body rear brown to blackish.
Size: 16 cm
Biology: At current-rich outer reef slopes and reef channels, 1–40 m. Not shy. Often in large congregations at drop-off edges and in front of steep slopes. Captures zooplankton in the open water.
Distribution: East Africa to Mauritius, the Maldives to Andaman Sea and W Sumatra.

Longnose Butterflyfish
Forciper flavissimus

Long snout, white breast without black dots.
Size: 22 cm
Biology: Prefers outreefs, 2–114 m. Common. Has the largest distribution area of all butterflyfish. Alone, in pairs or in small groups. Feeds on small crabs, also plucks feet from starfish, grapplers from sea urchins and tentacles from bristleworms.
Distribution: Red Sea and East Africa to SW Japan, Central America and Easter Islands.

Big Longnose Butterflyfish
Forcipiger longirostris

Extremely long tube snout, white breast with black spots.
Size: 22 cm
Biology: At coral-rich outreefs, preferably at steep slopes, 5–60 m. Uncommon, swims alone or in pairs through the reef and feeds on very small invertebrates, especially crustaceans, which it sucks in whole with its tube mouth.
Distribution: East Africa to SW Japan, Hawaii and French Polynesia.

Sixspine or Ocellated Butterflyfish
Parachaetodon ocellatus

Five dark to orange-brown vertical markings and a spot above at the penultimate marking.
Size: 18 m
Biology: Prefers protected, also silted coastal reefs. 5–50 m. Alone or in pairs, Adults occasionally also in groups.
Distribution: India, Sri Lanka to SW Japan, the Philippines, Fiji and E Australia.

Twospot Coralfish
Coradion melanopus

One eyespot each on rear dorsal and anal fin.
Size: 15 cm
Biology: In coastal and outreefs, usually at reef slopes in 10–30 m. Often swims in pairs and in the vicinity of sponges from which it feeds.
Distribution: Bali and Borneo to the Philippines and New Guinea.

Goldengirdled Coralfish
Coradion chrysozonus

Two broad, copper-brown vertical bands behind the head, black eyespot on the rear dorsal fin, black spot at the tail base.
Size: 15 cm
Biology: In coastal reefs with more or less coral growth, also in rocky and rubble areas, 3–60 m. Feeds on sponges.
Distribution: Andaman Sea and NW Australia to SW Japan, the Philippines, Solomons and GBR.

Copperband or Long-beaked Butterflyfish
Chelmon rostratus

Long tube snout, eyespot on rear dorsal fin.
Size: 20 cm
Biology: At coastal and interior reefs, also in sandy muddy areas with murky water, 1–25 m. Territorial species. Alone or in pairs. Feeds on small invertebrates, which are picked out with the tube snout from small crevices.
Distribution: Andaman Sea and NW Australia to SW Japan, the Philippines, PNG and GBR.

Schooling Bannerfish
Heniochus diphreutes

Forward-arched breast. Similar: *H. acuminatus*, breast not forward-arched, snout somewhat longer.
Size: 20 cm
Biology: In open water at outer reef slopes, 5–200 m. Prefers areas with rising deep water currents and current canals. Often clearly visible above or in front of the reef in open water where it feeds on zooplankton. Juveniles live in reef vicinity and can also work as cleanerfish.
Distribution: Red Sea and East Africa to S Japan, Hawaii, Australia and Vanuatu.

This species usually forms large schools which sometimes comprise thousands of fish and in open water move along the reef.

Singular Bannerfish
Heniochus singularius

Horn on the brow, white ring around snout, dark anal fin.
Size: 25 cm
Biology: In lagoons and outreefs, frequently also at wrecks, 2–50 m. Shy and uncommon. Juvenile often alone, adults usually in pairs, often only under about 15 m depth. Feeds on coral polyps, invertebrate bottom-dwellers and algae.
Distribution: the Maldives and NW Australia to SW Japan, Micronesia and Samoa.

Pennant Coralfish
Heniochus acuminatus

Breast does not bulge outward. Similar: *H. diphreutes* (breast bulges out, shorter snout).
Size: 25 cm
Biology: In lagoons and outer reef slopes, 2–75 m. Juveniles usually alone, adults often in pairs, rarely in small groups. Usually close by the reef. Feeds on zooplankton and invertebrate bottom-dwellers. Juveniles occasionally work as cleanerfish.
Distribution: Arabian Gulf and East Africa to the Philippines and French Polynesia.

Phantom Bannerfish
Heniochus pleurotaenia

White stripes in middle of body, frontal tubercle, a pair of little horns above the eyes. Similar to *H. varius*, without white middle stripe.
Size: 17 cm
Biology: Coral-rich lagoons, 1–25 m. In pairs (common in Indonesia) or in groups, such as is often the case around the Maldives.
Distribution: The Maldives and Sri Lanka to Gulf of Bengal, Andaman Sea and Java.

Masked Bannerfish
Heniochus monoceros

The black band begins to the rear of the streamer.
Size: 3 cm
Biology: Inhabits coral-rich lagoons and outreefs, occasionally also in dead reef areas, 2–25 m. Swims in pairs or in small groups. Feeds off invertebrate bottom-dwellers, such as bristleworms.
Distribution: East Africa to SW Japan and French Polynesia.

Arabian or Yellowbar Angelfish
Pomacanthus maculosus

Blueish white tail, yellow patch on side does not extend to the dorsal fin.
Size: 50 cm
Biology: In coral-rich outreefs as well as turbid bays, 2–60 m. Usually alone, occasionally also swims in pairs. Not shy. Its food includes sponges, leather coral and algae.
Distribution: Red Sea, Arabian Gulf and Gulf of Oman to Seychelles.

Angelfish
Pomacanthidae

All angelfish have a strong spine at the front gill lid and can thus be reliably distinguished from similar butterfly fish. As protogynic sequential hermaphrodites, angelfish sexually mature first as females and later in life go through a sex change to become male. They live in harem groups in which the male has two to eight females, depending on the species. They claim a variably sized territory (for the *Centropyge* species only a few square metres, for the *Pomacanthus* species more than 1,000 square metres). In the *Pomacanthus* species, the juveniles have a completely different colouration from the adults: the Indo-Pacific *Pomacanthus* juveniles are all dark blue with white line patterns. The majority of angelfish consume sponges, sea squirts, leather coral and other soft invertebrates as well as algae and fish eggs. *Geniacanthus* species feed on zooplankton, and *Centropyge* species on blanket-weed algae and small invertebrates.

Emperor Angelfish
Pomacanthus imperator

Alternate yellow and blue horizontal stripe.
Size: 40 cm
Biology: In coral-rich lagoons and outreefs, 3–70 m. Occupies large home territories and forms harems, but usually swims alone or in pairs. Feeds on sponges, sea squirts and cnidarians.
Distribution: Red Sea and East Africa to SW Japan, Micronesia, Hawaii and French Polynesia.

As with all Indo-Pacific *Pomacanthus* species, the Emperor Angelfish juveniles also show a completely different colouration from the adults with a characteristic blue-white pattern.

Semicircle Angelfish
Pomacanthus semicirculatus

A curved and a straight blue line from the spine at the front gill lid.
Size: 35–40 cm
Biology: Adults in coral-rich, protected reefs, 3–40 m. Usually alone. Its food sources include sponges and sea squirts.
Distribution: East Africa to SW Japan, Palau, GBR and Fiji.

Blue Ring Angelfish
Pomacanthus annularis

Blue temple ring, curved blue horizontal stripes.
Size: 45 cm
Biology: Prefers coastal reefs with moderate coral growth or rock areas, often in murky water, 5–45 m. Adults frequently in pairs, otherwise alone. Often rests in cavities and wrecks. Feeds on sponges and sea squirts.
Distribution: East Africa to SW Japan, the Philippines and Solomons.

Bluegirdled Angelfish
Pomacanthus navarchus

Blue pectoral fin, yellow tail. Dark blue area which extends in a U-shape over anal fin and abdomen to the brow.
Size: 25 cm
Biology: In clear lagoons and out-reefs, 3–40 m. Usually alone, often close to protection. Relatively shy. Its food sources include sponges and sea squirts.
Distribution: Indonesia to the Philippines, Palau, Yap, Solomons and GBR.

Yellowface Angelfish
Pomacanthus xanthometopon

Head blue with yellow eye mask. Dark spot at the back of the dorsal fin.
Size: 38 cm
Biology: Inhabits coral-rich lagoons and outer reef slopes, 5–35 m. Usually alone, sometimes also in pairs. Feeds on sponges and sea squirts.
Distribution: the Maldives to Indonesia, SW Japan, Western Micronesia, GBR and Vanuatu.

Sixbar Angelfish
Pomacanthus sexstriatus

Dark head with white vertical stripe behind eye. Dark vertical stripes on the sides.
Size: 46 cm
Biology: In lagoons and outer reef slopes, Both in clear coral-rich and muddier areas with coral-rubble mixed ground, 1–60 m. Frequently in pairs, also alone. Claims a large home territory.
Distribution: Malaysia, Indonesia to SW Japan, Palau and Yap, Solomons and GBR.

Regal Angelfish
Pygoplites diacanthus

Yellow-orange with pale blue, dark-edged vertical stripes.
Size: 25 cm
Biology: Denizens of coral-rich lagoons and outreefs, 1–80 m. Usually alone or in pairs. Common, however shy, rapidly flees from divers into crevices and holes. Feeds on sponges and sea squirts.
Distribution: Red Sea and East Africa to SW Japan, Micronesia and French Polynesia.

Threespot Angelfish
Apolemichthys trimaculatus

Luminous yellow. Blue lips. Two black patches on the brow. Grey temple spot. Anal fin with broad black edge fringe.
Size: 25 cm
Biology: Often at outer reef slopes and in clear lagoons, 3–50 m. Alone or in pairs, often also in small groups. Relatively shy. Feeds predominantly on sponges and sea squirts.
Distribution: East Africa, the Maldives to SW Japan and Samoa.

Yellowtail or Cream Angelfish
Apolemichthys xanthurus

Yellow caudal fin. Small yellow spot above the gill lid. Dorsal fin with white-edged fringe.
Size: 15 cm
Biology: Inhabits coral-rich regions, in some places also seen in rock areas, 5–25 m. Alone or in pairs. Shy.
Distribution: Réunion, Mauritius and Rodrigues to the Maldives, Sri Lanka, India and Andaman Sea.

Bicolour Angelfish
Centropyge bicolour

Front of its body and head yellow with a blue saddle over the eyes. Body rear blue. Tail yellow.
Size: 15 cm
Biology: Inhabits lagoons and outreefs, in coral-rich reef regions likewise over rock and rubble areas, 5–25 m. Alone, in pairs or in small groups.
Distribution: Malaysia to SW Japan, Phoenix Islands and Samoa.

Twospined Angelfish
Centropyge bispinosus

Sides with orange area and blue vertical stripes. The extent of the orange portion is extremely variable.
Size: 10 cm
Biology: Inhabits coral-rich lagoons and outer reef slopes, 5–50 m. In some places also in mixed zones with seagrass, coral blocks and rock. Common in some places, however shy and usually close to protection.
Distribution: East Africa to SW Japan, Micronesia and French Polynesia.

Blacktail Angelfish
Centropyge eibli

Thin orange vertical stripes. Tail black with blue fringe at the back edge. Orange eye-ring.
Size: 11 cm
Biology: Inhabits coral-rich areas in lagoons and protected outreefs, 3–25 m. Very similar: *Acanthurus tristis.* hybridized with *C. vroliki.*
Distribution: Sri Lanka, Andaman Sea and Indonesia to NW Australia.

Barred Angelfish
Paracentropyge multifasciata

Broad black vertical stripes. White interstices each one with a fine, weak yellowish line.
Size: 11 cm
Biology: Prefers steep outer reef slopes, 10–70 m. Alone, occasionally also in small groups. Usually at caves, overhangs or other shelters. Shy species.
Distribution: Cocos Keeling to SW Japan, the Philippines, PNG, GBR and French Polynesia.

Dusky or Brown Pygmy Angelfish
Centropyge multispinis

Dark brown. Fine, dark vertical stripes. Anal and ventral fin with pale blue edge.
Size: 10–14 cm
Biology: In lagoons and protected outreefs, above coral and rubble, 1–30 m. Has small hunting grounds in which it grazes on blanket-weed algae. Shy, quickly flees to hiding places.
Distribution: Red Sea, S Oman and East Africa to Mauritius, the Maldives and Andaman Sea.

Keyhole Angelfish
Centropyge tibicen

Dark blue (juvenile almost black) with a large white side spot. Anal fin with broad, yellow-edged fringe.
Size: 18 cm
Biology: In lagoons and outreefs, on coral and rubble areas, 3–35. Alone or in small groups.
Distribution: Malaysia, Christmas Islands to SW Japan, Palau and Yap, PNG and New Caledonia.

Halfblack Angel
Centropyge vroliki

Pale grey, flowing transition to black at the body rear.
Caudal fin with fine blue edge fringe. Gill lid with short
orange-brown line.
Size: 10–12 cm
Biology: Inhabits protected, coral-rich outreefs and
lagoons, 3–25 m. Alone or in small, loose groups.
Distribution: Christmas Islands and Bali to SW Japan,
Marshall Islands and Vanuatu.

Velvet Angelfish
Chaetodontoplus dimidiatus

Lower body area black, except for the head. Otherwise
very similar to *C. melanosoma*.
Size: 22 cm
Biology: Inhabits rock and coral reefs, 3–35 m.
Distribution: Indonesia, the Philippines to SW Japan.

Black-velvet Angelfish
Chaetodontoplus melanosoma

Adults: Yellow fringe along entire caudal fin as well
as back edge of back and anal fin. Juvenile with white
band at the head.
Size: 18 cm
Biology: Inhabits rock and coral reefs, 3–30 m. Feeds on
sponges and sea squirts.
Distribution: Andaman Sea, Indonesia, PNG, the Philippines to SW Japan.

Vermiculated Angelfish
Chaetodontoplus mesoleucus

Yellow tail, black eye stripes, blue lips.
Size: 18 cm
Biology: Inhabits coral-rich, protected reefs, 3–20
m. Usually swims in pairs. Feeds on sponges and sea
squirts as well as blanket-weed algae.
Distribution: Malaysia, Indonesia, to SW Japan, North
Australia, PNG and Solomons.

Zebra Angelfish
Genicanthus caudovittatus

Male with zebra pattern.
Size: 20 cm
Biology: Denizens of coral-rich outer reef slopes, 15–17 m, usually beneath 25 m. Usually in harem groups of one male and 5 to 9 females on about 25 sq.m territory. Feeds on zooplankton. The males can be observed higher in the water than the females.
Distribution: Red Sea to the Maldives and East Africa south to Mozambique.

Female: Black stripe above and below caudal fin.

Lamarck's Angelfish
Genicanthus lamarck

Both sexes with black stripes on the dorsal fin. Male with pale yellow brow spot.
Size: 25 cm
Biology: Inhabits coral-rich outer reef slopes, 10–50. Lives in small harems. Feeds on zooplankton in middle open water.
Distribution: Malaysia and Indonesia to SW Japan, GBR and Vanuatu.

On the female (lower photo), the upper horizontal stripe bends downwards and extends to the entire underside of the caudal fin.

Indo-Pacific Sergeant
Abudefduf vaigiensis

Five dark vertical markings, back often yellowish.

Size: 20 cm

Biology: At upper edges of rock and coral reefs. 0.5–12 m. In loose to large groups feeding on zooplankton near the reef in open water. Feeds on outgrowth algae. Guards and cares for the eggs laid on firm ground.

Distribution: Red Sea, East Africa to S Japan, Micronesia, GBR and French Polynesia.

Damselfish
Pomacentridae

This large family, which worldwide includes more than 320 species (of these three quarters in the Indo-Pacific) primarily populates all tropical waters. With its high species count and number of individuals in every coral reef, it plays a significant role in the reef community. Some feed on plankton (e.g. *Abudefduf, Chromis, Dascyllus*), others on algae (e.g. all *Stegastes*, some *Abudefduf*). There are also omnivorous specimens, like many *Pomacentrus*. At less than ten centimetres, the majority of species remain quite small. The typical breeding behaviour of reef perch includes the careful cleaning of a selected area of the firm seabed. Depending on species, more than a thousand sticky eggs are laid there. The clutch is guarded until the brood hatches and fanned with oxygen-rich water.

Sergeant Major
Abudefduf sexfasciatus

Tail with black edging stripes.
Size: 19 cm
Biology: At the upper slopes of lagoons and outreefs, 0.5–15 m. Common, not shy. Sometimes in large groups above or in the open water in front of the reef. Predominantly feeds on zooplankton, occasionally also on outgrowth algae.
Distribution: Red Sea and East Africa to S Japan, Micronesia and GBR.

Golden Damselfish
Amblyglyphidodon aureus

Usually uniformly yellow.
Size: 14 cm
Biology: Prefers steep outer reef slopes, 3–35 m. Feeds on zooplankton. Juveniles often at large sea whips or bushes of black coral. The eggs are often laid near sea whips.
Distribution: Andaman Sea, Cocos Keeling and NW Australia to SW Japan, Marshall Islands and Fiji.

Larger fish often have extended blueish parts.

Staghorn Damselfish
Amblyglyphidodon curacao

Middle of side is often yellowish, three irregular green vertical stripes.
Size: 11 cm
Biology: Coral-rich lagoons, bays and outreefs, 1–20 m. Usually in groups or large schools, feeds in the open water for zooplankton, also feeds on blanket-weed algae.
Distribution: Malaysia and Singapore to SW Japan, Micronesia, Samoa, NW Australia and GBR.

Yellowfin Damsel
Amblyglyphidodon flavilatus

Grey front, pale yellow rear.
Size: 10 cm
Biology: Inhabits protected outer and patch reefs with rich coral stock, 3–20 m. Swims alone or in small loose groups, often also along with the Maldives Damselfish, a short distance above the reef in open water in order to feed on zooplankton.
Distribution: Red Sea and Gulf of Aden.

Maldives Damselfish
Amblyglyphidodon indicus

Back blue greenish, flowing transition to white on underside.
Size: 13 cm
Biology: Clear, coral-rich lagoons and protected outreefs, 2–35 m. Common and not shy. Swims alone or in small groups just above the reef and snaps at zooplankton and drifting organic matter.
Distribution: Red Sea to Madagascar, Chagos Islands and Andaman Sea.

White-belly Damselfish
Amblyglyphidodon leucogaster

Yellow ventral fin.
Size: 13 cm
Biology: In clear lagoons and outreefs, 3–45 m. Alone or in small loose groups, feeds on zooplankton. Not shy.
Distribution: N Sumatra to SW Japan, Vanuatu and GBR.

Black-banded Demoiselle
Amblypomacentrus breviceps

Dark eye stripes. Two dark saddle spots, connected by a dark dorsal fin.
Size: 8 cm
Biology: In lagoons and coastal reefs, 2–35 m. On sand, rubble and mud. Often in small loose groups.
Distribution: Indonesia to the Philippines, Solomons and GBR.

Chocolatedip or India Half-and-half Chromis
Chromis dimidiata

Striking colouration, cannot be distinguished from its Pacific sister species (*C. iomelas*, GBR to Fiji).
Size: 7 cm
Biology: In lagoons and outreefs, 1–36 m. Usually in groups or large shoals at reef edges or exposed reef posts. Feeds on zooplankton in open water. Not shy.
Distribution: Red Sea and East Africa to Thailand, Java and Christmas Islands.

Doublebar Chromis
Chromis opercularis

One black spot each at the gill lid and pectoral fin base close together.
Size: 16 cm
Biology: Prefers outer reef slopes, 8–40 m. Usually in loose groups. Replaced by *C. xanthura* from Cocos Keeling to West Pacific.
Distribution: East Africa to Andaman Sea and Java.

Pemba Chromis
Chromis pembae

Brown with white or yellowish tail. Dorsal and anal fin predominantly black.
Size: 13 cm
Biology: In rock and coral reefs, 3–50 m. Prefers steep reef slopes, where in small groups it feeds on zooplankton just above the seabed in the open water. Not shy.
Distribution: Red Sea, Oman and East Africa to Seychelles and Chagos Islands.

Green Chromis
Chromis viridis

Metallic blue-green.
Size: 9 cm
Biology: Prefers coral-rich coastal reefs and bays, 1–15 m. Usually in groups above branched coral (Acropora). When disturbed, instantly flees between the coral branches.
Distribution: Red Sea and East Africa to SW Japan and French Polynesia.

Yellowtail Puller
Chromis xanthura

Adults: Dark metallic black-grey with dark-edged scales. Tail base and fin are white.
Size: 15 cm
Biology: Prefers steep outer reefs, 3–40 m. Usually in loose groups.
Distribution: Cocos Keeling to SW Japan, Line Islands and Pitcairn.

Juveniles are silvery-grey to blue-silver with yellow dorsal, anal and caudal fins. Frequently encountered in front of soft coral and sea whips.

Goldtail Demoiselle
Chrysiptera parasema

Luminous blue, tail stalk and fin yellow.
Size: 6–7 cm
Biology: Prefers protected, coral-rich reefs, 1–15 m. When disturbed, seeks protection between coral branches.
Distribution: Java and Borneo to the Philippines.

King Demoiselle
Chrysiptera rex

Whitish beige to pale yellowish. Very small dark ear mark.
Size: 7–8 cm
Biology: Prefers outer reefs and reef channels, 1–6 m. A relatively inconspicuous demoiselle, to be seen alone or in small groups. Feeds predominantly on algae.
Distribution: Indonesia (Bali) and the Philippines to SW Japan, Palau, New Caledonia and Vanuatu.

Rolland's Demoiselle
Chrysiptera rollandi

Dorsal front of body usually very
dark to blue-black, towards the
back whitish to yellowish. Often
with blue brow stripes. Always with
long white ventral fin.
Size: 5–6 cm
Biology: In lagoons and outer reefs,
above coral and rubble, 2–35 m.
Distribution: Andaman Sea to
the Philippines, Palau and New
Caledonia.

Talbot's Demoiselle
Chrysiptera talboti

Forehead and neck yellow. black spot
at middle base of the dorsal fin.
Size: 6 cm
Biology: Coral-rich areas in lagoons
and outer reefs, 5–35 m. Alone or in
small groups. Feeds on zooplankton.
Distribution: Andaman Sea to the
Philippines, Palau, GBR and Fiji.

Whitetail Dascyllus or Humbug
Dascyllus aruanus

Three black bands, black ventral fin.
Size: 8 cm
Biology: Shallow lagoons, protected patch reefs and bays, 0.5–20
m. Hovers in loose groups just
above branch coral such as Acropora and Pocillopora and feeds on
zooplankton from the water. When
disturbed, instantly flees between
the coral branches.
Distribution: Red Sea and East
Africa to SW Japan, Micronesia, Line
Islands and French Polynesia.

Marginate or Threespot Dascyllus
Dascyllus marginatus

Dorsal fin with black edge.
Size: 6 cm
Coral branches. Feeds on zooplankton from the water just above the coral.
Distribution: Red Sea to Gulf of Oman.

Two Stripe Damselfish
Dascyllus reticulatus

Tail region usually somewhat brown-grey.
Size: 8 cm
Biology: In lagoons and outer reefs, 1–50 m. In small to large groups over branched coral with which it is closely associated and on danger it flees between the branches.
Distribution: Cocos Keeling to SW Japan, Micronesia, Line Islands, Samoa and East Australia.

Threespot Dascyllus
Dascyllus trimaculatus

Can change its colouration in a matter of seconds from light grey or black-brown.
Size: 14 cm
Biology: In rock and coral reefs, 1-30 m. Usually in small groups. Juveniles often in the host anemone of anemone fish, and like these, are not stung.
Distribution: Red Sea, East Africa to S Japan, Line Islands and Pitcairn.

Honey-head Damsel
Dischistodus prosopotaenia

Shoulder spot. Fine blue line on head.
Size: 18 cm
Biology: In lagoons, protected coastal and patch reefs, 2–12 m. Prefers sand and muddy ground near coral. Male watches over and cares for the eggs.
Distribution: Andaman Sea to SW Japan, the Philippines, GBR and Vanuatu.

Cross' Damsel
Neoglyphidodon crossi

Brow marking and blue horizontal stripe. Adults uniformly dark brown with golden iris.
Size: 13 cm
Biology: Protected rock and coral reefs, lagoons and bays, 1–10 m.
Distribution: Bali, Komodo, Flores to Sulawesi, the Moluccas and Raja Ampat.

Black-and-gold Chromis
Neoglyphidodon nigroris

Adults with dark stripes on gill lid and pale-dark stripes under the eye. Rear of body and tail yellow. Juveniles yellow with two black stripes.
Size: 11–13 cm
Biology: In coral-rich lagoons and outreef slopes, 2–25 m. Feeds on zooplankton and algae.
Distribution: Andaman Sea to SW Japan, Palau, Vanuatu and GBR.

Chinese Demoiselle
Neopomacentrus bankieri

Grey, tail and back edge from the
dorsal and anal fin yellow. Black spot
at the base of upper pectoral fins.
Size: 7–8 cm
Biology: Inhabits rock and coral
reefs, 3–13 m. Above coral, rubble
and sandy areas.
Distribution: Java Sea to S China,
PNG and GBR.

Regal Demoiselle
Neopomacentrus cyanomos

Dark brown, back edge of tail, dorsal and anal fins yellow. Luminous
yellow to white spot at rear base of
the dorsal fin.
Size: 10 cm
Biology: Prefers protected coastal
reefs and bays, 5–20 m. Usually
in small groups not far from coral
formations. Feeds on zooplankton
in the water.
Distribution: Red Sea, Oman and
East Africa to SW Japan, Solomons,
Vanuatu and GBR.

Blackbar Damsel or Devil
Plectroglyphidodon dickii

Black vertical band in front of white
tail.
Size: 11 cm
Biology: In coral-rich, clear lagoons
and outer reefs, 1–12 m. Rests
usually close to branch coral (e.g.
Acropora and *Pocillopora*). Territorial. Grazes on blanket-weed algae,
also feeds on small invertebrates
and occasionally small fish.
Distribution: East Africa to SW
Japan, Line Islands and French
Polynesia.

Whitespotted Devil or Jewel Damsel
Plectroglyphidodon lacrymatus

Green-brown to brown with blue spots. Yellow Iris.

Size: 11 cm

Biology: In clear lagoons and outer reefs, 1–40 m. Very territorial, aggressively defends a small territory where blanket-weed algae grows on hard ground. Also undismayed by divers. Apart from algae from its "garden", it also feeds on small invertebrates and fish eggs.

Distribution: Red Sea and East Africa to SW Japan, Marshall Islands and French Polynesia.

Ambon Demoiselle or Damsel
Pomacentrus amboinensis

Variable colouration. Usually bright base with pale, somewhat wavy-yellowish or blue-greenish transverse lines. Cheeks and snout with very pale light blue markings. Juveniles with eyespot in back of the dorsal fin.

Size: 10 cm

Biology: Prefers protected reefs with coral-sand mixed zones, 2–40 m.

Distribution: Andaman Sea to SW Japan, Micronesia and Fiji.

Goldbelly Demoiselle or Damsel
Pomacentrus auriventris

Head and dorsal body metallic blue. Body rear and underneath up to the pectoral fins yellow.

Size: 7 cm

Biology: Usually just above rubble of lagoons and outer reefs, 2–15 m. Partly alone, frequently however in small loose groups. Often also along with the Neon Demoiselle.

Distribution: Christmas Islands, Bali and Borneo to Micronesia and Solomons.

Speckled Damselfish
Pomacentrus bankanensis

Colouration is variable. Usually brow and back are red with blue stripes, eyespot at back of the dorsal fin. Whitish tail.
Size: 10 cm
Biology: In lagoons and protected outer reefs, 1–12 m. Usually above coral-rubble mixed zones. Feeds on algae, also on zooplankton.
Distribution: Andaman Sea and Christmas Islands to SW Japan, Palau and Yap, Australia and Fiji.

Lemon Demoiselle
Pomacentrus moluccensis

Luminous yellow. Snout and cheeks with pale blue markings (partly not clearly visible).
Size: 7 cm
Biology: At clear lagoons and outer reefs, 1–15 m. Often in small, loose groups in front of coral formations. Feeds on zooplankton and algae.
Distribution: Andaman Sea to Rowley Shoals, SW Japan, Palau, Yap and Fiji.

Sulphur Demoiselle
Pomacentrus sulfureus

Continuously yellow up to a black spot at the pectoral fin base.
Size: 11 cm
Biology: At coral-rich, protected patch and fringe reefs, 1–12 m. Alone or in loose groups near coral outcrop, likes also to be near fire corals. In some places common.
Distribution: Red Sea and East Africa to Mauritius and Seychelles.

Ocellate Demoiselle
Pomacentrus vaiuli

White edged, black eyespot at the back of the dorsal fin.
Size: 10 cm
Biology: Inhabits lagoons and outer reefs, 1–40 m. In some places common, feeds on blanket-weed algae and small invertebrates.
Distribution: Bali and Rowley Shoals to SW Japan, Micronesia, Samoa.

Pink Anemonefish
Amphiprion peridaraion

Pink to orange, back stripe and narrow head stripes.
Size: 10 cm
Biology: lagoons and outer reefs, 3–20 m. Usually Inhabits the Magnificent Sea Anemone *Heteractis magnifica*, less often together with three other anemone fish.
Distribution: Parts of Malaysia and Sumatra, Gulf of Thailand to SW Japan (Ryukyu Islands), Cocos Keeling, NW Australia, Micronesia and New Caledonia.

Anemone Fish
Amphiprioninae

All species of this subfamily of the damselfish live in close symbiosis with the sea anemone, without which it would be easy prey for numerous predators. They aquire an immunity to the stings when they are juveniles by touching the tentacles for short periods at a time. They also spend the night there vigorously defending their anemone against fish that wish to feed on the tentacles. The largest and socially dominant fish in an anemone is always a female – the next largest a male. The two form a long-term pair. If the female dies, within about one week the highest-ranking male performs a sex change and becomes the dominant female.

Skunk Clownfish
Amphiprion akallopisos

Narrow, white back stripe extends from the tail to the brow, not to the lip.
Size: 10 cm
Biology: In lagoons and outer reefs, 2–25 m. Associated with the anemones *Heteractis magnifica* and *Stichodactyla mertensii*.
Distribution: East Africa (Horn of Africa to Comoro Islands and Madagascar), Seychelles, west coast of Thailand to Sumatra, Java and Bali.

Saddle or Red Saddleback Anemonefish
Amphiprion ephippium

Orange-red with black region at the rear of body of varying size.
Size: 12 cm
Biology: Inhabits protected coastal reefs and bays, 2–15 m. Very common in the Bubble Anemone *Entacmaea quadricolor*, also in the Sebae Anemone *Heteractis crispa*.
Distribution: West Malaysia, Sumatra and Java.

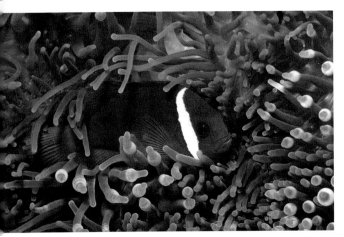

Barber's Anemonefish
Amphiprion barberi

Body and fin red-orange, back usually darkish. A white head stripe.
Size: 13 cm
Biology: In lagoons and outer reefs, 2–10 m. First identified as a species only in 2008 by Allen, Drew and Kaufmann. Regularly occurs in the distribution area with anemones *Entacmaea quadricolor* and *Heteractis crispa*. Usually in groups, swimming a short distance above its anemone.
Distribution: Fiji, Tonga and Samoa.

Yellow or Orange Clownfish
Amphiprion sandaracinos

Broad white back stripe, extends from the upper lip to the tail root.
Size: 13 cm
Biology: Lagoons and outreefs, 3–20 m. Associated with two anemone species, usually with Mertens Anemone (*Stichodactyla mertensii*), less often with Sebae Anemone (*Heteractis crispa*).
Distribution: NW Australia to SW Japan, the Philippines and Solomons.

Cinnamon or Red and Black Clownfish
Amphiprion melanopus

Red-orange, large black region at the rear of the body, which can also extend to head stripes.
Size: 13 cm
Biology: In lagoons and outer reefs, 1–18 m. Lives together with three anemone species: *Heteractis magnifica, H. crispa* and *Entamaea quadricolour.*
Distribution: Bali und East Kalimantan to the Philippines, Marshall Islands, Fiji and Society Islands in French Polynesia.

Twoband Anemonefish
Amphiprion bicinctus

Basic colouration is variable, yellow to dark brown, two white to blue-white stripes.
Size: 14 cm
Biology: At fringe and patch reefs, bays and outer reefs, 0.5–30 m. Common. Lives with five anemone species: *Heteractis magnifica, H. crispa, H. aurora, Entamaea quadricolour* and *Stichodactyla gigantea.*
Distribution: Red Sea, Gulf of Aden and Chagos Islands.

Clark's Anemonefish
Amphiprion clarkii

Many versions of the basic colouration of almost entirely orange or black, as well as white, yellow, orange or black caudal fin (rarely).
Size: 14 cm
Biology: Lagoons and outreefs, 1–55 m. Occurs in all ten anemone species, which are known as hosts for anemone fish. Has the largest distribution area of all anemone fish.
Distribution: Arabian Gulf to the Maldives to S Japan, Fiji and New Caledonia.

Orangefin Anemonefish
Amphiprion chrysopterus

Body predominantly brown to black. Two white to blue-white stripes, the front broader than the rear. Fin is orange, caudal fin, however, often whitish. Variant in Melanesia with black anal and ventral fin.
Size: 15 cm
Biology: Lives together with six anemone species.
Distribution: Micronesia, the Philippines, PNG, Solomons, NE Australia, Fiji, Samoa to French Polynesia.

Maldives or Black-finned Anemonefish
Amphiprion nigripes

Narrow white head stripe, anal and ventral fins black.
Size: 11 cm
Biology: Lagoons and outer reefs, 1–25 m. Has a very small distribution area. Lives exclusively with Magnificent Sea Anemone *Heteractis magnifica*. Frequently in larger groups.
Distribution: the Maldives, Sri Lanka.

Saddleback Clownfish
Amphiprion polymnus

Broader head stripe, second stripe saddle-shaped towards the back, drawn to the dorsal fin. Caudal fin black with white edges.
Size: 12 cm
Bioloilargy: Lives together with two anemone species, usually observed as in Haddons Anemone on sandy bottom.
Distribution: Gulf of Thailand to SW Japan, N Australia and Solomons.

Sebae Anemonefish
Amphiprion sebae

Broader head stripes, second stripes broad towards the back and drawn to the dorsal fin. Caudal fin totally or partially yellow.
Size: 14 cm
Biology: In lagoons, bays and outer reefs, 2–35 m. Inhabits Haddon's Anemone (*Stichodactyla haddoni*), often on sand or rubble.
Distribution: Gulf of Aden and Gulf of Oman to Sri Lanka, the Maldives and Java.

False Clown Anemonefish
Amphiprion ocellaris

Three white stripes, the middle with bulge forwards.
Size: 9 cm
Biology: Lagoons, coastal and protected outer reefs, 1–15. Often in small groups on an anemone. Inhabits the three anemones, *Heteractis magnifica*, *Stichodactyla gigantea* and *S. mertensii*.
Distribution: Andaman Sea and Nikobar to SW Japan, the Philippines and NW Australia.

Maroon Clownfish
Premnas biaculeatus

Luminous red to brown-red, large female is usually dark reddish-brown to black-red. Only anemone fish with a spine protruding from its gill cover.
Size: 8 cm (male), 16 cm (female)
Biology: In lagoons and protected outer reefs, 1–18 m. Lives exclusively with Bubble Anemone *Entacmaea quadricolour*.
Distribution: Burma, Thailand, Malaysia and Sumatra to the Philippines, GBR and Vanuatu.

Whitebonnet Anemonefish
Amphiprion leucokranos

Orange to yellowish-brown. White spot on the head ("bonnet"), white, somewhat curved spot on cheeks and usually with a small white dorsal spot.
Size: 11 cm
Biology: Inhabits lagoons and outer reefs, 2–10 m. Lives along with Sebae Anemone (*H. crispa*), Magnificent Sea Anemone (*H. magnifica*) and Mertens Anemone (*Stichodactyla mertensii*).
Distribution: Northern PNG and Solomons.

Humphead or Napoleon Wrasse
Cheilinus undulatus

TP blue-green, with frontal tuber-cle. IP paler and without frontal tubercle.

Size: 2.3 m

Biology: Lagoons, bays and outreefs, 1–60 m. Uncommon. Shy, but sometimes can be curious in regions frequented by divers but without stress from fishing. Usually alone. Feeds on hard-shelled inver-tebrates such as snails, crustaceans, sea urchins and starfish (also crown of thorns), also fish, e.g. boxfish. It usually finds its prey on rubble and sand surfaces. In some areas greatly depleted by reckless fishing. Expensive edible fish and in strong demand from SE Asian restaurants.

Distribution: Red Sea and East Africa to SW Japan, Micronesia, New Caledonia and French Polynesia.

Wrasse
Labridae

This large family comprises more than 500 species, among which there is a wide variety of size, behavioural patterns and nutrition. All have a characteristic way of swimming: propulsion is generated with the pectoral fins, the caudal fin is employed only for high speeds, for escape for instance. Wrasse are day-active fish, often splendidly co-loured; smaller species are also often agile swimmers. For their night's rest, they burrow into sandy ground, especially the small species, larger ones usually seek protected shelters. Wrasse are protogynic hermaphrodites: upon ageing, the female changes into a so-called secondary male. There is also a primary male which develops directly from a juvenile to a sexually mature male. Age and sex are frequently expressed by different colouration. These are termed Initial Phase (IP) or Initial Colouration (IC) for the primary male and female and Termi-nal Phase (TP) or Terminal Colouration (TC) for the usually particularly spectacular colouring of the secondary male. If the colouration of juveniles is clearly different from the initial colouration, this is termed the Juvenile Phase (JP).

Floral Wrasse
Cheilinus chlororus

Colouration very variable from light grey-blueish to green with red parts; usually with small white dots arranged in horizontal rows, also often white irregular patches along the back.
Size: 36 cm
Biology: In lagoons and coastal reefs, 2–30 m. Usually in mixed zones with sand, rubble and coral. Always swims near seabed, feeds on various invertebrate bottom-dwellers.
Distribution: East Africa to SW Japan, Micronesia and French Polynesia.

Broomtail Wrasse
Cheilinus lunulatus

Ragged caudal fin. Yellow, dark-edged spot on gill lid. Yellow pectoral fin.
Size: 50 cm
Biology: Usually at coral-rich reef edges above areas with sand and rubble patches, 0.5–30 m. Cautious, shy species. Predominantly feeds on bottom-dwelling invertebrates such as crustaceans, mussels and snails.
Distribution: Red Sea and Gulf of Aden.

Redbreasted Wrasse
Cheilinus quinquecinctus

Large adults with ragged tail. A forked white stripe is drawn above lower and upper jaw from the corner of the mouth. Very similar to *C. fasciatus* without the ragged tail.
Size: 36 cm
Biology: Prefers mixed coral, sand and rubble zones, 4–40 m. Relatively common and not shy. Feeds on bottom-dwelling invertebrates.
Distribution: Red Sea.

Blue-spotted Wrasse
Anampses caeruleopunctatus

TP with yellow-green stripes on the front of the body, IP with horizontal rows of small blue dots.
Size: 42 cm
Biology: Denizens of clear outreefs, 1–30 m. Usually in upper areas. Feeds on small invertebrates, bristleworms and molluscs. Male alone and territorial. Female in loose harem groups. At night, burrows into sandy soil.
Distribution: Red Sea and East Africa to S Japan, Line Islands, French Polynesia and Easter Islands.

Yellowtail Wrasse
Anampses meleagrides

IP with white spots arranged in horizontal rows. One eyespot each at the back on dorsal and anal fin.
Size: 22 cm
Biology: Prefers mixed coral, rubble, and sandy areas, 3–60 m. Adult male usually alone, juveniles and females often in small, loose groups. Feeds on small bottom-dwelling invertebrates.
Distribution: Red Sea and East Africa to S Japan, Micronesia and French Polynesia.

Yellow-breasted Wrasse
Anampses twistii

TP without, IP with eye spots at the back on the dorsal and anal fins.
Size: 18 cm
Biology: In lagoons, bays and outreefs, 2–30 m. Usually in areas with mixed coral, rubble and sand surfaces. Feeds on small bottom-dwelling invertebrates.
Distribution: Red Sea and East Africa to SW Japan, Micronesia and French Polynesia.

Cigar Wrasse
Cheilio inermis

Long extended body, variable colouration, brown, green or yellow.
Size: 50 cm
Biology: In protected areas of rock and coral reefs or above seagrass, 1–35 m. Shy. Likes to swim along with goatfish and other wrasse in order to snatch exposed prey from the sand. Its food sources include molluscs, crustaceans (crabs and shrimps) and also sea urchins. Generally shy.
Distribution: Red Sea and East Africa to SW Japan, Hawaii, Micronesia and Polynesia.

Top photo: Terminal phase (large male), about 50 cm long, with brilliant colouration on the flanks in yellow, orange, black and white. Bottom photo: Initial phase (female).

Lyretail Hogfish
Bodianus anthioides

Adults: brown-red front of body, white with reddish brown spots rear of body.
Size: 21 cm
Biology: In deep lagoons, bays and outreefs, 5–60 m. Adults in search of bottom-dwelling invertebrates are often over sand and rubble ground of the reef.
Distribution: Red Sea and East Africa to S Japan, Line Islands and French Polynesia.

Juveniles are differently coloured. They frequently rest in close proximity to sea whips, soft coral and black coral bushes.

Axilspot Hogfish
Bodianus axillaris

Adults (TP): each with an eyespot at the pectoral fin base ("shoulder") and back of dorsal and anal fin.
Size: 20 cm
Biology: Clear lagoons, bays and outreefs, 3–40 m. Swims alone and close to the bottom. Adults and juveniles occasionally work as cleanerfish.
Distribution: Red Sea, East Africa and S Oman to S Japan, Micronesia, French Polynesia and Pitcairn.

Juveniles are black with large white patches. Can usually be seen in the shelter of cavities.

Splitlevel or Blackbelt Hogfish
Bodianus mesothorax

Adults (TP): Black, wedge-shaped to triangular band on the front of body. Similar: *B. axillaris* (black patches in dorsal and anal fin).
Size: 20 cm
Biology: In coral-rich outer reef slopes, 5–30 m.
Distribution: Christmas Islands to S Japan, Western Micronesia, PNG and GBR.

Juveniles are dark purple with large yellow patches. They keep near hiding-places such as crevices and overhangs.

Diana's Hogfish
Bodianus diana

TP: Black spot at tail root. Dorsal side with 4–5 white, ventral and anal fins with red patches.
Size: 25 cm
Biology: In rock and coral reefs, 3–50 m. Common in some places, especially at coral-rich slopes.
Distribution: Red Sea and East Africa to S Japan, Micronesia and Samoa.

Juveniles with numerous white spots and short lines. They also work as cleanerfish and like to keep close to sea whips.

Redfin Hogfish
Bodianus dictynna

TP: Black spot at tail root, black patches in ventral and anal fins.

Size: 20 cm

Biology: Prefers coral-rich outer reef slopes, 5–25 m. Swims alone or in pairs in areas with good coral growth. Feeds on invertebrates such as crustaceans, mussels and snails.

Distribution: Malaysia and Indonesia to the Philippines, Western Micronesia, GBR, Samoa and Tonga.

Juveniles are reddish-brown with numerous white markings. Black patches on the fins. Can often be seen at fan sea whips and black coral.

Neil's Hogfish
Bodianus neilii

The front of body is pale reddish-brown, and towards the rear it becomes gradually brighter to white. Elongated red to red-black spot on the dorsal and anal fin.

Size: 20 cm

Biology: Inhabits lagoons and shallow coastal reefs, also likes areas with murky water and low coral growth, 2–15 m. Loner, combs the seabed for small animals.

Distribution: The Maldives, Sri Lanka and Andaman Sea.

Blueside Wrasse
Cirrhilabrus cyanopleura

TP: With blue region on the front of body, snout and brow usually dirty green, dorsal side whitish.

Size: 15 cm

Biology: In lagoons and outreefs, in coral-rich areas and over mixed coral and rubble, 2–30 m. Frequently swims in small groups, feeds on zooplankton.

Distribution: Andaman Sea and Christmas Islands SW Japan, NW Australia, PNG and GBR.

Lubbock's Wrasse
Cirrhilabrus lubbocki

TP: With yellow pectoral fins. As distinct from the one shown, there is a variant with yellow back and ruddier side.
Size: 8 cm
Biology: Prefers outreefs, over coral and rubble, 3–35 m. Alone, often also in small loose groups, feeds on zooplankton.
Distribution: E Indonesia, the Philippines, Palau.

Exquisite Wrasse
Cirrhilabrus exquisitus

Black spot in the upper region of the tail stalk.
Size: 12 cm
Biology: Prefers outer reef slopes, 5–35 m. Often in current-exposed areas, also over rubble, feeds on zooplankton.
Distribution: East Africa to S Japan, Palau, GBR and French Polynesia, and Ducie Islands.

Blackstripe Coris
Coris pictoides

Light belly and dark back. Beginning over the eye, a thin white line extends to the tail.
Size: 12 cm
Biology: Prefers sand near the reef and rubble, 10–35 m. Swims alone or in small groups.
Distribution: Malaysia and Indonesia to the Philippines and SE Australia.

Batu Coris
Coris batuensis

TP: Upper body half with short dark vertical bands. Small black shoulder spot. An eyespot in the middle of the dorsal fin. IP with three eye spots on the dorsal fin and red spots on the head.
Size: 18 cm
Biology: In lagoons and outreefs, 1–20 m. Loner, usually just above sand and rubble.
Distribution: East Africa to S Japan, Micronesia and Tonga.

Clown Coris
Coris aygula

TP: (male, above) with frontal tubercle and ragged tail, olive-green and usually with whitish cross markings. IP (middle) and juveniles (below) with black spots on the front of body, juveniles also with two eye spots on the dorsal fin.

Size: 1 m

Biology: In lagoons and outer reef slopes, 2–40 m. Swims alone, frequently in reef areas with mixed coral, sand and rubble zones. Feeds on bottom-dwelling invertebrates, especially hard-shelled species, such as mussels, snails, sea urchins as well as hermit crabs and shrimps which it cracks with the grinding teeth in its gullet.

Distribution: Red Sea and East Africa to S Japan, Micronesia, Line Islands, French Polynesia.

African Coris
Coris gaimard

TP: Yellow tail, luminous blue dots at rear on tail base and body.

Size: 38 cm

Biology: In lagoons and outreefs, 2–50 m. Prefers to swim near coral above sand and rubble. Feeds predominantly on hard-shelled invertebrates such as snails, mussels, sea urchins, crustaceans.

Distribution: Christmas Islands and Bali to S Japan, Micronesia, Hawaii and French Polynesia.

IP: (middle) with a ruddy head. This specimen is already beginning the colour change to an adult male, discernible from the vertical greenish strip starting to form at the front of its body.

JP (below) is red-orange with white black-edged patches.

Spottail Coris
Coris caudimacula

Whitish with olive-reddish brown, rectangular patches on upper body half, colouration is pale to vivid.
Size: 20 cm
Biology: In lagoons, bays and protected outreefs, 2–25 m. Prefers to be above sand and rubble near corals. Alone and always near the bottom. Feeds on hard-shelled bottom-dwellers. Often accompanied by other fish when foraging.
Distribution: Red Sea, East Africa and Golf of Oman to Bali and NW Australia.

Queen Coris
Coris formosa

Male (TP) with cross bands. Female (IP, photo) with black spots, caudal fin is red in front, semi-transparent in the rear area.
Size: 60 cm
Biology: In coral-rich, usually exposed reefs, 3–30 m. Alone, above mixed zones with sand, coral and rubble. Feeds on hard-shelled invertebrates.
Distribution: Southern Red Sea, East Africa, the Mascarenes, Seychelles, Chagos Islands, the Maldives and Sri Lanka.

Green Birdmouth Wrasse
Gomphosus caeruleus

Characteristic tube snout. Similar to *G. varius*, but with different colouration.
Size: 28 cm
Biology: Inhabits coral-rich lagoons, bays and outreefs. Not uncommon, but shy and an agile, rapid swimmer. Feeds on small invertebrates, can also pick them up from branch coral and narrow crevices with its long, narrow snout.
Distribution: Red Sea to Mauritius, South Africa, Oman and Andaman Sea.

Male (TP, upper photo) coloured dark blue and is a loner, female (IP, lower photo) is yellowish-brown on the belly and usually swims in small groups.

Slingjaw Wrasse
Epibulus insidiator

TP: (Male) with white face and orange-coloured neck.
Size: 35 cm
Biology: Inhabits coral-rich lagoons and outreefs, 2–40 m. Loner, possibly in small harem groups, relatively shy. Feeds on shrimps, crustaceans and fish. It can rapidly thrust out its slingjaw tube and also suck in prey that live in-between the corals.
Distribution: Red Sea and East Africa to S Japan, Micronesia, Hawaii and French Polynesia.

IP: (Female) is cream-coloured to dark brown, also luminous yellow variant often seen.

Tail-spot Wrasse
Halichoeres melanurus

TP: (Male) with large, black spot on the back edge of the caudal fin, head with red stripes on green to blueish ground.
Size: 12 cm
Biology: Prefers protected reefs, 1–15 m. Swims alone or in small groups. Feeds off small invertebrates such as crustaceans and bristleworms.
Distribution: Indonesia to SW Japan, Micronesia, Samoa and GBR.

IP: With eyespot at upper tail base, an additional eyespot in the dorsal fin middle and a small black spot in front. The initial phases of *H. richmondi*, *H. purpurascens* and *H. vrolikii* (Indian Ocean) are very similar.

Checkerboard Wrasse
Halichoeres hortulans

Checkered pattern, TP (above) with one, IP (middle) with two to three yellow back spots. Juveniles (below) alternately with silvery-white and black bands and eyespot in the middle of the dorsal fin.

Size: 27 cm

Biology: In clear lagoons and outreefs, 1–30 m. Agile swimmers, always in movement during the day and not shy. Male occupies a large territory. Feeds on small bottom-dwelling invertebrates, frequently swims above rubble and sandy patches near coral.

Distribution: Red Sea, S Oman and East Africa to S Japan, Micronesia, Line Islands and French Polynesia.

Nebulous Wrasse
Halichoeres nebulosus

Complex pattern, colouration variable.
Size: 12 cm
Biology: In rock and coral reefs, 1–40 m. Shy, always close to the seabed, also on surfaces overgrown with algae and in the vicinity of hiding places. It is therefore frequently overlooked despite being common. Feeds on invertebrate bottom-dwellers.
Distribution: Red Sea, S Oman and East Africa to S Japan, Solomons and East Australia.

Canary Wrasse
Halichoeres chrysus

Lemon yellow. TP (male) has a black spot on the dorsal fin.
Size: 12 cm
Biology: Prefers to be above sand and rubble at reef edges and slopes, 2–60 m. Usually swims in small, loose groups.
Distribution: Christmas Islands and Bali to S Japan, Marshall Islands, Solomons, NW and East Australia.

Initial phase with two or three black patches on the dorsal fin. Juvenile phase (lower photo) with three black patches. Of these, the one on the middle back is a large eyespot. In the fish shown, the third front spot is obscured by the dorsal fin.

Adorned or Cosmetic Wrasse
Halichoeres cosmetus

Blueish-green with orange horizontal stripes. Juveniles (JP) and females (IP) with two eye spots on the dorsal fin.
Size: 13 cm
Biology: In lagoons and outreefs, 3-30 m. Usually in mixed zones of coral, rock and rubble.
Distribution: East Africa, Mauritius, Seychelles, the Maldives to Andaman Sea and Sumatra.

Twotone Wrasse
Halichoeres prosopeion

TP and IP: Head and parts of the body front are grey-blue with a flowing transition to a whitish-yellow to yellow rear of body. Black spot in front on the dorsal fin.
Size: 13 cm
Biology: In lagoons and outreefs with rich coral growth, 2–40 m. Swims alone or in small, loose groups.
Distribution: Indonesia to SW Japan, Palau, Samoa and SE Australia.

Juvenile phase with dark horizontal stripes and black spot in front on the dorsal fin.

Richmond's Wrasse
Halichoeres richmondi

TP: Caudal fin with blue-bordered fringe and blue horizontal stripes. Head with blue horizontal stripes.
Size: 19 cm
Biology: Shallow lagoons, protected reef channels and coastal reefs, 2–15 m. Shy, swims alone or in small groups.
Distribution: Indonesia (Java) to SW Japan, Marshall Islands, PNG and Vanuatu.

Green Wrasse
Halichoeres solorensis

TP (photo): Head yellowish-green with pale stripe pattern. Body mauve-coloured to grey.
Size: 18 cm
Biology: Lagoons and coastal reefs, above coral as well as on sand and rubble zones, usually in low depths to about 10 m. Female often in groups. Feeds on bottom-dwelling invertebrates.
Distribution: Indonesia to the Philippines and the Moluccas.

Blackeye Thicklip
Hemigymnus melapterus

Bright front and dark green-black back of body, large adults are predominantly olive-green.
Size: 50 cm
Biology: Inhabits lagoons and protected outreefs, 1–30 m. Prefers to swim above mixed zones with coral, sand and rubble in search of hard-shelled invertebrates on which it predominantly feeds.
Distribution: East Africa to S Japan, Micronesia and French Polynesia.

Juvenile phase with different, very high-contrast colouration, dark eyes and yellow tail.

Barred Thicklip
Hemigymnus fasciatus

Broad dark vertical strips.
Size: 50 cm
Biology: In lagoons and outreefs, 1–25 m. Prefers protected reefs and mixed zones with sand, rubble and coral. Alone, occasionally in small groups. Feeds on invertebrate bottom-dwellers, among them bristle-worms, crustaceans, brittle starfish and molluscs.
Distribution: East Africa to S Japan, Micronesia, Line Islands, French Polynesia and Ducie Islands.

Tubelip Wrasse
Labrichthys unilineatus

Thick, fleshy lips. TP greenish with light, broad vertical stripe behind head.
Size: 17 cm
Biology: Inhabits coral-rich, protected reefs, 1–20 m. Swims constantly between the coral. Feeds on coral polyps, especially on branched forms such as Acropora coral, where it will also withdraw when disturbed.
Distribution: East Africa to SW Japan, Micronesia, Samoa and Australia.

The initial phase is black with a white horizontal line. Like the adults, they are also already very agile and tireless swimmers.

Allen's Tubelip
Labropsis alleni

TP: Head brownish, yellowish to the body middle and becoming white toward the tail. Large black light-bordered spot at the pectoral fin base. A smaller spot in front on the dorsal fin and on the belly above the anal fin.
Size: 10 cm
Biology: At coral-rich lagoons and outer reef slopes, 4–50 m.
Distribution: Indonesia to the Philippines, Marshall Islands and Solomons.

Ring Wrasse
Hologymnosus annulatus

TP: Dark green with vertical stripes.
Size: 40 cm
Biology: Clear lagoons, bays and protected outer reefs, 5–35 m. Frequently in areas with alternating coral, rubble and sand surfaces. Male (TP) roams a large home territory. Predominantly feeds on fish, also supplemented by small crustaceans.
Distribution: Red Sea and East Africa to S Japan, Line Islands to French Polynesia and Pitcairn.

Juvenile phase with pale yellow back and dark brown to blackish lower body half. Always swims near seabed, usually above sand and rubble.

Pastel Ringwrasse
Hologymnosus doliatus

TP and IP with numerous blue vertical stripes. TP: an additional whitish crossband at the front of its body.
Size: 38 cm
Biology: In lagoons, outreefs and bays above mixed zones of coral, sand and rubble, 3–30 m. Male with large territory and harem females.
Distribution: Southern Red Sea, S Oman and East Africa to S Japan, Micronesia, Line Islands, Samoa and SE Australia.

Juveniles are cream-coloured with three red horizontal stripes. Frequently keep close together in small groups.

Bicolour Cleaner Wrasse
Labroides bicolor

Snout and parts of the head dark blue, front body black with abrupt transition to the pale yellowish body rear. Juveniles black with yellow back stripe.
Size: 14 cm
Biology: Coral reefs, 2–25/30 m.
Distribution: East Africa to S Japan, Micronesia, Line Islands and French Polynesia.

Bluestreak Cleaner Wrasse
Labroides dimidiatus

TP: Blueish-white. Black, from snout to tail increasingly broader horizontal stripe.
Size: 12 cm
Biology: In all reef ecosystems, 1–40 m. Operates cleaner stations, entices numerous fish species with conspicuous waving swim behaviour. Feeds exclusively on skin parasites, mucus and skin residues from its cleaning customers. Adults often in pairs.
Distribution: Red Sea, Arabian Gulf and South Africa to S Japan and French Polynesia.

Blackspot Cleaner Wrasse
Labroides pectoralis

Yellowish head. Dark horizontal stripe to the body rear is black and covers the entire top of the body. Black pectoral spot.
Size: 8 cm
Biology: Prefers to inhabit clear, coral-rich outreefs, also in lagoons, 2–28 m. Like other cleaner wrasse, feeds on skin parasites of other fish.
Distribution: Cocos Keeling and Christmas Islands to S Japan, Micronesia, Line Islands and Pitcairn.

Fourline Wrasse
Larabicus quadrilineatus

Male dark blue, IP: striped light dark blue and large black spot on caudal fin.
Size: 11 cm
Biology: In coral-rich bays, fringe and patch reefs, 0.5–20 m. Adults are territorial and feed on coral polyps. Juveniles and sub-adults work as cleanerfish, usually in small groups, but have no fixed stations.
Distribution: Red Sea and Gulf of Aden.

Leopard or Rare Wrasse
Macropharyngodon bipartitus

TP: male with green stripes at the front of its body
Size: 13 cm
Biology: In lagoons and outreefs beneath the surf areas, 2–30 m. Prefers mixed zones of sand, rubble and coral. Always swims near the bottom in search of small invertebrates. Males are territorial, each with a large territory and a harem of several females.
Distribution: Subspecies *M. b. marisrubri* in the red Sea, subspecies *M. b. bipartitus* from Oman to the Maldives, Mauritius and South Africa.

IP: Female reddish with white spots. Breast black with pale blue spots or mottled.

Ornate Wrasse or False Leopard
Macropharyngodon ornatus

IP (female upper photo): head orange to reddish with short, green, black-edged stripes. Body dark with blueish-green spots. TP: (male) very similar, but head greenish, the stripes and body dots blueish.
Size: 12 cm
Biology: In lagoons and protected outreefs, 3–30 m. Swims alone or in small groups, usually above mixed zones of coral, sand and rubble.
Distribution: Sri Lanka, Andaman Sea to SW Japan, Samoa and GBR.

Juveniles (lower photo): head with white basic colouration and net-like orange stripes. Black body with rows of large white patches.

Blackspotted or Guineafowl Wrasse
Macropharyngodon meleagris

IP: Black with very numerous small white spots. Transparent tail and whitish dorsal fin. TP with short head stripes.
Size: 12 cm
Biology: Inhabits mixed areas of sand, rubble and coral, 5–30 m. Alone or in small groups of a few fish. Small juveniles have a black eyespot at the back on the dorsal fin.
Distribution: The Maldives, Andaman Sea to SW Japan, SE Australia and Samoa.

Sharpnose Wrasse
Wetmorella nigropinnata

Red to brownish-red with one yellow band behind each eye and at the tail base. Dorsal, anal and ventral fin with one white-edged black spot each.
Size: 8 cm
Biology: In lagoons and outer reef slopes, 1–50 m. Lives hidden in caves and crevices. Very shy. Is often overlooked.
Distribution: Red Sea to SW Japan and Pitcairn.

Rockmover Wrasse
Novaculichthys taeniourus

White vertical stripe on tail root.
Size: 30 cm
Biology: In lagoons and outreefs, 2–45 m. Can usually be observed alone and above mixed sand-coral areas near reef. Feeds on bottom-dwelling invertebrates and also turns rubble over in order to uncover them.
Distribution: Red Sea, East Africa, S Oman to SW Japan, Hawaii, Panama and Polynesia.

Juveniles are brown with light speckles and imitate drifting seaweed in colouration and movement above the seabed.

Peacock Razorfish
Iniistius pavo

TP: (top): light greyish-blue with small, black back flecks.

Size: 40 cm

Biology: Near the reef, free sand surfaces in lagoons and at outreefs, 2–100 m. Adults usually below 20 m depth, alone or in loose groups. Feeds on hardshell invertebrates, such as shelled snails and crustaceans. Very shy, dives quickly into the sand when disturbed.

Distribution: Red Sea and East Africa to S Japan, Hawaii, Mexico and French Polynesia.

Juvenile (middle and lower photos, two colour variants) imitate drifting seaweed or dead leaves with their un-dulations. They are often observed in shallows. Usually not so shy as the adults.

Whitepatch Razorfish
Iniistius aneitensis

TP (top): large whitish spot rear of the pectoral fin. Occasionally shows 3–4 vertical stripes, which however contrast only weakly with the basic colouration.
Size: 24 cm
Biology: On open sand surfaces near the reef in lagoons and at outreefs, 10–90 m. At night, sleeps buried in the sand like other razorfish.
Distribution: Chagos Islands to SW Japan, Hawaii, Micronesia.

The photos below and in the middle show the juvenile phase in two colour variants.

Fivefinger Wrasse
Iniistius pentadactylus

TP: With 4–5 individual, often also overlapping, red patches towards the back of the eye.
Size: 25 cm
Biology: At coasts with sand and mud slopes, 1–30 m. Swims alone or in loose groups, always near to the bottom. When disturbed, dives rapidly into the soft ground, also sleeps at night in the sand.
Distribution: Red Sea and East Africa to SW Japan, Guam, Solomons and GBR.

IP: A whitish spot above the belly with red lines (red scale edges).

Two-spot Wrasse
Oxycheilinus bimaculatus

The caudal fin has an unusual angular form.
Size: 15 cm
Biology: In lagoons and outreefs, 2–110 m. Usually in areas with rubble, sand, seagrass and isolated stony corals with algae growth. Males are territorial, live with harem females, defending their spawning territory against other males.
Distribution: Gulf of Aden and South Africa to S Japan, Hawaii, Micronesia and French Polynesia.

Mental Wrasse
Oxycheilinus mentalis

Dark horizontal stripe on the side, white spot on the tail root.

Size: 24 cm

Biology: In lagoons, bays and outreefs with rich coral growth, 1–25 m. Not shy, sometimes even curious. Swims leisurely between small coral formations and always close to the seabed.

Distribution: Red Sea to Madagascar and the Maldives.

Bandcheek Wrasse
Oxycheilinus diagrammus

Variable colouration, however always with diagonal cheek stripes.

Size: 30 cm

Biology: In coral-rich lagoons, bays and outreefs, 3–60 m. Loner, not shy, occasionally even curious. Sometimes swims close above and between coral blocks, sometimes also a good distance above the seabed. As a predator, it feeds on small fish.

Distribution: Red Sea and East Africa to SW Japan, Micronesia, New Caledonia and Samoa.

This species occurs in very different basic colouration, from light whitish-grey to greenish with red to dark red belly.

Blue Flasher Wrasse
Paracheilinus cyaneus

TP: Small dots and lines on the head.

Size: 5 cm

Biology: On rubble ground of fringe reefs and outer reef slopes, 5–20 m. In the mating ritual, the male swims back and forth extremely fast and jerkily over a small area, while rapidly changing its colouration: the dorsal fin switches from red to white, the front body, especially on the upper side, from red to light blue-green.

Distribution: Borneo to Raja Ampat.

Chiseltooth Wrasse
Pseudodax mollucanus

TP: Yellow upper lip, whitish vertical stripe at tail base.
Size: 25 cm
Biology: Coral-rich lagoons, bays and outreefs, 2–40 m. Agile, fast swimmers, usually alone. Feeds on hardshell invertebrates.
Distribution: Red Sea and East Africa to S Japan, Micronesia and French Polynesia.

Juveniles with light stripes along back and belly. They keep predominantly to reef slopes with lots of crevices and cavities for hiding places. They occasionally act as cleanerfish.

Sixline Wrasse
Pseudocheilinus hexataenia

Six orange horizontal stripes. Tail root with small spot.
Size: 8 cm
Biology: Lagoons, bays and protected outreefs, 2–35 m. Common in many regions, however often overlooked because usually hidden between coral and coral branches. Feeds on small invertebrates.
Distribution: Red Sea, East Africa and Oman to SW Japan, Micronesia and French Polynesia.

Cryptic Wrasse
Pteragogus cryptus

Approximately oval eyespot on the gill lid, white stripe behind eye.
Size: 9.5 cm
Biology: Inhabits lagoons and shallow, protected fringe reefs, 1–20 m. Alone or in pairs, lives hidden and therefore frequently overlooked. Rests usually in the cover of coral branches, soft coral, seagrass or algae.
Distribution: Red Sea, East Africa and Oman to the Philippines, New Caledonia and Samoa.

Cockerel Wrasse
Pteragogus enneacanthus

Side line with small dark patches which can form large continuous stripes.
Size: 12 cm
Biology: On coral, algae-covered rock and sand surfaces, 3–30 m. Alone and quite shy, can only be rather rarely observed.
Distribution: Indonesia to Mariana Islands, Coral Sea, Tonga and SE Australia.

Sixbar Wrasse
Thalassoma hardwicke

Body with black, saddle spot-like vertical stripes on the back, which are shorter towards the back.
Size: 20 cm
Biology: In shallow lagoons and outreefs, 1–15 m. Also swims in shallow water on reef roofs and at reef edges. Not shy, sometimes curious. Feeds predominantly on bottom-dwelling invertebrates as well as plankton, crustaceans and small fish.
Distribution: East Africa to S Japan, Line Islands and French Polynesia.

Jansen's Wrasse
Thalassoma janseniii

Yellowish-white with three exten-
ded black areas.
Size: 20 cm
Biology: In lagoons and outreefs,
1–15 m. Alone or in groups. Very
quick and agile swimmers.
Distribution: The Maldives to S
Japan and Fiji.

Crescent Wrasse
Thalassoma lunare

TP: Blue to blue-green with blue
head. IP: predominantly greenish.
Size: 27 cm
Biology: Lagoons and outreefs,
1–20 m. Alone or in groups. Very
quick swimmers, always in rapid
movement. Not shy, sometimes
curious. Male is territorial and lives
with a harem of females. Feeds
on invertebrate bottom-dwellers,
especially crustaceans, also small
fish.
Distribution: Red Sea, Arabian Gulf
and South Africa to S Japan and
Line Islands and New Zealand.

Klunzinger's Wrasse
Thalassoma rueppellii

TP with more intense colour than IP.
Size: 20 cm
Biology: In coral-rich bays,
fringe and patch reefs, 0.5–20 m.
Common species, not at all shy,
often even curious enough to swim
towards the diver. Feeds on small
invertebrates, also small fish. Large
males have a territory with harem
females.
Distribution: Red Sea.

Parrotfish
Scaridae

Parrotfish are herbivores and use their beak-like teeth to scrape tiny algae from rock and coral making scratching noises heard over large distances. They also sometimes scratch at living stony corals for the symbiotic algae in these upper skeleton layers. They take up large quantities of indigestible calcium, which they eliminate in the form of conspicuous finely ground sand clouds. This contributes to the bio-erosion of the reef and is an important producer of coral sand. Like the related wrasse, parrotfish swim with the aid of pectoral fins while the caudal fin is employed only for flight or for the mating ritual when they rise rapidly to the water surface in pairs for spawning. Likewise, similar to wrasse (see page 185), many parrotfish switch their sex and colouration as they age. At night they rest in holes and crevices of the reef. Some also excrete a transparent mucous cocoon which probably forms an odour barrier to protect from nocturnal predators such as moray eels.

Bumphead Parrotfish
Bolbometapon muricatum

Olive to grey-green, adults with pronounced frontal tubercle with high vertical brow.
Size: 130 cm
Biology: In coral-rich lagoons and outreefs, 1–50 m. Largest species of the family, at least 70 kg. Feeds on living coral, bites off entire branches or noisily rams and breaks them off with its frontal tubercle. Day-active, usually moves in fixed groups which collect early in the morning over a reef. Sleeps at night in groups in large crevices and caves. Rare and shy in the majority of regions.
Distribution: Red Sea (rare) and East Africa to SW Japan, Taiwan, Line Islands and French Polynesia.

Bluemoon Parrotfish
Chlorurus atrilunula

Female with several (usually four) vertical bands of white rectangular patches. Male with dark blue tail sickle.
Size: 30 cm
Biology: Inhabits protected reefs, 1–20 m. Over coral, sand and rubble areas. Scrapes small algae growth from substrate.
Distribution: East Africa (Kenya to South Africa) to Chagos Islands, the Maldives and Seychelles.

Bleeker's Parrotfish
Chlorurus bleekeri

Adult male with large pale region on the cheek. Initial phase green-brown with light vertical stripes.
Size: 50 cm
Biology: Inhabits protected clear outreefs and lagoons, 2–30 m. Adult male is a loner, IP animals frequently swim in groups.
Distribution: Indonesia to the Philippines, Marshall Islands, Solomons, Fiji and GBR.

Indian Parrotfish
Chlorurus capistratoides

TP: (Male) with green stripes around eye, yellow spot on the pectoral fin base and long tail filaments. Juveniles and IP (female) dark grey with pink tail and snout.
Size: 55 cm
Biology: Prefers upper areas of coral-rich reef slopes, even in surf regions.
Distribution: East Africa to Seychelles, Andaman Sea, Bali and Flores.

Bicolour or Indian Parrotfish
Cetoscarus bicolour

Juveniles (below), female (middle) and male (above) with their own colouration.

Size: 80 cm

Biology: Prefers upper reef slopes of clear lagoons and outreefs, 1–30 m. The males are territorial and usually have several harem females.

Distribution: Red Sea and East Africa to Mauritius, S Japan, Micronesia and French Polynesia.

The juveniles usually swim over small sandy areas between the coral blocks and can – unlike many other juvenile parrotfish – be frequently observed by divers.

Heavybeak Parrotfish
Chlorurus gibbus

TP: Small brow hump, long tail filaments. IP: yellow
with green tail border and green chin. Very similar to *C.
strongylocephalus* of the Indian Ocean.
Size: 70 cm
Biology: Regularly along upper fringe reef slopes with
rich coral growth, 1–35 m. Male (TP) patrols a large
territory, frequently also a good distance above the
seabed. Belongs to those species which sleep at night in
a self-made mucous cocoon.
Distribution: Red Sea.

Middle: IP (female) typical yellow colouration. Bottom:
IP: in the process of a colour change to male (TP).

Purplestreak Parrotfish
Chlorurus genozonatus

TP: (Male) with green cheek stripes, among them a broad blueish-purple band. Initial phase reddish-brown.
Size: 30 cm
Biology: Inhabits coral-rich bays and slopes of fringe reefs, 5–25 m. Male alone and with large territory. Shy and relatively fast swimmers. In the initial phase, the fish usually move in small groups.
Distribution: Red Sea and Gulf of Aden.

Daisy or Bullethead Parrotfish
Chlorurus sordidus

Colouration and intensity variable. TP: (upper) usually with visible yellow-orange region on the cheek and a paler colouration of the tail stalk.
Size: 40 cm
Biology: Inhabits lagoons and outreefs, 1–30 m. Common and very widely disseminated species (with geographic forms). Adults usually above coral, Juveniles also above neighbouring rubble and seagrass surfaces. IP: often in smaller or larger touring groups. Sleeps in a mucous cocoon at night.
Distribution: Red Sea and East Africa to SW Japan, Hawaii, Line I and Ducie Islands

Juveniles or IP (lower) dark with white spots on the side and pale tail with dark spot.

Steephead Parrots
Chlorurus microrhinos

Usually intense greenish-blue, lower head area pale blue. A less frequent variant is dusky reddish with yellow fins. Both with high head profile.
Size: 70 cm
Biology: Inhabits lagoons and outreefs, 3–40 m.
Distribution: Bali to the Philippines and SW Japan, Line Islands, SE Australia and Pitcairn.

Sheephead Parrotfish
Chlorurus strongychephalus

TP (male): Yellow cheek spots, steep head profile. Blue caudal fin with long filaments.
Size: 70 cm
Biology: Inhabits lagoons and outreefs, 2–35 m. Relatively common. Usually swims alone. Rarely, adults roaming in schools are also encountered.
Distribution: Gulf of Aden and East Africa to Andaman Sea and SW Indonesia.

IP (Female): lower body area reddish, yellow caudal fins with blue back edge and short filaments.

Longnose Parrotfish
Hipposcarus harid

Elongated head. TP with long, IP with short tail filaments.
Size: 75 cm
Biology: In deep lagoons and semi-protected outreefs, 3–25 m. Commonly swims above near-reef sand and rubble ground. Often in groups of one male and several females. Grazes on algae growth.
Distribution: Red Sea and East Africa to Andaman Sea, Java and Cocos Keeling.

Common or Palenose Parrotfish
Scarus psittacus

TP: With grey-blue "snout cap", short stripes on the chin. IP: reddish-brown.
Size: 33 cm
Biology: In lagoons and outreefs, 1–25 m. At slopes and low-lying reef flats with hard ground and scattered coral formations. Produces a mucous cocoon for sleeping. Females often in schools with other species.
Distribution: Red Sea, East Africa to S Japan, Hawaii, and French Polynesia.

Yellowbarred Parrotfish
Scarus dimidiatus

TP: With blue-green region on the head and on the upper front of its body. Yellowish-pale diagonal stripe behind eye. IP: yellowish with three diffuse grey saddle spots.

Size: 30 cm

Biology: Inhabits coral-rich lagoons and outreefs, to about 20 m.

Distribution: Indonesia to SW Japan, the Philippines, Micronesia and Samoa.

IP: (Female): frequently pale yellowish and sometimes show three diffuse, grey saddle spots.

Rusty Parrotfish
Scarus ferrugineus

TP: (Male): Very broad green marking around the snout. IP: brownish with yellow tail.

Size: 40 cm

Biology: Prefers coral-rich fringe reef slopes and patch reefs. Common species, not shy. Males are territorial with a harem of several females. Can produce a mucous cocoon for sleeping.

Distribution: Red Sea to Arabian Gulf.

IP: (Female): brown with yellow tail.

Forsten's or Bluepatch Parrotfish
Scarus forsteni

TP: Green marking around the snout, with horizontal runners to rear of eyes. IP: with multi-coloured iridescent side-bands, additionally sometimes with a white spot.
Size: 40 cm
Biology: Lives in clear lagoons and outer reefs, 3–30 m.
Distribution: Cocos Keeling to Indonesia to SW Japan, Micronesia, GBR and French Polynesia.

Bridled Parrotfish
Scarus frenatus

TP: Abrupt transition from dark to light green just in front of the tail base.
Size: 47 cm
Biology: At clear outer reef slopes, frequently at reef tops and edges, 0.3–25 m. Grazes on algae growth, also in shallow water on the reef top.
Distribution: Red Sea, Oman and East Africa to SW Japan, Line Islands, SE Australia and French Polynesia.

IP: With dark diamond-shaped markings, often merging to a horizontal stripe.

Blue-barred Parrotfish
Scarus ghobban

Blueish-green with blue pectoral fins and significant scale markings. IP: yellow with blue, several bands forming patches.
Size: 75 cm
Biology: Inhabits protected rock and coral reefs, often also in murky and muddy water, 1–35 m. Juveniles also in groups above seagrass fields.
Distribution: Red Sea and East Africa to SW Japan, Galapagos, Panama and French Polynesia.

Redbarred Parrotfish
Scarus caudofasciatus

IP: (Female): Dark brown body front and three white bands on the back half of body.
Size: 50 cm
Biology: On steep outer reef slopes, 3–50 m. Shy. Always swims alone.
Distribution: East Africa to Mauritius, the Maldives and Andaman Sea.

Tricolour Parrotfish
Scarus tricolour

TP: Caudal fin with blueish base, green back edge and pink-coloured filaments. One green stripe above and below the eye.
Size: 55 cm
Biology: Inhabits coral-rich lagoons and outer reef slopes, 5–40 m. Usually swims alone.
Distribution: East Africa to the Philippines, Palau, Line Islands and PNG.

Swarthy Parrotfish
Scarus niger

TP: Dark greenish-blue with red eye and yellow-green spot behind the eye.
Size: 40 cm
Biology: Lives in coral-rich outreefs, lagoons and bays, 1–20 m. A common species in some places. Females often in small harem groups. Male territorial behaviour is occasionally observed.
Distribution: Red Sea and East Africa to SW Japan, GBR and French Polynesia.

JP: Red head and wavy light and dark side strip. The specimen shown is already undergoing the colour change to male (IP).

Ember or Redlip Parrotfish
Scarus rubroviolaceus

TP: Striking nose hump, long tail filaments, two chin stripes.
Size: 75 cm
Biology: In rock and coral reefs, 1–30 m. Prefers outer reef slopes. Swims alone or in groups and grazes on algae growth on the substrate.
Distribution: Red Sea and East Africa to SW Japan, Hawaii, Panama, SE Australia and French Polynesia.

IP: Light to dark reddish-brown, often with darker front and bright body rear. Chin, lips and ventral fin red, also sometimes the other fins.

Yellowband Parrotfish
Scarus schlegeli

A yellowish spot on the back which extends further to the ventral side as a pale crossband.
Size: 38 cm
Biology: Inhabits coral-rich lagoons and outreefs, 1–50 m. Often above mixed areas with coral and rubble.
Distribution: E Indonesia (e.g. Flores) to SW Japan, Micronesia, Australia and French Polynesia.

IP: (Female): Grey-brown with light sides stripes. Occasionally moves in larger groups through the reef in search of food.

Speckled Sandperch
Parapercis hexophthalma

Both sexes with large black tail spot. Male (upper photo) with stripes, female (lower photo) with spots on the cheek.
Size: 28 cm
Biology: Inhabits sand and rubble in lagoons and semi-protected outreefs, 2–25 m. Male is territorial, with a harem of 2–5 females. Feeds on bottom-dwelling invertebrates.
Distribution: Red Sea and East Africa to SW Japan, GBR and Fiji.

Sandperch
Pinguipedidae

Sandperch have long, thin bodies and are bottom-dwelling, lurking for prey. They usually lie on sand or rubble, less often also on dead stony coral. Supported on their ventral fins and the head a little raised for an improved overview, they await invertebrates and small fish which they capture with short, rapid thrusts. Some species make a sex change from female to male as they age. The latter are territorial and have a harem of several females.

Blackflag Sandperch
Parapercis signata

Grey back flecks, pale orange patches along the lower half. Side of head with dark markings.
Size: 13 cm
Biology: On sand and rubble near the reef and frequently on overgrown stony coral (as in photo), 8–30 m.
Distribution: The Maldives.

Black Dotted Sandperch
Parapercis millipunctata

White, often stipe-shaped spot on the caudal fin. Olive-brown patches on the side as well as on brow and snout.
Size: 18 cm
Biology: On rubble and sand surfaces near the reef, also on dead stony coral, 3–40 m.
Distribution: Mauritius and the Maldives to SW Japan, Micronesia, GBR and French Polynesia, Pitcairn.

Nosestripe Sandperch
Parapercis lineopunctata

Whitish with olive-grey back saddles and vertical stripes on the side. Striking black stripes from the snout tip through the eye.
Size: 12 cm
Biology: In coral reefs on fine and coarse sandy surfaces, often covered with dead stony coral, 3–35.
Distribution: Indonesia to the Philippines and Solomons.

Cylindrical or Sharpnose Sandperch
Parapercis cylindrica

Dark, vertical to slightly diagonal stripes below the eye. Lower side of body with broad, dark patches coursing vertically.
Size: 18 cm
Biology: On sand, rubble and rock grounds of coral and rock reefs, 1–20 m.
Distribution: The Maldives, Gulf of Thailand to S Japan, Marshall Islands and SE Australia. Variant with a yellow tail: Bali and East Indonesia.

Harlequin Sandperch
Parapercis maculatus

A double row of approximately rectangular, reddish-brown patches on the side. Short blueish-white lines on the cheek.
Size: 20 cm
Biology: Prefers protected coastal reefs on sand and rubble. 3–35 m.
Distribution: East Africa and Oman to Japan.

Latticed Sandperch
Parapercis clathrata

A row of pale brown to orange-brown patches along the lower side of the body. Always with a blackish centre. Male with eye-spot on either side of the neck.
Size: 18 cm
Biology: On sand and rubble of lagoons and outreefs, 3–50 m.
Distribution: Andaman Sea to SW Japan, Micronesia, Phoenix Islands, Samoa and GBR.

Redflecked Sandperch
Parapericis schauinslandi

Side with double row of red patches. First dorsal fin with red-black marking. Very pale and vivid red colour variants.
Size: 13 cm
Biology: On sand and rubble near the reef, 10–50 m. Often at outreefs, also where there's a slight current. Often floats some distance above the seabed and feeds on plankton.
Distribution: East Africa to S Japan, Guam, Hawaii and French Polynesia.

Blackfin Sandperch
Parapercis snyderi

About five reddish-brown, irregular saddle spots. Back edge of the caudal fin is dark. First dorsal fin is black. Yellow spot at pectoral fin base.
Size: 10 cm
Biology: Inhabits sand and rubble grounds near the reef, 5–35 m.
Distribution: Andaman Sea to S Japan, PNG and GBR.

Reticulated Sandperch
Parapercis tetracantha

Very high-contrast pattern of white and black-brown patches. An indistinct eyespot on the upper back of the head.
Size: 25 cm
Biology: In lagoons and protected outreefs, 5–25 m. Inhabits sand and rubble near the reef.
Distribution: India (Gulf of Bengal) and Andaman Sea to S Japan, Palau and PNG.

Yellowbar Sandperch
Parapercis xanthozona

Cheeks with white and orange diagonal stripes. Bright stripe from the pectoral fin to the tail base.
Size: 23 cm
Biology: On sandy grounds and overgrown rock near the reef, 8–30 m.
Distribution: East Africa to SW Japan, East Australia and Fiji.

Blennies
Blenniidae

About 350 species belong to this family. Blennies have no or only tiny, smooth scales, and instead have a protective mucous layer. They typically occupy small hunting grounds on hard ground and a tube-like burrow. The eggs are deposited on the seabed, as well as in crevices or below stones. The male commonly guards the clutch, sometimes also both parents. Two groups are common in the coral reef. Blennies have lots of small teeth for rasping tiny blanket-weed algae from the hard bottom, they also feed on small invertebrates. Fangblennies are predators, usually active swimmers and have a long, curved canine tooth on both sides of the lower jaw. Some specialist species bite off the scales, skin mucus or pieces of fin from larger fish. The genus *Meiacanthus* has poisonous canine teeth.

Blackflap or Eared Blenny
Cirripectes auritus

Light to dark brown with "ear" spot at the neck.
Size: 9 cm
Biology: Inhabits reef slopes with good coral growth, 2–20 m. Can usually be seen in shallower reef areas.
Distribution: East Africa to the Philippines, Taiwan, Palau and Line Islands.

White-lined Combtooth Blenny
Ecsenius pictus

Yellowish tail root with faded dark bands. Body with fine white horizontal stripes, the upper and the middle stripe broken by white spots.
Size: 5 cm
Biology: Inhabits reef slopes, 10–40 m. Often in the open, squatting on living coral.
Distribution: The Moluccas to the Philippines and Solomons.

Aron's Blenny
Ecsenius aroni

Dusty ochre, blue-grey head, black spot at the tail stalk.
Size: 5.5 cm
Biology: Spot and fringe reefs, 2–35 m. Uncommon. Shy species, bolts into small holes on approach.
Distribution: Red Sea.

Bath's Combtooth Blenny
Ecsenius bathi

Body whitish-grey with a dark horizontal stripe, short yellow stripe through the eye.
Size: 4 cm
Biology: In reefs with good coral growth, 3–20 m.
Distribution: Borneo and Bali to Western New Guinea.

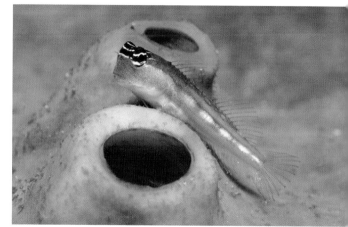

Red Sea or Many-toothed Blenny
Ecsenius dentex

Pale greyish to light brown. Dark chin stripe. Diffuse light patches on the body, pale yellow at the cheek.
Size: 6 cm
Biology: In protected fringe reefs, 1–15 m. Common species, not shy and can often be observed squatting in the open on coral or stony coral. Withdraws into small living holes when disturbed.
Distribution: Northern Red Sea.

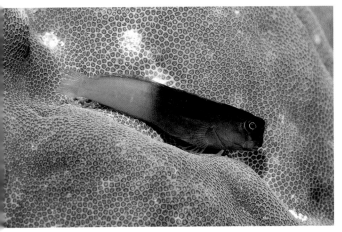

Bicolour Blenny
Ecsenius bicolour

This species occurs in two colour variants. The more common has a dark, blueish-grey body front and a yellow-orange coloured body rear (upper photo).
Size: 10 cm
Biology: Inhabits clear lagoons and outreefs, 2–25 m. On living coral and stony ground.
Distribution: The Maldives to SW Japan, Micronesia, Phoenix Islands, GBR and Fiji.

In the second variant, the lower body is half white, the upper dark brown, often turning yellow towards the tail.

Smooth-fin Blenny
Ecsenius frontalis

Occurs in three colour variants. Apart from the one shown (dark brown with white tail, *albicaudatus form*), there is also a light variant with black side stripe (*nigrivittatus form*) as well as a yellow form. Rarely in the Northern Red Sea, more common to the south.
Size: 8 cm
Biology: Inhabits coral, rock and rubble, 3–25 m.
Distribution: Red Sea and Gulf of Aden.

Red Sea Mimic Blenny
Ecsenius gravieri

Blue-yellow with black horizontal stripe behind the eye. The steep brow distinguishes it from the poisonous Blackline Fangblenny, which it imitates.
Size: 8 cm
Biology: In coral-rich areas from relatively protected fringe reefs, 2–25 m. Common species, often observed dormant on dead stony coral or living coral.
Distribution: Red Sea and Gulf of Aden.

Persian or Midas Blenny
Ecsenius midas

Swallowtail. Orange-yellow (shown) and grey-blue variant.
Size: 13 cm
Biology: In coral-rich reef slopes, 2–35 m. Yellow variant imitates the Sea Goldie, mixes in with their shoals. Feeds on plankton. Inhabits a small burrow, often with head protruding on the look out.
Distribution: Red Sea and East Africa to the Philippines, GBR and French Polynesia.

Yellowtail Blenny
Ecsenius namiyei

Dark brown to olive, with pale or yellow tail. Variant with high-contrast white markings on the head.
Size: 10 cm
Biology: In lagoons and outreefs, 3–30 m. Squats on coral, rock and sponges. Shy.
Distribution: Sulawesi and the Moluccas to the Philippines, Taiwan and Solomons.

Schroeder's or Spoke-eye Blenny
Ecsenius schroederi

Pale grey-brown, with a row white dashes on the back and the side.
Size: 5 cm
Biology: Inhabits protected lagoons and outreefs, 3–10 m.
Distribution: NW Australia to the Moluccas.

Shirley's Coral Blenny
Ecsenius shirleyae

Light brown. White stripe begins behind eye, extends to roughly middle of body. Two yellow stripes through the eyes.
Size: 4 cm
Biology: In coral reefs, 2–15 m.
Distribution: Indonesia.

Tail Spot Blenny
Ecsenius stigmatura

White-bordered black spot on the tail root. Yellow eye, orange-bordered.
Size: 5 cm
Biology: Inhabits coral-rich lagoons and outreefs, 3–30 m. Only moderately shy. This particularly attractive species can be observed alone and often also in small, loose groups.
Distribution: The Moluccas, Raja Ampat, the Philippines.

Yaeyama Blenny
Ecsenis yaeyamaensis

Two dark, short, close dashes at the rear of the eye. Black chin stripe.
Size: 6 cm
Biology: In lagoons and outreefs, 3–15 m. On dead and living coral. Squats usually in the open, flees into its burrow upon danger.
Distribution: Sri Lanka to SW Japan, Taiwan and Vanuatu.

Triplespot Blenny
Crossosalarias macrospilus

A conspicuous spot in front of the first dorsal fin, usually olive-green to brown.
Size: 8 cm
Biology: Inhabits coral-rich lagoons and outreefs, 1–25 m. Usually observed in lower depths. Not very shy.
Distribution: Indonesia to SW Japan, Palau, Tonga and GBR.

Leopard Blenny
Exallias brevis

Numerous reddish-brown patches.
Size: 14 cm
Biology: In coral-rich reefs, 0.3–20 m. Near short-branched coral such as *Acropora* and *Pocillopora*, feeds on their polyps. Shy; when disturbed, withdraws immediately into the protection of the coral branches. Male territorial, guards the eggs laid at the coral base.
Distribution: Red Sea and East Africa to SW Japan, Hawaii and French Polynesia.

False Cleanerfish
Aspidontus taeniatus

Snout juts beyond the mouth.
Size: 12 cm
Biology: In lagoons and protected outreefs, 1–25 m. Imitator of (mimics) the normal cleanerfish (page 202). Bites off pieces of skin, fin parts or scales from other fish. Often in a small burrow during the day, where its head is visible.
Distribution: Red Sea and East Africa to S Japan, SE Australia and French Polynesia.

Forktail or Yellowtail Blenny
Meiacanthus atrodorsalis

Blue-grey at the front, merging to yellow towards the back. Line from the eye diagonally up to the dorsal fin.
Size: 11 cm
Biology: In lagoons and outreefs, 1–30 m. Is imitated by *Escenius bicolour* and *Plagiotremus laudandus*. Usually stays a short distance above the seabed. Feeds on plankton and bottom-dwelling invertebrates.
Distribution: Bali and NW Australia to the Philippines, SW Japan, GBR and Samoa.

Striped Poison-fang Blenny
Meiacanthus grammistes

Three black horizontal stripes. Head yellowish. A row of black patches on the dorsal fin form a broken band. Black dots on the tail.
Size: 12 cm
Biology: Inhabits protected reef slopes and lagoons, 1–25 m. Can be observed fairly frequently. Not shy.
Distribution: Indonesia to SW Japan, Solomons and GBR.

Blackline Fangblenny
Meiacanthus nigrolineatus

Pale blue-grey, transitioning to pale yellow towards the rear. Black line behind eye to the tail.
Size: 10 cm
Biology: Inhabits protected fringe reefs and bays, 1–25 cm. Usually rests just above coral or the seabed. Remains largely unmolested because of its poison fangs.
Distribution: Red Sea and Gulf of Aden.

Bluestriped Fangblenny
Plagiotremus rhinorhynchus

Light to very dark brown with two blue stripes.
Size: 12 cm
Biology: Prefers clear, coral-rich lagoons and outreefs, 1–40 m. In rapid attacks, it bites off small skin flakes, scales or fin parts from other fish from which it feeds. Juveniles imitate the cleanerfish *Labroides dimidiatus.* When disturbed, flees into small rock holes or empty worm burrows. The eggs are also laid in such burrows and the male stands guard nearby.
Distribution: Red Sea and East Africa to S Japan, Line Islands, SE Australia and French Polynesia.

A variant is continuously orange with two blue stripes.

Piano Fangblenny
Plagiotremus tapeinosoma

Sideband of dark vertical stripes.
Size: 14 cm
Biology: In lagoons and outreefs, 1–20 m. Swims with winding movements, usually a short distance above the seabed. Bites skin, scales and pieces of fin off fish in surprise attacks. Seeks safe retreat in rock holes or empty worm burrows.
Distribution: Red Sea and East Africa to S Japan, Line Islands and French Polynesia.

Shorthead Fangblenny
Petroscirtes breviceps

Whitish to pale yellowish with three dark horizontal stripes.
Size: 12 cm
Biology: Inhabits protected reefs, preferably above sandy muddy or algae-covered surfaces, 1–15 m. Alone, in pairs or in small groups. Resembles the poisonous three-striped blennies and thereby obtains greater protection from predators. Inhabits small rock holes, empty worm burrows, in bays with civilization waste.
Distribution: East Africa to SW Japan, Yap, Solomons and New Caledonia.

Triplefins
Tripterygiidae

Triplefins derive their name from their three dorsal fins, however this characteristic is usually difficult to recognise because the fins are placed close behind each other. These bottom-dwelling fish are most commonly present in subtropical and temperate seas such as the Mediterranean. Apart from the Striped Triplefins, they are only very rarely observed by divers in the coral reef. In addition, the species represented here are usually less than 5 cm long. They feed on small bottom-dwelling invertebrates.

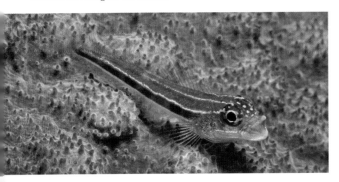

Striped Triplefin
Helcogramma striatum

Three white stripes. Brow with spots.
Size: 5 cm
Biology: In lagoons and outreefs, 5–25 m. Common, not shy. Often exposed on coral, sponges and rock. Alone or in small groups.
Distribution: Andaman Sea to SW Japan, Micronesia and Australia.

Volcano Triplefin
Helcogramma vulcanum

Male reddish-brown. Lower half of head dark with white to blueish horizontal stripe beneath the eye. Pectoral fin base with blueish-white spots.
Size: 4 cm
Biology: On hard ground in a few metres water depth.
Distribution: Bali to East indonesia.

Female with a row of dark patches or shorter bands along the side.

Mandarin Fish
Synchiropus splendidus

Unmistakable colour pattern of orange, green and blue.

Size: 6 cm

Biology: Sometimes common, though hidden in small groups on soft ground with dense coarse rubble or between coral branches, 2–20 m. While mating in the twilight, they swim a short distance in pairs into the open with body contact. Very shy, immediately flee into their shelters from the light of diving lamps.

Distribution: Indonesia to the Philippines, SW Japan, Caroline Islands, PNG and New Caledonia.

Dragonets
Callionymidae

Dragonets are a relatively large family with about 125 species. The majority of dragonets remain well below ten centimetres in length. All species stay close to the bottom, frequently living on sand or muddy grounds, some on hard ground. They feed on small bottom-dwelling invertebrates. Many species are adapted to the colour of the seabed, hence well camouflaged. The male dragonets are usually more colourful, and their first dorsal fin is enlarged and intensively coloured. Before mating, they perform an extended mating ritual.

Spotted Mandarin Fish
Synchiropus picturatus

Basic colouration is light brown to intensive green with large dark, orange-edged patches.
Size: 6 cm
Biology: Inhabits protected coastal reefs, 1–10 m. On hard ground such as coarse rubble and dead stony coral. Secluded lifestyle.
Distribution: Borneo to East Indonesia, NW Australia and the Philippines.

Fingered Dragonet
Dactylopus dactylopus

Free-standing first ray of the ventral fin ("finger") is used for walking. Front dorsal fin of the male with long filaments and a blue spot in the anterior region.
Size: 15 cm
Biology: Inhabits sand and muddy grounds along protected coastal reefs, 2–55 m. Alone or in pairs. During the day often partially buried.
Distribution: Andaman Sea to SW Japan, the Philippines, Palau, East Indonesia and North Australia.

The females are speckled or mottled light and dark brown.

Orange and Black Dragonet
Dactylopus kuiteri

First dorsal fin very tall, flag-like and with large eyespot at the base. Anal fin with blackish-blue luminous blue patches. Caudal fin with yellow and blue markings.
Size: 15 cm
Biology: Inhabits protected coastal reefs with sand and muddy grounds, 2–40 m. Alone or in pairs.
Distribution: Bali to East Indonesia and the Philippines.

Ocellated Dragonet
Synchiropus ocellatus

Greenish to brownish with spotted camouflage pattern. Fine blue dots on the head. End of the gill lid has small "plaques" in blue-white-ochre.
Size: 7 cm
Biology: On sand and rubble, shallow area to about 25 m. Alone or in small, loose groups.
Distribution: East Indonesia to SW Japan, the Philippines, Micronesia, GBR and French Polynesia.

Morrison's Dragonet
Synchiropus morrisoni

Male red with several small blue spots. Black spot to the rear of the pectoral fin base.
Size: 5 cm
Biology: In outreefs, 8–30 m. Usually on stony ground or rubble with algae upgrowth.
Distribution: Western Australia to Fiji, Samoa and Micronesia.

Moyer's Dragonet
Synchiropus moyeri

Adults whitish with irregular red jagged patches. Upper photo: female with transparent yellowish pectoral and ventral fins. In the male, the first dorsal fin is enlarged like a flag.
Size: 7 cm
Biology: On algae-covered rock and rubble ground, 5–30 m. Alone or in small groups.
Distribution: Indonesia to SW Japan, Palau, Solomons and GBR.

Juveniles (lower photo) with red bands around the eye and large white patches on the body.

Dartfish
Ptereleotridae

Dartfish are elongated fish with two dorsal fins and a small, diagonal, upwards-pointing mouth. They inhabit sand, gravel, rubble or mud grounds. They typically live in pairs, some also in small or larger groups. They never move far from their shelter to which they rapidly flee upon imminent danger. Dartfish feed on zooplankton which they snatch from the flowing water while suspended above the seabed.

Twotone Dartfish
Ptereleotris evides

Blueish-white on the adult front body, black rear of body.
Size: 14 cm
Biology: Prefers clear lagoons and outer reef slopes, 2–25 m. Usually in pairs and encountered up to two metres above the seabed. On approach, tends to swim away instead of fleeing into its burrow. Feeds on zooplankton. Juveniles in groups.
Distribution: Red Sea and East Africa to SW Japan, Micronesia, SE Australia and French Polynesia.

Fire Dartfish
Nemateleotris magnifica

White front, red body rear, dark tail root.
Size: 8 cm
Biology: Prefers outer reef slopes, 5–60 m. Adults usually in pairs. Usually hovers a half-metre above sand or rubble ground and feeds on plankton. Frequently snaps the long first fin ray up and down.
Distribution: East Africa to SW Japan, Hawaii, New Caledonia and French Polynesia.

Spottail Dartfish
Ptereleotris heteroptera

Light greenish-blue. Yellow tail with black spot.
Size: 12 cm
Biology: Inhabits lagoons and outreefs, 7–46 m. Alone, adults often in pairs, Juveniles in groups. Above sand and rubble. Swims to about 3 m above the seabed, feeds on zooplankton.
Distribution: Red Sea and East Africa to SW Japan, Micronesia, SE Australia and French Polynesia.

Brazilian Dartfish
Ptereleotris randalli

Pale blue with dark blue stripe along the side.
Size: 12 cm
Biology: On sandy bottom in protected bays and coastal reefs, 8–25 m.
Distribution: Widely distributed in the West Pacific.

Gobies
Gobiidae

Gobies are the largest family of sea fishes with more than 1,500 species in about 220 genera. They have an elongated, cylindrical body. They typically lie on the seabed or glide a short distance above it. They have developed different ecosystems. They can be frequently seen in reefs on sand surfaces. Many live here in symbiosis with snapping, rock-boring shrimp with which they share a burrow (see page 10). Some inhabit branched coral (*Gobiodon, Paragobiodon*) or sea whips and black coral (*Bryaniops*). Gobies usually live alone or in pairs. A Goby (*Trimmaton natans*) from the Maldives at only eight millimetres long is the smallest vertebrate in the world.

Aurora Shrimpgoby
Amblyeleotris aurora

Cream-coloured with five orange-brown stripes. Caudal fin yellow with red, blue-edged patches.
Size: 10 cm
Biology: Inhabits sand surfaces in lagoons and outreefs, 5–40 m. Alone or in pairs. Lives in a common burrow along with the snapping shrimp *Alpheus randalli*.
Distribution: East Africa to the Maldives, Seychelles and Andaman Sea.

Arcfin Shrimpgoby
Amblyeleotris arcupinna

Cream-coloured with five reddish-brown stripes and dark speckles in the interstices. Arching brown marking on the first dorsal fin.
Size: 8 cm
Biology: On sand and fine rubble in protected reefs. Shares a burrow with the partner shrimp *Alpheus bellulus* (see photo).
Distribution: Bali to Raja Ampat, PNG, Solomons and Fiji.

Giant Shrimpgoby
Amblyeleotris fontanesii

Whitish with 5 brown stripes. Small orange-yellow speckles on the head. Because of their unusual size, adults are distinguishable from species of similar colour.
Size: about 18 cm
Biology: Inhabits sandy to muddy grounds of lagoons and protected coastal reefs, 3–30 m.
Distribution: Sumatra and Gulf of Thailand to SW Japan, Palau and PNG.

Spotted Shrimpgoby
Amblyeleotris guttata

Pale with orange patches on head and body. Ventral fin as well as underside of body front is black, with vertical offshoots in front and rear of the pectoral fins.
Size: 9 cm
Biology: On sand and fine rubble grounds of clear lagoons and out-reefs, 3–35 m. Inhabits a sand pipe along with the snapping shrimp *Alpheus ochrostriatus.*
Distribution: The Philippines to SW Japan, Micronesia, East Indonesia, Australia and Samoa.

Masked or Nakedhead Shrimpgoby
Amblyeleotris gymnocephala

Whitish with 5 brown stripes and brown markings in their interstices. Often with a dark line from the back edge of eye to the first vertical stripe.

Size: 10 cm

Biology: Inhabits sandy as well as rubble areas in lagoons and outer reef slopes, 3–35 m. In burrow along with partner shrimp *Alpheus ochrostriatus.*

Distribution: NW Australia and Eastern Indonesia to the Philippines and Marshall Islands.

Broadbanded Shrimpgoby
Amblyeleotris periophthalma

Five to six orange-brown to dark orange bands. Interstices with same colour speckles. Dark-edged, orange dots on the head.

Size: 10 cm

Biology: Inhabits sand and rubble grounds of lagoons and outer reef slopes, 3–30 m. Lives along with various snapping shrimp, often with *Alpheus ochrostriatus.*

Distribution: East Africa to SW Japan, Micronesia, GBR and Samoa.

Randall's Shrimpgoby
Amblyeleotris randalli

Unmistakable, with six to seven orange vertical stripes and a large first dorsal fin with light-edged black eyespot.

Size: 9 cm

Biology: On sandy bottom, often below overhangs, prefers clear outreefs, 10–50 m. Lives along with snapping shrimp such as *Alpheus djeddensis* or *A. ochrostiatus.*

Distribution: Indonesia, the Philippines to SW Japan, Palau and Fiji.

Steinitz' Shrimpgoby
Amblyeleotris steinitzi

Whitish with five brown stripes. Tiny yellow dots on the dorsal fin.
Size: 8 cm
Biology: Inhabits sandy areas in lagoons and outreefs, 6– 30 m. Common in some places, but shy. Lives in symbiosis with various Alpheus snapping rock-boring shrimp (e.g. *A. djeddensis*).
Distribution: Red Sea and East Africa to SW Japan, Micronesia, GBR and Samoa.

Gorgeous Shrimpgoby
Amblyeleotris wheeleri

Six broad, red to brown-red bands, interstices light to yellowish with pale blue spots.
Size: 10 cm
Biology: Inhabits fine to coarse sandy grounds in clear lagoons and outer reef slopes, 3–30 m. Common in some places. Lives along with snapping shrimp (*Alpheus djeddensis* or *A. ochrostiatus*).
Distribution: Red Sea and East Africa to SW Japan, Marshall Islands, GBR and Fiji.

Flagtail Shrimpgoby
Amblyeleotris yanoi

Broad, diffuse-edged brownish-orange stripes. Caudal fin very conspicuous: orange and yellow with blue lines.
Size: 13 cm
Biology: In lagoons and outer reef slopes, 3–30 m. Inhabits sand pipes along with *Alpheus randalli*.
Distribution: Bali and Flores to SW Japan, Palau and Solomons.

Dracula Shrimpgoby
Stonogobiops dracula

Four black vertical bands, the second draws upwards to the back edge of the first dorsal fin. One fine brownish slash each between the bands.
Size: 6 cm
Biology: On protected sand and fine rubble near the reef areas, 6–40 m. Alone or in pairs, very shy. Often along with the snapping shrimp *Alpheus randalli*.
Distribution: Seychelles, the Maldives.

Black-rayed Shrimpgoby
Stonogobiops nematodes

Yellow face. Four dark bands, the anterior three diagonal. First dorsal fin with long, black filaments.
Size: 6 cm
Biology: On sand slopes in lagoons and outreefs, 5–40 m. Usually in pairs. Always close to the entrance of the burrow, which is shared with the snapping shrimp *Alpheus randalii*.
Distribution: Andaman Sea, Indonesia to the Philippines, Palau, E Australia and Samoa.

Whitebarred or Banded Goby
Amblygobius phalaena

Variable colouration from very pale to olive-brownish to blackish-brown. Red patches above the head. Dark spot on the first dorsal fin.
Size: 14 cm
Biology: On sand and rubble ground of protected reefs, 2–20 m. Alone or in pairs, often with a burrow dug by itself below a stone or rock.
Distribution: Cocos Keeling to SW Japan, Micronesia and French Polynesia.

Miller's or Blue-dot Goby
Asterropteryx ensiferus

Dark brown to blackish. Several rows of luminous blue dots along the entire side and on the anal fin.
Size: 3.5 cm
Biology: Inhabits larger, current-exposed rubble ground, 5–40 m. Frequently floats at an angle very close to the seabed.
Distribution: Red Sea to SW Japan, Marshall Islands, GBR and French Polynesia.

Pink-eye Goby
Bryaninops natans

Transparent, violet eye, yellowish gleaming ventral region.
Size: 2.5 cm
Biology: In lagoons and outreefs, 7–25 m. Usually hovers close above branches of Acropora branch coral. Occasionally also rests on them. Usually collects in small groups.
Distribution: Red Sea to SW Japan, Micronesia, GBR and Cook Islands.

Whip Coral Goby
Bryaninops yongei

Upper body is half transparent with about seven rust-brown patches.
Size: 3.5 cm
Biology: Exclusively inhabits spiral wiry corals *Cirripathes* anguinea. These prefer to grow at current-rich outer reef slopes between 3 and 50 m depth. The species lives in pairs on the coral, occasionally also with some juveniles.
Distribution: Red Sea to SW Japan, Hawaii, GBR and French Polynesia.

Blotched Goby
Coryphopterus inframaculatus

Semi-transparent, numerous orange patches along top of entire body. Tail root with dark spot and a white spot in front of it. Front dorsal fin with long first ray.
Size: 7 cm
Biology: On sand or silted stony coral of outreefs, 5–20 m. Takes sand in its mouth and sifts it for tiny invertebrates.
Distribution: Indonesia to Guam, GBR, Solomons and Tonga.

Beautiful Goby
Exyrias bellissimus

Diffuse broad side bands, partially merged. High dorsal fin with markings.
Size: 13 cm
Biology: Prefers fine sandy or muddy grounds in turbid bays, coastal and lagoons reefs, 1–20 m. Not shy. Takes fine sediment into its mouth and sifts for small invertebrates.
Distribution: Red Sea and East Africa to SW Japan, Micronesia, GBR and Samoa.

Citron Goby
Gobiodon citrinus

One pair of light blue horizontal stripes on the head, another pair beneath the eye.
Size: 6.5 cm
Biology: Prefers protected, coral-rich reefs, 1–20 m. Often in small loose groups of differently sized fish on Acropora or Millepora fire corals.
Distribution: Red Sea and East Africa to S Japan, GBR and Samoa.

Curious Wormfish
Gunnellichthys curiosus

Broad orange horizontal stripes. Black tail spot.
Size: 12 cm
Biology: On sand and rubble ground, 7–60 m. Floats or swims with undulating movements close to the seabed. Extremely vigilant and shy. When disturbed, rapidly dives head first into its narrow burrow.
Distribution: Madagascar, Seychelles to the Philippines, Palau, Hawaii and French Polynesia.

Decorated Goby
Istigobius decoratus

Whitish with numerous dark patches, often in a reticulated pattern.
Size: 12 cm
Biology: In protected outreefs, bays and lagoons, 1-20 m. Sifts sand for tiny invertebrates. Loner, not shy. In search of food, often makes short stops lying on the sand.
Distribution: Red Sea, East Africa, Madagascar to Taiwan and New Caledonia.

Hector´s Goby
Koumansetta hectori

Dark with yellow horizontal stripes. One black spot each on the first dorsal fin and at upper tail root as well as one eyespot on the second dorsal fin.
Size: 6 cm
Biology: In lagoons and outreefs, 3–25 m. Territorial, inhabits small sand patches, always near reef formations that offer shelter. Usually observed alone and below overhangs.
Distribution: Red Sea and East Africa to SW Japan, Caroline Islands.

Old Glory
Koumansetta rainfordi

Five orange, dark-edged horizontal stripes. A row of white flecks on the back. Eyespot on the back of the dorsal fin and black spot above the tail root.
Size: 6 cm
Biology: Above coral and stony coral in bays and outreefs, 3–30 m.
Distribution: Indonesia and the Philippines to Marshall Islands, NW Australia, GBR and Fiji.

Redhead Goby
Paragobiodon echinocephalus

Rear of body black. Head is red with closely-placed skin papillas, which make it look furred. With colour variants, the head or even the entire body is yellowish-green.
Size: 3.5 cm
Biology: Like all species of its genus, inhabits short-branched coral such as *Pocillopora*, *Seriatopora* and *Stylophora*. Often in small groups. In low depths up to about 10 m.
Distribution: Red Sea and East Africa to SW Japan and French Polynesia.

Signal Goby
Signigobius biocellatus

Two large eye spots on the dorsal fins, green-brown vertical stripe under the eye. Unmistakable.
Size: 6.5 cm
Biology: Inhabits sand and mud flats in protected coastal reefs, lagoons and bays, 2–30 m. Usually hovers very close to the seabed. Takes sand into its mouth and filters out tiny living creatures.
Distribution: Indonesia to the Philippines, Palau, GBR and Vanuatu.

Frogface Sleepergoby
Oxyurichthys papuensis

Tawny, irregular patches along the side.
Size: 18 cm
Biology: Inhabits muddy grounds in bays, protected coastal areas, 1–50 m. Has a mud burrow, but when disturbed it can also rapidly dig itself head first into muddy ground.
Distribution: Red Sea to SW Japan, Micronesia and New Caledonia.

Twostripe Goby
Valenciennea helsdingenii

Two reddish-brown horizontal stripes. Large black spot on the first dorsal fin.
Size: 15, max. 20 cm
Biology: On fine sand to gravel ground, 3–40 m. Usually in pairs. Digs a burrow into the sand with its mouth.
Distribution: Red Sea and East Africa to SW Japan, Palau and Marquesas in French Polynesia.

Orange-dash Goby
Valenciennea puellaris

Pale blue cheek spot. Yellow-orange coloured patches along the side. Colour intensity can be very different depending on bottom surface.
Size: 15 cm
Biology: In clear lagoons, bays and outreefs, 3–30 m. Inhabits self-made caves, often below pebbles on sandy bottom. Usually in pairs before the burrow entrance. Feeds on tiny invertebrates taken with the sand into its mouth and sifted through the gills.
Distribution: Red Sea to Madagascar, S Japan, Palau and Samoa.

Sixspot Goby
Valenciennea sexguttata

Black spot at the top of the first dorsal fin. Pale blue cheek spot.
Size: 14 cm
Biology: In protected bays, lagoons and coastal reefs, 1–10 m. On fine sandy to muddy ground. Adults always in pairs, inhabit burrows they dig themselves below a stone or a piece of dead coral.
Distribution: Red Sea and East Africa to SW Japan, Marshall I, Line Islands and Tonga.

Blueband Goby
Valenciennea strigata

Face yellow, turquoise head stripe.
Size: 18 cm
Biology: Usually on sand and rubble, also on hard ground, in clear lagoons and outreefs, 1–20 m. Monogamous, almost always in pairs, glide a short distance above the seabed. Shared burrow in hard or soft ground.
Distribution: East Africa to SW Japan, Micronesia, Line Islands, SE Australia and French Polynesia.

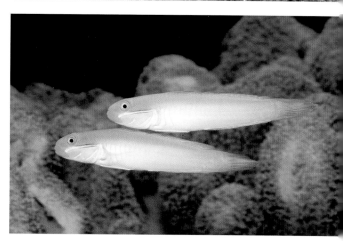

Barracudas
Sphyraenidae

Barracudas are active, strong predators that hunt various fish. With their powerful jaws and sharp teeth, they can easily split a fish as large as themselves into two halves in a single bite. It has an extremely fast acceleration from stationary and hits its prey in a split-second thrust. Long pursuits are not its business. Juveniles as well as adults of various species can live in large schools. Barracudas are represented worldwide in all tropical and subtropical seas. Barracudas have a bad reputation outside of diver circles which is unfounded. Attacks on humans are exceedingly rare and are then almost always based on mix-ups, feeding activities, or self-defence when feeling threatened.

Great Barracuda
Sphyraena barracuda

Caudal fin with white tips and frequently with two large dark patches. Often some dark speckles on the body.
Size: 180 cm
Biology: In lagoons, bays, outreefs and river deltas, one to more than 100 metres, usually in the upper 20 metres. Often stands motionless in open water near the reef. Juveniles frequently in groups, adults are usually loners. Curious, can approach divers.
Distribution: All tropical seas.

Pickhandle Barracuda
Sphyraena jello

Pale yellowish tail. Side with slightly curved markings.
Size: 150 cm
Biology: In deep lagoons and at current-rich protrusions of outreefs. Uncommon. Also intrudes into muddier waters. Occurs alone or in small schools.
Distribution: Red Sea, Arabian Gulf and East Africa to SW Japan and Fiji and Tonga.

Blackfin Barracuda
Sphyraena qenie

Vertical angular markings. Dark notched caudal fin with black fringe.
Size: 140 cm
Biology: Prefers current-rich outreefs, also in deep lagoons, 1–50 m. In large, semi-stationary schools during the day, sticking to the same location sometimes for months. At night, shoals dissolve probably in search of food.
Distribution: Red Sea and East Africa to Panama and French Polynesia.

Yellowtail Barracuda
Sphyraena flavicauda

Back and tail yellowish-green, likewise lateral horizontal stripe. Especially in older fish, this colouration usually only appears as a pale shimmer on the basic silvery colouration.
Size: 40 cm
Biology: In deep lagoons and at outer reefs. In schools during the day which disperse at night.
Distribution: Red Sea and East Africa to SW Japan, Samoa and GBR.

Tuna and Mackerel
Scombridae

Tunas have a spindle-shaped body, rigid in the front with a slender tail base and a high, sickle-shaped caudal fin. Some species are among the fastest of all swimmers and achieve top speeds of up to 95 kilometres per hour. They manage large distances in search of food tirelessly and must feed up to a quarter of their body weight daily. Almost all bony fish are "cold-blooded". Only a few dozen species can keep parts of their body warm. These species also include various tuna species. They warm their head with special vascular lines that take up warmth generated by the swimming muscles before it is lost in the circulation to the gills. Tuna stocks have declined worldwide because of over-fishing and some species are greatly endangered.

Dogtooth Tuna
Gymnosarda unicolor
Whitish tips of dorsal and anal fins.
Size: 200 cm
Biology: In deep lagoons, reef channels and at outreefs, 1–100 m. Alone or in small loose groups, patrolling in the open water along reef slopes. Fast hunting fish, especially of fusiliers and other plankton-feeding fish in open water. Occasionally swims curiously past divers. Probably the most common tuna species sighted along coral reefs.
Distribution: Red Sea, Gulf of Oman and East Africa to SW Japan, Micronesia, New Caledonia and French Polynesia.

Barred Spanish Mackerel
Scomberomorus commerson

Silvery with slightly wavy vertical stripes along the side.
Size: 245 cm
Biology: Pelagic lifestyle, 1–200 m. Migrates over longer distances, thereby occasionally crossing near reefs. Feeds predominantly on sardines, anchovies and fusiliers.
Distribution: Red Sea and East Africa to SW Japan, Palau, SE Australia and Fiji.

Indian or Long-jawed Mackerel
Rastrelliger kanagurta

Black spot behind the pectoral fins.
Size: 38 cm
Biology: In bays, lagoons and along protected outreefs, 1–70 m. Swims along the reef in large dense schools and thereby filters plankton from the water with wide-open mouth. Can be attracted to light at night.
Distribution: Red Sea and East Africa to SW Japan, GBR and Samoa.

Flatfish
Order *Pleuronectiformes*

Flatfish have an asymmetrical body that is laterally extremely compressed. Initially their larval stage retains the normal fish form. In the transformation process, one eye migrates in the direction of the other which lies on the opposite side, which later becomes the upper side. Only this eye is pigmented and can quickly adapt its colour to the relevant bottom surface. Flatfish are bottom-dwelling predators that feed on invertebrates and fish. Can dig into the soft ground so that only the eyes are visible.

Flowery or Peacock Flounder
Bothus mancus

Eyes far apart. Blue dots. Partially broken rings. Male has long pectoral fin rays.
Size: 42 cm
Biology: On sand and hard grounds 0.5–80 m. Frequently on reef tops.
Distribution: Red Sea, East Africa to SW Japan, Micronesia, Hawaii and Ducie Islands.

Leopard Flounder
Bothus pantherinus

Eyes close together.
Size: 39 cm
Biology: On soft and rubble grounds, 1-60 m. Male directs long pectoral fin rays upwards during courtship, disturbance and territorial behaviour.
Distribution: Red Sea, East Africa to S Japan and French Polynesia.

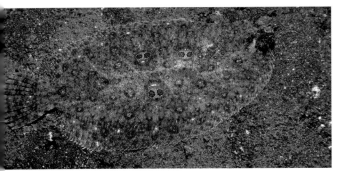

Eyespot or Ocellated Flounder
Pseudorhombus dupliciocllatus

2–4 pairs of eye spots.
Size: 40 cm
Biology: Inhabits sand and mud ground in coastal vicinity, 5–150 m. Usually in lower depths. Feeds on fish and small invertebrates on the seabed.
Distribution: Andaman to the Philippines, S Japan, North Australia, East indonesia.

Finless Sole
Pardachirus marmoratus

Pale mottled. Numerous black dots.
Size: 26 cm
Biology: On sandy areas near the reef, 1–15 m. Usually mostly buried. Secretes a milky, poisonous substance from pores at the base of the pectoral and anal fin.
Distribution: Red Sea, Arabian Gulf and East Africa to Sri Lanka.

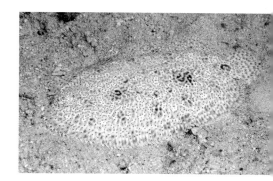

Peacock Sole
Pardachirus pavoninus

Numerous different large, bright patches. The larger usually with a dark dot in the middle.
Size: 30 cm
Biology: Inhabits sand and mud flats in reef vicinity, 1–40 m. Often buried up to their eyes and nostrils. Predominantly feeds on bottom-dwelling invertebrates. Secretes a milky poison from pores at the base of the back and anal fin.
Distribution: Sri Lanka to S Japan and Tonga.

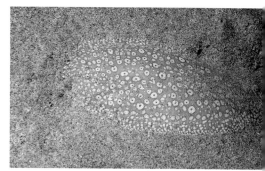

Banded Sole
Soleichthys heterorhinos

Dark vertical bands. Fin edges often blueish.
Size: 16 cm
Biology: On sand areas near the reef, less often on hard ground, 1–15 m. At night, it may swim a short distance above the seabed. With their blue edge fringe, juveniles possibly imitate poisonous flatworms.
Distribution: Red Sea and East Africa to S Japan, Marshall Islands, SE Australia and Samoa.

Zebra Sole
Zebrias fasciatus

Light grey-brown with darker vertical stripes, often with several light, diffuse patches. Tail is black with yellow patches and often with a blue edge.
Size: 25 cm
Biology: Inhabits sand and mud grounds of protected coasts, bays and estuaries, 5–25 m. Probably active at night.
Distribution: Indonesia to the Philippines, China and Korea.

Spadefish
Ephippidae

Longfin Spadefish
Platax teira

Broad dorsal and anal fins. Black spot diagonally beneath the pectoral fin.

Size: 60 cm

Biology: In deep lagoons, bays and at outer reef slopes, 2–30 m. Often in schools, sometimes also alone or in small groups. Juveniles of this species prefer to keep to low depths in protected reef areas and can more often be observed than juveniles of other *Platax* species.

Distribution: Red Sea and East Africa to SW Japan, Kosrae in Micronesia, GBR and Fiji.

Juvenile, about 14 cm high, with greatly extended dorsal, anal and ventral fins. Animals this size can usually be encountered at protected locations near coral formations.

Golden Spadefish
Platax boersi

Head profile slightly curved.
Size: 40 cm
Biology: In deep lagoons and at outreefs, 2–30 m. Frequently in large schools, sometimes also alone or in pairs, usually along steep reef slopes.
Distribution: Red Sea and East Africa to SW Japan, Palau, Solomons and GBR.

Humpback or Batavia Batfish
Platax batavianus

Frequently with speckled black patches on the belly.
Size: 50 cm
Biology: Prefers lagoons and protected coastal reefs, 5–45 m. Usually alone or in loose small groups. Rare compared to other *Platax* species. Juveniles with white-black stripe pattern and extended pectoral, anal and ventral fins.
Distribution: Malaysia to North Australia and PNG.

Circular Spadefish
Platax orbicularis

Yellowish pectoral fins.
Size: 50 cm
Biology: In deep lagoons and at outreefs, 2–35 m. In pairs or in schools. Often swims along steep slopes or in the open water of deep lagoons and bays.
Distribution: Red Sea and East Africa to SW Japan, Micronesia, New Caledonia and French Polynesia.

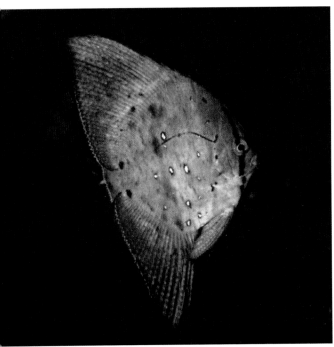

Juveniles keep to protected areas at very low depth, also close to shore in bays. They imitate dead leaves in colouration as well as in their swaying or drifting movements. They occasionally lie on their side on the seabed. The specimen shown is about 4 cm high.

Dusky Batfish
Platax pinnatus

Characteristicly protruding mouth.
Size: 35 cm
Biology: At protected reef slopes,
2–40 m. In contrast to other *Platax*
species usually alone and prefers to
stay at protected places in the reef.
Distribution: Thailand and Sumatra
to SW Japan, Palau, Salomons,
Vanuatu and New Caledonia.

Juveniles are black and have a
luminous orange edge fringe all
around. They are rather shy and
usually stay in the protection of
caves, crevices and overhangs. It is
assumed that with their colouration, they imitate large, poisonous
flatworms. The specimen shown is
about 9 cm long.

Rabbitfish
Siganidae

It is rare to see rabbitfish at rest during the day. They tirelessly cruise above the reefs and seagrass fields in search of food, moving in pairs or in small, sometimes also larger, groups depending on species. About half of the approximately 30 species live as juveniles in schools, but later form pairs. The others remain in schools, which can comprise several hundred fish, for life. Rabbitfish feed primarily on algae and seagrass, some species also occasionally feed on invertebrates like sea squirts and sponges. When feeding, they make characteristic mumbling movements with their small mouths which have a thickened upper lip, a characteristic to which they owe their name. It is hard to believe that this harmless-looking fish is abundantly armoured with poisonous fin rays. They serve exclusively for defence and can cause painful wounds. At night they take on a diffuse camouflage colouration and lie on their side in an open area.

Forktail Rabbitfish
Siganus argenteus

Caudal fin clearly forked and usually somewhat blueish.

Size: 43 cm

Biology: Adults often at outer reef slopes, 1–30 m. Usually moves through the reef in small and sometimes also in large groups, often above mixed coral rubble zones or algae-covered areas.

Distribution: Red Sea and East Africa to SW Japan, GBR and French Polynesia.

Coral Rabbitfish
Siganus corallinus

Yellow with numerous small pale blue spots.
Size: 30 cm
Biology: Adults in coral-rich lagoons and protected coastal reefs, 2–20 m. Feeds on algae growth. Juveniles in seagrass fields and between horn corals (*Acropora sp.*)
Distribution: Seychelles to SW Japan, Palau and Guam, GBR and New Caledonia.

Dusky Rabbitfish
Siganus fuscescens

Grey with numerous small pale blue to blueish-white spots. Greenish from the brow over the top of the back to the tail.
Size: 30 cm
Biology: In bays, lagoons and less often along outer reef slopes, 1–10 m. Juveniles in schools, adults usually in smaller groups, sometimes also in pairs.
Distribution: Andaman Sea to SW Japan, Micronesia, Australia, Vanuatu and New Caledonia.

Golden Rabbitfish
Siganus guttatus

Numerous orange-yellow body spots. Large, golden yellow spot beneath the rear dorsal fin base.
Size: 40 cm
Biology: In lagoons and coastal reefs, coral and rock areas, 2–30 m. Often in small groups, sometimes also in pairs. Swims over coral-rich surfaces as well as over sand.
Distribution: Andaman Sea to SW Japan, Palau, Bali and Irian Jaya.

Java Rabbitfish
Siganus javus

Tail predominantly or totally dark grey to black. Body with numerous light spots. Often only a few horizontal stripes on the belly, but can cover the bulk of the side.
Size: 53 cm
Biology: In coral and rock reefs along coasts, also in estuaries and mangrove regions, 1–15 m. Alone or in small groups.
Distribution: Arabian Gulf to Andaman Sea, the Philippines, NE Australia and Vanuatu.

Dusky Spinefoot or Squaretail Rabbitfish
Siganus luridus

Pale olive-green to dark brown.
Size: 24 cm
Biology: In lagoons, bays and protected outreefs, 2–18 m. Swims alone or in small groups above silted or algae areas and grazes on algae growth.
Distribution: Red Sea and Arabian Gulf to Mozambique and Mauritius. Migrated by way of the Suez Canal into the Mediterranean.

Masked Rabbitfish
Siganus puellus

Yellow with wavy blue lines and spots. Dark horizontal band from the chin to the eye, grey with black patches above this.
Size: 30 cm
Biology: Inhabits coral-rich reefs, 2–25 m. Usually in pairs, feeds on sea squirts and sponges.
Distribution: Cocos Keeling to SW Japan, Micronesia and Gilbert Islands, GBR, Vanuatu and New Caledonia.

Goldspotted Rabbitfish
Siganus punctatus

Numerous dark-edged orange dots (below water from a distance they appear brown).
Size: 35 cm
Biology: In lagoons and outreefs, 2–35 m. Above coral and sandy grounds near the reef. Swim in pairs.
Distribution: Cocos Keeling and Sumatra to SW Japan, Micronesia, Australia and New Caledonia.

Marbled Spinefoot
Siganus rivulatus

Very pale olive colour with irregular, sometimes broken orange lines on the side (can only be recognised easily from close up).
Size: 30 cm
Biology: In protected outreefs and bays, 1–15 m. Moves in groups or large schools over areas with dead coral as well as sandy and algae surfaces.
Distribution: Red Sea and Gulf of Aden; Migrated by way of the Suez Canal into the Mediterranean.

Stellate Rabbitfish
Siganus stellatus laqueus

Dense black honeycomb-shaped dot pattern. Neck and back olive-coloured and without dots. Edges of the caudal fin and back edge of the dorsal fin are yellow.
Size: 35 cm
Biology: In clear, coral-rich bays and outreefs, 1–35 m. Adults almost always in pairs. Ranges extensive distances through the reef and grazes on algae growth.
Distribution: Red Sea and Gulf of Aden.

Honeycomb Rabbitfish
Siganus stellatus

On cream-coloured to light brown background, numerous densely-placed dots, also on neck and back. Caudal fin with narrow white edge fringe.
Size: 35 cm
Biology: In lagoons and outreefs, 1–30 m. Almost always in pairs, ranges through coral-rich zones as well as through algae reef areas with rubble and dead coral.
Distribution: East Africa to the Maldives, Andaman Sea and Bali.

Barhead Spinefoot or Virgate Rabbitfish
Siganus virgatus

Two dark diagonal bands on the head, one of these through the eye. Upper body with blue spots. Similar to *S. doliatus* with fine yellow traverse lines.
Size: 30 cm
Biology: In rock and coral reefs, 2–20 m. Swims in pairs or in small groups.
Distribution: India to the Philippines, SW Japan, North Australia and Irian Jaya.

Foxface Rabbitfish
Siganus vulpinus

Head with black-white "fox face". Rest of body solid yellow. Similar to *S. unimaculatus* but with the addition of a large, black spot on the side.
Size: 24 cm
Biology: Inhabits coral-rich lagoons and outreefs, 2–30 m. Juveniles often seek protection between the branches of horn corals (*Acropora* species). Adults swim in pairs.
Distribution: Sumatra to Taiwan, Gilbert Islands, GBR and New Caledonia.

Surgeonfish
Acanthuridae

The family is subdivided into surgeonfish, unicornfish and sawtails. All bear razor sharp bone blades on both sides of the tail base – hence their name. Scalpel surgeonfish have an adjustable blade on each side. Unicornfish have one or two, the sawtails have three to six fixed blades on each side. They only use their blades as defensive weapons, occasionally also for intra-species fights. Scalpel surgeonfish usually graze on tiny blanket-weed algae on rock. Others, such as the majority of the *Naso* species, feed on zooplankton. Grazing surgeonfish have an important function for the ecological equilibrium of the reef because they prevent algal blooms.

Powderblue Surgeonfish
Acanthurus leucosternon

Black head, white throat, yellow dorsal fin.

Size: 23 cm

Biology: Interior and outreefs, 0.5–25 m. Adults usually in groups, sometimes in very large schools which move as a feeding consort usually in low depths above the reef. Grazes on algae. Can cross-breed with *A. nigricans*. The hybrids have no white throat spot.

Distribution: East Africa to Burma and Andaman Sea, Christmas Islands, Bali and Komodo.

Sohal Surgeonfish
Acanthurus sohal

White side strip, black caudal fin seamed blue.

Size: 40 cm

Biology: At exposed outreefs with heavy seas, 0.2–10 m. Nimble, sturdy swimmer, prefers to stop at the reef roof and reef edge, where it grazes on algae. Very territorial: male aggressively defends its small feeding grounds with several harem females.

Distribution: From Red Sea along the Arabian Peninsula to Gulf of Oman and Arabian Gulf.

Yellowmask Surgeonfish
Acanthurus mata

Yellow upper lip, yellow eye mask, very fine horizontal stripes.

Size: 50 cm

Biology: In lagoons, bays and outreefs, also in turbid water, 3 to more than 30 m. Often also swims in schools in front of reef slopes and catches zooplankton high above the seabed. Can rapidly change colour, especially at cleaner stations.

Distribution: Southern Red Sea to South Africa, SW Japan, Marshall Islands and French Polynesia.

Lined Surgeonfish
Acanthurus lineatus

Yellow with blue, black-seamed horizontal stripes; blueish belly.
Size: 38 cm
Biology: Frequently in the surf regions of outer reef roofs and exposed reef edges, 0.2–6 m. Very territorial, large males have feeding grounds and harems which they aggressively defend. Grazes on algae.
Distribution: East Africa to SW Japan, Micronesia and French Polynesia.

Chocolate or Mimic Surgeonfish
Acanthurus pyroferus

Adults brown with red spot above pectoral fin base, and black band from the chin to eye rear. Juveniles in two colour variants: solid yellow or blackish in back, greyish in front.
Size: 25 cm
Biology: in lagoons and outreefs, 2–60 m. Adults usually swim alone in mixed areas of coral, sand and rock.
Distribution: Cocos Keeling to SW Japan, Hawaii, Micronesia and French Polynesia.

Depending on the region, juveniles are imitators of the yellow Lemonpeel Angelfish *Centropyge flavissima* or the Pearlscale Angelfish (*C. vroliki*). The juvenile fish in this photo is a mimic of the latter. However, it is already beginning to show the colour change to an adult. Instead of the blue, it already has a yellow tail fringe and the start of a black band at the chin.

Roundspot Surgeonfish
Acanthurus bariene

White lips, yellow dorsal fin, blue spot and yellow-orange vertical stripe to the rear of the eye.
Size: 42 cm
Biology: In coastal and outreefs with clear water, 6–50 m. The brow protrusion enlarges on ageing. Ranges alone or in small groups above the reef and grazes on algae growth on hard ground.
Distribution: East Africa to SW Japan, Palau, Solomons and GBR.

Ringtail Surgeonfish
Acanthurus blochii

Small, orange-yellow spot to the rear of the eye, tail base usually with white ring, caudal fin blue.
Size: 45 cm
Biology: Inhabits lagoons and outreefs usually by 2–15 m. Swims alone or in small groups and grazes on algae growth on rock, dead coral and other firm substrates.
Distribution: East Africa to SW Japan, Marshall Islands, Hawaii and French Polynesia.

Epaulette or Blackstreak Surgeonfish
Acanthurus nigricaudus

Horizontal stripe to the rear of the eye, tail base whitish.
Size: 40 cm
Biology: Inhabits clear lagoons outreefs as well as murky, sandy lagoons, 3–30 m. Ranges alone, often also in groups of other surgeonfish, near reef areas with sand and rubble ground and stringy algae growth. Can switch its basic colouration rapidly from dark grey brown to pale grey.
Distribution: East Africa to SW Japan, GBR and French Polynesia.

Yellowfin Surgeonfish
Acanthurus xanthopterus

Yellow at the pectoral fins. Yellow
band above the eye.
Size: 60 cm
Biology: Lagoons and outreefs,
3–90 m. Largest species of its genus. Alone or in loose groups above
the reef sand, rubble and stony
ground. Grazes predominantly on
thread algae and diatoms as well as
detritus, occasionally also hydrozoa.
Can rapidly switch colour pattern.
Distribution: East Africa to SW
Japan, Hawaii, Panama and New
Caledonia.

Whitecheek Surgeonfish
Acanthurus nigricans

Back and anal fin with yellow base
line. Yellow vertical stripe on caudal
fin, yellow tail blade.
Size: 21 cm
Biology: Prefers outreefs, 1–60 m.
Frequently in low depths beneath
the surf regions. Territorial, grazes
on blanket-weed algae on hard
ground.
Distribution: Cocos Keeling, Christmas Islands, Western Australia to
SW Japan, Hawaii, Panama and
French Polynesia.

Palelipped Surgeonfish
Acanthurus leucocheilus

White tail blade. Pale band at the
chin. Whitish mouth. Black shoul-
der spot. Basic colouration often
dark brown to blackish, can rapidly
become significantly brighter (see
photo).
Size: 45 cm
Biology: At clear outreefs, often in
the vicinity of steep drops, 4–30 m.
Alone or in small groups.
Distribution: East Africa, the
Maldives, Seychelles to Andaman
Sea, Indonesia, the Philippines,
Palau and Line Islands.

Convict Surgeonfish
Acanthurus triostegus

Pale green with five to six black vertical stripes.
Size: 26 cm
Biology: In lagoons and outer reefs, 2 to above 20 m. Usually in shallow areas above coral reefs and rock substrates. Often moves in large shoals, sometimes with more than 1,000 fish, over reef and grazes on blanket-weed algae.
Distribution: East Africa to SW Japan, Micronesia, Hawaii, Panama and French Polynesia.

Pallete Surgeonfish
Paracanthurus hepatus

Cobalt blue, laterally with unmistakable black "pallet" markings.
Size: 26 cm
Biology: Prefers clear, current-rich outreefs, 2–40 m. Swims in small, loose groups 1–3 metres above the seabed and feeds on plankton.
Distribution: East Africa to SW Japan, Line Islands and Samoa.

Juveniles, about 4 cm long, swim immediately above branched coral and flee between the coral branches upon imminent danger.

Yellowtail Tang
Zebrasoma xanthurum

Body blue, caudal fin and outer edge of the pectoral fin yellow.
Size: 22 cm
Biology: In coral and rock reefs, 0.5–22 m. Alone or in small, loose groups. Prefers highly structured areas and feeds on blanket-weed algae that it grazes from rock and dead stony coral.
Distribution: Red Sea to Arabian Gulf and Sri Lanka.

Indian Sail-fin Surgeonfish
Zebrasoma desjardinii

Caudal fin with pale blue spots.
Size: 40 cm
Biology: Inhabits deep lagoons and semi-protected outreefs with moderate to rich coral growth, 1–30 m. Usually in pairs or small groups, juveniles live alone and usually in the protection of branch coral.
Distribution: Red Sea and East Africa to Andaman Sea, Cocos Keeling and NW Sumatra.

A dark variant often occurs in the same area next to the light variant (upper photo). The blue dots on the caudal fin are also present on very dark fish, however from some distance cannot be so clearly recognised.

Sailfin Tang
Zebrasoma veliferum

Caudal fin straw yellow to dark brown and without dots.
Size: 40 cm
Biology: In deep lagoons and semi-protected outreefs, 1–40 m. Juveniles with enlarged dorsal and anal fin, yellowish colouration with light and dark vertical stripes and transparent caudal fin.
Distribution: Christmas Islands and Malaysia to SW Japan, Hawaii and French Polynesia.

Twotone Tang
Zebrasoma scopas

Body yellowish-brown, becoming dark toward the back with an almost black caudal fin. White tail blade.
Size: 20 cm
Biology: In coral-rich lagoons and outreefs, 2–50 m. Alone or in groups. Spawning usually takes place in groups.
Distribution: East Africa and Oman to SW Japan, the Philippines, Micronesia, Indonesia, GBR and French Polynesia.

Juveniles are about 3 cm long with light transverse lines and tall dorsal and anal fins. It is frequently observed among branched coral.

Striated Surgeonfish or Lined Bristletooth
Ctenochaetus striatus

Very fine horizontal stripes, brow region with small orange spots.
Size: 26 cm
Biology: In lagoons and outreefs, 1–30 m. Alone or in groups. Grazes off sand and hard grounds on blue and diatom algae, is thereby frequently ciguatoxic.
Distribution: Red Sea to South Africa, SW Japan, Micronesia and French Polynesia.

Indian Gold-ring Bristletooth
Ctenochaetus truncatus

Yellow eye-ring, light to dark brown with numerous small, light dots.
Size: 18 cm
Biology: Interior and outreefs, 1–20 m. Grazes on algae growth on hard ground. Juveniles can have a solid yellow colouration.
Distribution: S Oman and East Africa from Kenya to Natal to the Andaman Sea, the Maldives, Chagos Islands, Cocos Keeling and Christmas Islands.

Lower photo: The juveniles are lemon yellow. The specimen shown is about 6 cm long.

Elegant Unicornfish
Naso elegans

Dorsal and anal fin are orange with a narrow, blue edge fringe. Males with long caudal fin filaments.
Size: 45 cm
Biology: In lagoons and outreefs, 1–90 m. Sometimes in small, loose groups. Grazes on algae on dead coral, rock and rubble grounds. Large males occasionally claim territory.
Distribution: Red Sea to South Africa, S Oman, Andaman Sea and Bali.

Orangespine Unicornfish
Naso lituratus

Dorsal fin black with broad whitish edge fringe.
Size: 45 cm
Biology: In lagoons and outreefs, 1–90 m. Swims alone or sometimes in larger groups, usually above 30 m. Grazes predominantly on leafy brown algae on dead coral or rock grounds.
Distribution: Gulf of Thailand to SW Japan, Hawaii, French Polynesia and Pitcairn.

Bluespine Unicornfish
Naso unicornis

Blue tail blades, on ageing, the forehead horn becomes longer, however does not extend beyond the snout.
Size: 70 cm
Biology: In lagoons, bays and outreefs, 1–80 m. Common species, often in exposed surf regions. Also swims alone, usually however in loose groups. Feeds on leafy algae and sargasso seaweed.
Distribution: Red Sea, S Oman and East Africa to SW Japan, Hawaii and French Polynesia.

Humpback Unicornfish
Naso brachycentron

Back with striking hump; long horn.
Size: 70 cm
Biology: Prefers outer reef slopes, 1–30 m. Alone or in small groups. Rare in the majority of regions and therefore difficult to approach. In the male, the horn is very long, the female only develops a very small protuberance.
Distribution: East Africa to SW Japan, Guam, Palau and French Polynesia.

Bignose Unicornfish
Naso vlamingii

Blue lips, blue horizontal band on the snout between the eyes.
Size: 55 cm
Biology: Inhabits deep lagoons and outer reef slopes, 4–50 m. Usually swims in groups some metres above the reef. Feeds on large plankton.
Distribution: East Africa to SW Japan, Micronesia and French Polynesia.

Very rapid colour changes between very light and dark. Such colour changes take place for instance at cleaner stations and during the mating ritual.

Elongate Unicornfish
Naso lopezi

Slim body, upper half with numerous grey to black spots.
Size: 60 cm
Biology: Prefers current-rich, steep outer reef slopes, 6–50 m. Alone, frequently however in groups and often hunting plankton quite deep in open water. Lies on the reef floor to rest.
Distribution: Andaman Sea to the Philippines, Palau, Solomons and New Caledonia.

Sleek Unicornfish
Naso hexacanthus

White lips, black gill lid edge. Can rapidly change colour.
Size: 75 cm
Biology: Lives in deep lagoons and outer reef slopes, 6–137 m. Common and not shy. Usually swims in groups, sometimes in large schools a short distance above the reef and hunts large plankton.
Distribution: Red Sea to SW Japan, Hawaii, Micronesia and French Polynesia and Pitcairn.

Spotted Unicornfish
Naso brevirostris

Light blue-grey to dark olive-brown, narrow dark vertical stripes. Horn becomes longer with age.
Size: 60 cm
Biology: In deep lagoons and at outer reef slopes, 1–50 m. Usually in groups in the open water where it feeds on plankton. Juveniles and sub-adults graze on algae growth. Can abruptly change colouration, e.g. during the mating ritual the male displays a broad, pale-blue crossband at the front of its body.
Distribution: Red Sea to South Africa, SW Japan, Hawaii and Ducie Islands.

Moorish Idol
Zanclidae

Briefly seen, it could pass as a bannerfish from the butterflyfish family. However, it is not even distantly related to this family. Rather, it is close to the surgeonfish. The family of the *Zanclidae* consists of only a single species, the Moorish Idol.

Moorish Idol
Zanclus cornutus

Long dorsal fin filaments. extended snout with yellow saddle.
Size: 22 cm
Biology: Inhabits rock and coral reefs, 1–145 m. Alone, in pairs or in groups, less often also in large schools. Predominantly feeds on sponges. The very wide distribution is based on the long larval stage.
Distribution: Gulf of Aden, Oman and East Africa to SW Japan, Hawaii, Mexico, Galapagos, Polynesia.

Clown Triggerfish
Balistoides conspicillum

White spotted pattern. Juveniles with a yellow dorsal region.
Size: 50 cm
Biology: In clear, coral-rich out-reefs, 3–75 m. Alone. Uncommon. Often at steep reef slopes with terraces. Juveniles usually in caves or shelters beneath 15 m. Feeds on sea urchins, crustaceans, mussels, snails and sea squirts.
Distribution: East Africa to S Japan, Micronesia, Line Islands and Samoa.

Triggerfish
Balistidae

Triggerfish have a characteristic style of swimming using the second dorsal and the anal fin, the caudal fin generally serving as a rudder and employed only for rapid thrust propulsion and escape. The name is derived from a special mechanism of its first dorsal fin. The first ray resting in a dorsal groove can be erected upright and locked into place by the second ray. On depressing the third ray, the first is once again unlocked. In case of imminent danger, triggerfish flee into rock crevices and wedge there with the erected dorsal fin ray. They also spend the night anchored in such reef crevices. They crack mussels, snails, coral, sea urchins and crustaceans with their powerful jaws and chisel-like teeth.

Orange-lined Triggerfish
Balistapus undulatus

Dark green with orange stripe.
Size: 30 cm
Biology: Prefers coral-rich lagoons and outreefs, 1–50 m. Feeds on branched coral tips, sea urchins, crustaceans, bristleworms, sponges and other invertebrates as well as small fish and algae. When spawning, it creates shallow nest troughs in sand or rubble.
Distribution: Red Sea and East Africa to S Japan, Hawaii and French Polynesia.

As an exception among the triggerfish, the sexes of this species can be externally distinguished: adult males (lower photo) have no stripes or dots on the snout.

Starry Triggerfish
Abalistes stellatus

3–4 white patches on the back; narrow tail stalk.
Size: 60 cm
Biology: Prefers mud and sandy grounds, 5–120 m. Adults occasionally also keep in vicinity of reef.
Distribution: Red Sea and East Africa to S Japan, Palau, New Caledonia and Fiji.

Older juvenile.

Titan Triggerfish
Balistoides viridescens

Basic colouration of light yellow-green to dark olive-green, however always with broad dark band ("moustache") above the upper lip.

Size: 75 cm

Biology: In bays, lagoons and outreefs, 3–40. Its food includes sea urchins, coral, crustaceans, mussels, shelled snails. Usually alone, the pair cares for the brood. Eggs are laid on sand or rubble ground in nest troughs and are aggressively guarded, also from divers. Feint attacks, but also strong ramming blows as well as bites with painful injuries have frequently been described.

Distribution: Red Sea and East Africa to S Japan, Micronesia and French Polynesia.

A juvenile about 4 cm long.

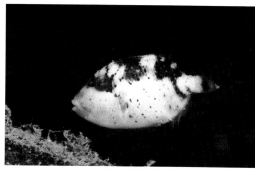

Indian Triggerfish
Melichthys indicus

Base of the dorsal and anal fin with white band, caudal fin white edged.
Size: 25 cm
Biology: At coral-rich outer reef slopes, 5–50 m. Swims alone or in loose groups, often a short distance above the seabed. Feeds on zooplankton drifting in open water. Flees on disturbance into small reef crevices.
Distribution: Red Sea, Oman and East Africa to Andaman Sea and West Indonesia.

Redtoothed Triggerfish
Odonus niger

Sickle tail, red teeth.
Size: 40 cm
Biology: Prefers current-rich outer reef slopes and reef terraces, 3–55 m. Frequently forms large, sometimes colossal schools and catches zooplankton in open water, often high above the reef. In case of imminent danger, it flees to the reef and hides in small crevices, from where the caudal fin often slightly protrudes.
Distribution: Red Sea and East Africa to S Japan, Micronesia and French Polynesia.

Juvenile specimen, about 8 cm long.

Pinktail Triggerfish
Melichthys vidua

Dorsal and anal fin seamed black.
Size: 35 cm
Biology: Inhabits clear outer reef slopes, 4–60 m.
Alone or in loose groups, up to a few metres above the
seabed. Feeds on algae, various invertebrates such as
crustaceans and sponges, as well as small fish.
Distribution: East Africa to S Japan, Hawaii, Galapagos
and French Polynesia.

Yellow-margin Triggerfish
Pseudobalistes flavimarginatus

Pastel yellowish to pink around the snout, fin edges
yellow to orange.
Size: 60 cm
Biology: Inhabits deep bays, lagoons, canals and sandy
areas of outreefs, often also in areas with seagrass,
2–50 m. Feeds on tips of branched coral, shelled snails,
crustaceans and sea squirts. Frequently blows on sandy
ground standing head first to free prey. Creates large
nest troughs in sand or rubble grounds and cares for
the brood. Aggressive in the vicinity of the nest, also
to divers.
Distribution: Red Sea and East Africa to S Japan, Micronesia and French Polynesia.

The middle photo shows a juvenile about 7 cm long, the
lower is a juvenile about 3 cm long.

Yellow-spotted or Blue Triggerfish
Pseudobalistes fuscus

Blue to blue-grey with small yellow patches.
Size: 55 cm
Biology: Inhabits lagoons, bays and outreefs, prefers reefs with sand, rubble or seagrass surfaces, 1–50 m. Feeds on various bottom-dwelling invertebrates and spends much time blowing these free from the sand. It is frequently accompanied by wrasse and other fish which snatch exposed prey. Shy, but can be aggressive when watching over its nest.
Distribution: Red Sea and East Africa to S Japan, Micronesia and French Polynesia.

This fish has erected its first dorsal fin, which triggerfish can use to wedge themselves into crevices.

Lagoon or Blackbar Triggerfish
Rhinecanthus aculeatus

Yellow horizontal stripe from the snout to the cheek. Two pairs of white to blueish diagonal stripes at the lower body rear. An orange-brown diagonal stripe on the back.
Size: 25 cm
Biology: Inhabits lagoons and shallow reef roofs, 0.3–5 m. Above sand, rubble and stony coral. Territorial, alone or in pairs. Apart from numerous invertebrates, it also feeds on small fish and algae.
Distribution: East Africa to SW Japan, Micronesia, Hawaii and French Polynesia.

Picasso Triggerfish
Rhinecanthus assasi

Yellow lips, three black horizontal stripes on the rear of the body.
Size: 30 cm
Biology: In protected, shallow out-reefs and lagoons, usually in areas with sand, rubble and stony coral, 1–25 m. Not rare in certain areas, but shy. Territorial and always swims close to hiding places.
Distribution: Red Sea to Arabian Gulf.

Wedgetail Triggerfish
Rhinecanthus rectangulus

V-shaped marking at the back.
Size: 25 cm
Biology: In lagoons and outreefs, 1-18 m. Territorial and shy. Prefers mixed coral, rock, rubble and sandy areas. Juveniles are often on shallow reef roofs. Like the other species of this genus, it feeds on in-vertebrate bottom-dwellers such as crustaceans, worms, brittle starfish, sea urchins, sponges, as well as fish and algae.
Distribution: Southern Red Sea and East Africa to SW Japan, Hawaii and Ducie Islands.

Blackpatch Triggerfish
Rhinecanthus verrucosus

Large black, roundish oval spot towards the rear of the lower body.
Size: 23 cm
Biology: Inhabits lagoons and coastal reefs, 1–20 m. Prefers pro-tected mixed zones with seagrass, coral and rubble grounds, also likes less clear water. Alone or in loose groups, shy and uncommon in the majority of regions.
Distribution: Seychelles, Chagos Islands and Sri Lanka to S Japan, Yap, Solomons, GBR and Fiji.

Bluethroat Triggerfish
Sufflamen albicaudatus

Caudal fin ochre-yellow with white border. Males with blue breast. Similar to *S. chrysopterus*.
Size: 22 cm
Biology: In lagoons and protected outreefs, 2–20 m. Shy, if disturbed flees rapidly into small reef crevices. Prefers areas with coral, sand and rubble ground.
Distribution: Red Sea.

Juvenile, about 4 cm long.

Boomerang or Scythe Triggerfish
Sufflamen bursa

Two characteristic brown or yellow, slightly curved stripes ("scythes") behind the eye.
Size: 24 cm
Biology: Inhabits outreefs, 3–90 m. Prefers steep reef slopes beneath the surf regions, in coral-rich areas as well as in mixed zones of coral, sand and rubble ground. Can change colour very rapidly, especially also the "scythe" stripes. Feeds on various invertebrate bottom-dwellers.
Distribution: East Africa to S Japan, Hawaii, Micronesia and French Polynesia.

The upper photo shows a specimen with bright basic colouration and yellow "scythes", the lower one with darker body and dark brown "scythes".

Halfmoon or Flagtail Triggerfish
Sufflamen chrysopterus

Bright vertical stripe behind the eye; caudal fin with white edge. The similar *S. albicaudatus* has a root that is also white.
Size: 22 cm
Biology: In shallow lagoons and outreefs, 1–30 m. Territorial, prefers free surfaces with scattered coral and hard and sandy ground. In turbid as well as in very clear areas. Feeds on invertebrate bottom-dwellers.
Distribution: East Africa to S Japan, Micronesia and Samoa.

Bridled Triggerfish
Sufflamen fraenatus

Light to dark brown. Juveniles pale with fine black lines and darker back.
Size: 38 cm
Biology: Prefers open, sparsely overgrown areas with sand and rubble ground, 8–180 m. Juveniles in low depths. Feeds on invertebrates such as mussels, snails, crustaceans, sea urchins, brittle starfish, bristleworms, also fish and algae. Photo: sub-adult.
Distribution: East Africa to S Japan, Hawaii and French Polynesia.

Gilded Triggerfish
Xanthichthys auromarginatus

Rows of white scale dots, only the males with yellow edge fringe on the tail, anal and dorsal fin as well as a blue spot above chin and throat.
Size: 22 cm
Biology: Prefers outer reef slopes, 15–150 m. Frequently swims in loose groups some metres above the reef and hunts zooplankton in open water.
Distribution: Mauritius to SW Japan, Micronesia, Hawaii and French Polynesia.

Filefish
Monacanthidae

Filefish are slow, deliberate swimmers that have great manoeuvrability and often hover motionless in one place. Smaller species usually live hidden or camouflaged near the bottom. The majority of filefish live alone or in pairs, sometimes also in small groups, and have a broad diet that includes algae, seagrass, sponges, worms and crustaceans. But some species are true food specialists. Filefish are closely related to triggerfish. Like these they have an extended first dorsal fin spine, which can be erected or folded down.

Scrawled Filefish
Aluterus scriptus

Small pale blue dots and short stripes. Large "broom tail".
Size: 100 cm
Biology: Prefers lagoons and protected outer reef slopes, 2–80 m. Loner, uncommon and relatively shy. Feeds on bottom-dwelling invertebrates.
Distribution: Worldwide in tropical waters.

Bristle-tail Filefish
Acreichthys tomentosus

Can adapt colouration to the bottom surface. Typically with V-shaped marking in the middle of the side but not always easily discernible.

Size: 10 cm

Biology: In protected reefs, bays and seagrass fields, 1–20 m. Usually alone.

Distribution: East Africa to SW Japan, Fiji and Tonga.

This species is similar to many kinds of triggerfish that can change their colour pattern like a chameleon. The specimen in the upper photo has adapted to the bottom surface of dark sand with orange sponges, and the fish in the lower photo has taken the pattern of the grey-brown patchwork of its surroundings.

Whitespotted or Barred Filefish
Cantherhines dumerili

Two pairs of yellowish barbs on the tail stalk. Yellow eye-ring.

Size: 38 cm

Biology: Inhabits clear lagoons and outreefs, 1–35 m. Frequently swims in pairs. Feeds predominantly on the tips of branched coral, also on various invertebrate bottom-dwellers.

Distribution: East Africa to S Japan, Hawaii, Mexico and Ducie islands.

Honeycomb or Wirenet Filefish
Cantherhines pardalis

Greenish-brown to blueish-yellow, always with honeycomb net pattern. Usually with white spot on the tail root.
Size: 25 cm
Biology: In clear, coral-rich lagoons and outer reef slopes, also in seagrass fields, 2–25 m. Loner, relatively shy.
Distribution: Red Sea and East Africa to S Japan and Ducie Islands.

Pig-faced Leather Jacket or Whitebar Filefish
Paramonacanthus choirocephalus

Variable in colour, usually with dark spot beneath the second dorsal fin.
Size: 12 cm
Biology: In protected outreefs, above sandy ground and above seagrass fields, to about 20 m. Alone or in small groups.
Distribution: from India, Thailand and Malaysia to Indonesia, the Philippines, PNG and Vanuatu.

Strapweed Filefish
Pseudomonacanthus macrurus

Colouration very variable. Numerous small dark dots on the body.
Size: 18 cm
Biology: Inhabits lagoons and outreefs, to about 12 m depth. Often above sand and rubble ground as well as in seagrass fields.
Distribution: Parts of the Indian Ocean, Thailand, Malaysia, Indonesia, to the Philippines and PNG.

Blackbar Filefish
Pervagor janthinosoma

Head area brownish, turning into olive-green towards the rear. Caudal fin orange-coloured.
Size: 14 cm
Biology: In shallow lagoons and coral reefs, to about 20 m. Shy, with a very secluded lifestyle in and near small crevices and cavities.
Distribution: East Africa to SW Japan, Mariana Islands, GBR, Samoa and Tonga.

Redtail or Blackheaded Filefish
Pervagor melanocephalus

Dark brown to blueish-black head, remainder of body is orange.
Size: 10 cm
Biology: Prefers clear, coral-rich, protected outreefs, 5–40 m. Alone or in pairs. Shy, always remains near shelters.
Distribution: Andaman Islands and Sumatra to SW Japan, Marshall Islands, Fiji and Tonga.

Harlequin Filefish
Oxymonacanthus longirostris

Rows of orange dots. Small black spot on caudal fin. Replaced by *O. halli* (slightly larger tail spot) in the Red Sea.
Size: 9 cm
Biology: In coral-rich, clear lagoons and outreefs, 1–30 m. In pairs or small groups, always swims just above or between coral. Exclusively feeds on *Acropora* coral polyps.
Distribution: East Africa to S Japan, Samoa and Tonga.

Blacksaddle or Mimic Filefish
Paraluteres prionurus

Rear dorsal fin much broader than the very similar Valentin's Sharpnose Puffer, for which it is often mistaken.
Size: 11 cm
Biology: Lives in clear lagoons and outreefs, 2–25 m. Imitates the poisonous pufferfish. Alone or in small groups; males are territorial.
Distribution: Gulf of Aden and East Africa to S Japan, Marshall Islands, GBR and New Caledonia.

Rhinoceros Leatherjacket or Rhino Filefish
Pseudaluttarius nasicornis

Two olive-brownish horizontal stripes at the side. Caudal fin with large dark spot.

Size: 18 cm

Biology: Prefers protected coastal areas, 1–55 m. Swims alone, in pairs or in small groups near the seabed. Usually observed above sand, rubble or seagrass.

Distribution: East Africa to S Japan, Guam and East Australia.

A couple in the upper photo (below left the slightly higher-backed male, above right the more slender female). In the lower photo, a female Rhinoceros Leatherjacket with erected first spine ray, which for this species starts well in front on the head, significantly in front of the eye.

Minute Filefish
Rudarius minutus

Cream-coloured to light grey with numerous light brown to olive-coloured, roundish patches.

Size: 4 cm

Biology: In lagoons and protected coastal reefs, 2–15 m. Alone or in small groups, between the branches of fire, horn or soft coral. The males with a dark, light-edged eyespot above the base of the anal fin.

Distribution: Malaysia and Borneo to Palau and GBR.

Spotted Boxfish
Ostracion meleagris

Female (below): dark brown with white spots. Male (above): back blackish with white spots, side blue with yellow spots.

Size: 16 cm

Biology: In clear lagoons and outreefs, usually in protected areas, 1–30 m. Feeds on various small invertebrates, sea squirts and sponges.

Distribution: East Africa to S Japan, Hawaii, Galapagos, Mexico and French Polynesia.

Boxfish
Ostraciidae

Boxfish have a hard, angular external armour formed from polygonal, usually hexagonal, bony plates. For some species, these honeycomb-shaped plates are easy to recognise. This protective exoskeleton is only broken through at the mouth, anus, eyes, gills and fin bases. As another protection against predators, it can emit poisonous secretions (ostracitoxine) with skin jets. These protection and warning substances frighten many predators away. Boxfish are slow swimmers, but are masters of precise manoeuvring. They can turn on the spot like a helicopter and also swim backwards. The caudal fin serves as rudder and is otherwise only employed for escape. During the mating ritual and spawning, they rise in pairs to the surface.

Yellow Boxfish
Ostracion cubicus

Juveniles bright yellow with black spots, in the course of growth there is a change of colouration (see small photos), large males blue-grey and with bulge on tip of the snout.

Size: 45 cm

Biology: In lagoons and not too exposed areas of outreefs, usually in coral-rich areas, 1–40 m. A loner. Juveniles at protected places, e.g. below small overhangs, between rocks or branched coral. Adults also swim above open areas. Feeds on various small bottom-dwelling invertebrates also from algae growth. A relatively common boxfish, only moderately shy.

Distribution: Red Sea, Arabian Gulf, Gulf from Oman and East Africa to SW Japan, French Polynesia and New Zealand.

Solor Boxfish
Ostracion solorensis

Males with dark blue side and pale blue spots.
Size: 11 cm
Biology: Prefers outreefs with good coral growth, 2–20 m. Swims alone or in pairs, usually near shelters, quite shy.
Distribution: Christmas Islands and NW Australia to S Japan, Palau, PNG, Fiji and Northern. GBR.

Female with beige-coloured to dark brown sides and irregular light and line patterns.

Bluetail Trunkfish
Ostracion cyanurus

Males with olive-coloured back, side and tail dark blue with black spots. Female yellow with black spots.
Size: 15 cm
Biology: In lagoons, bays and outreefs, 3–25 m. Frequently in areas with moderate coral growth. Loner, always near hiding places and exceptionally shy. Comparatively rare species.
Distribution: Red Sea to Arabian Gulf.

Horn-nosed Boxfish
Rhychostracion (Ostracion) rhi-norhynchos

In adults, the snout is rounded and arched forward like a nose; juveniles with smaller bulge on the snout.
Size: 35 cm
Biology: Lives near coral rubble and sand surfaces in deep lagoons and protected areas of outreefs, 3–40 m. Rather rare in the majority of regions, feeds on small bottom-dwelling invertebrates.
Distribution: East Africa to S Japan, Palau and NW and North Australia.

Longhorn Cowfish
Lactoria cornuta

A pair of long horns both on the brow and at the lower body ends.
Size: 46 cm
Biology: In shallow lagoons and coastal reefs, inhabits sand, mud, rubble, algae rock and seagrass zones, 1–100 m. Loner, grazes the seabed for small invertebrates which it can also blow free with a water jet. Very long caudal fin, usually narrowly folded together, can be displayed like a fan.
Distribution: Red Sea, Gulf of Oman and East Africa to S Japan, Mariana Islands Islands and French Polynesia.

Juvenile, about 3 cm long.

Thornback Cowfish
Lactoria fornasini

A pair of shorter horns both at the brow and at the lower body ends, a backwards-curved spike on the middle back.

Size: 15 cm

Biology: Lives on sand rubble grounds and in zones with algae growth, 3–30 m. Usually alone, typically swims very close to the seabed.

Distribution: East Africa to S Japan, Hawaii and French Polynesia.

Middle photo: juvenile.

Humpback Turretfish
Tetrasomus gibbosus

Back not flattened, but rather roof-shaped and with large spike in the middle.

Size: 30 cm

Biology: In lagoons and coastal reefs above shallow sand and seagrass grounds, 1–20 m, also on muddy offshore grounds in depths to 110 m. Feeds on bottom-dwelling invertebrates which it uncovers with a water jet.

Distribution: Red Sea, Arabian Gulf and East Africa to the Philippines, PNG and New Caledonia.

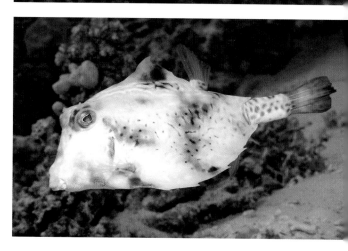

Pufferfish
Tetraodontidae

Pufferfish are sedate, but very manoeuvrable swimmers. Like boxfish they can turn on the spot and swim backwards. They crack hardshell animals such as crustaceans and shelled snails with their powerful beak teeth. In case of imminent danger, they can suck water into a side chamber of the stomach and expand like a balloon, thus deterring attackers and making them too big for the predators' mouth. Pufferfish contain tetrodotoxin, one of the strongest natural poisons. Its consumption causes muscle paralysis, including the respiratory muscles which can lead to death by suffocation. The family is divided into the larger pufferfish (*Tetraodontinae*) and the smaller sharpnose puffer (*Canthigasterinae*).

Star Puffer
Arothron stellatus
Numerous closely-placed black dots. Lower photo: juvenile.
Size: 100 cm
Biology: Deep lagoons and outreefs, 2–55 m. Largest pufferfish. Often rests on sandy bottom. Often glides during the day in middle open water above the reef. Feeds on sea urchins, crustaceans, starfish, coral and fire corals.
Distribution: Red Sea, Arabian Gulf, East Africa to S Korea, Micronesia, French Polynesia and New Zealand.

Blue-spotted Puffer
Arothron caeruleopunctatus

Small, closely-placed blue patches; forms broken rings around the eyes.
Size: 80 cm
Biology: Inhabits lagoons, canals and outreefs, 2–45 m. Rather rare. Leisurely swimming loner. Usually hovers close to the seabed or pauses below overhangs.
Distribution: Réunion and the Maldives to SW Japan, Marshall Islands and New Caledonia.

Middle photo: variant.

Masked Puffer
Arothron diadematus

Dark eye mask, extends to the pectoral fin.
Size: 30 cm
Biology: In coral-rich bays and fringe reefs, 3–25 m. Common species, often seen dormant on the seabed. Forms groups during reproduction periods.
Distribution: Red Sea.

White-spotted Puffer
Arothron hispidus

White patches, white rings around the eyes. A large dark spot with white to yellow markings and fine white border around the pectoral fin base.

Size: 50 cm

Biology: Inhabits lagoons, bays and outreefs with mixed coral, sand and rubble ground; also on seagrass fields, 1–50 m. Common species, often found dormant on the seabed. Feeds on sponges, sea squirts, crabs, coral, starfishes, mussels and algae.

Distribution: Red Sea to S Japan, Hawaii, Panama and French Polynesia.

At first, juveniles have very few white dots. A characteristic is the large, dark, brightly-bordered spot around the pectoral fin base.

Narrow-lined or Striped Puffer
Arothron manilensis

Primary colour beige to light brown or grey-green, dark horizontal stripes.

Size: 31 cm

Biology: In lagoons, bays and pro-tected outreefs, 1–20 m. Inhabits seagrass fields and sandy areas near reef.

Distribution: Borneo and Bali to the Philippines, SW Japan, Micronesia, Samoa and East Australia.

Map Puffer
Arothron mappa

Pale with black, maze-like pattern; radial around the eyes. Adult (above), older juvenile (middle), juvenile (below).

Size: 60 cm

Biology: In lagoons and outer reefs, 4–40 m. Feeds on sponges, sea squirts, snails and algae. Only moderately shy. Usually near the bottom in areas rich in hiding places. Larger specimens occasionally also travel through the reef during the day in the open.

Distribution: East Africa to SW Japan, Samoa, New Caledonia and Tonga.

Immaculate Puffer
Arothron immaculatus

Whitish, light brown or grey, depending on environment. Skin with small, slightly raised nodules. Caudal fin with dark seam. Iris is luminous yellow.

Size: 30 cm

Biology: On seagrass fields, sandy and muddy areas, in estuaries and mangrove regions, 2–30 m.

Distribution: Red Sea and East Africa to SW Japan, (the Philippines) and Indonesia.

Blackspotted Puffer
Arothron nigropunctatus

Very variable in colour: pale cream-coloured, grey, blue-grey, greenish, brownish, yellow, also in colour combinations such as olive and orange or blueish and yellow (see lower photo). Always with isolated black patches, these are likewise variable in number.

Size: 30 cm

Biology: Inhabits coral-rich lagoons and outreefs, 1–35 m. Feeds on coral, sponges, sea squirts and algae.

Distribution: East Africa and Gulf of Aden to SW Japan, Line Islands and Cook Islands.

Guineafowl Puffer
Arothron meleagris

Black with numerous small white spots (photo above). There is a relatively common, partly or almost completely yellow variant (middle photo), which can be very regularly observed in some places.
Size: 60 cm
Biology: Usually in clear, coral-rich lagoons and outreefs, 1–73 m. Feeds on the tips of branch coral, additionally also on sponges, snails and algae.
Distribution: East Africa to S Japan, Galapagos, Panama and French Polynesia.

Juvenile about 2 cm long: black with yellow spots and almost as round as a ball.

Pacific Crown Toby
Canthigaster axiologus

Saddle spots seamed with yellow dots and dashes.
Size: 10 cm
Biology: On rubble and sand areas of protected outreefs, 5–80 m.
Distribution: Indonesia, the Philippines to SW Japan, Marshall Islands, Australia, New Caledonia and Tonga.

Blue-spotted Toby
Canthigaster cyanospilota

Saddle spots. Blue dots. Brown spot below the pectoral fins.
Size: 10 cm
Biology: On seagrass, rubble and sand areas of protected outreefs, 5 to probably 80 m. This species, newly described in 2008, was previously designated as *C. coronata*. This name actually, however, covered three closely-related species: *C. coronata* (Hawaii), *C. axiologus* and *C. cyanospila*.
Distribution: Red Sea, Oman, East Africa to Réunion, Mauritius, the Maldives.

Bennett's Sharpnose Puffer or Whitebelly Toby
Canthigaster bennetti

Whitish dorsal side and light brown back, a soft-edged dark brown horizontal band in between.
Size: 10 cm
Biology: In protected coastal reefs and lagoons above sand and rubble grounds, 1–15 m. Feeds on algae and small invertebrates.
Distribution: East Africa to S Japan, Micronesia and French Polynesia.

Fingerprint Toby
Canthigaster compressa

Upper side brown, underside pale.
Side with very fine spots and lines
("fingerprint").
Size: 10 cm
Biology: In lagoons and coastal
reefs, bays and harbours, often
above rubble and soft ground,
2–20 m.
Distribution: Bali to SW Japan,
Guam and Mariana in Micronesia,
Solomons and Vanuatu.

Honeycomb Toby
Canthigaster janthinoptera

Dark brown, entire body covered
with closely-placed white spots.
Size: 9 cm
Biology: Inhabits lagoons and
outreefs, 1–30 m. Alone or in pairs,
usually near hiding places such as
crevices and cavities.
Distribution: East Africa to S Japan,
Line. Islands and French Polynesia.

Pearl Toby
Canthigaster margaritata

Dark to olive-brown with pale blue
spots and lines.
Size: 12 cm
Biology: Inhabits protected reef
areas with mixed zones of coral,
sand and rubble ground, 1–30 m.
Alone or in pairs. Imitated by the
filefish *Paraluteres arqat*.
Distribution: Red Sea.

Papuan Toby
Canthigaster papua

Orange snout. Fine pale blue to greenish dots, also on the tail. Some thin lines on the back.

Size: 9 cm

Biology: Prefers clear, coral-rich as well as muddier lagoons and outreefs, 3–40 m. Swims alone or in pairs.

Distribution: The Maldives, Andaman Sea and Indonesia to the Philippines, Palau, GBR and Vanuatu.

Pygmy Toby
Canthigaster pygmaea

Brown to pink-brown with blue stripes on the snout and on the eye as well as blue spots on the body. Brow and back without markings.

Size: 6 cm

Biology: Inhabits protected, coral-rich areas from fringe reefs and bays, 1–30 m. Shy species. Lives well hidden, usually in crevices and holes.

Distribution: Red Sea.

Spotted Sharpnose or Indian Toby
Canthigaster solandri

Orange-brown with yellow-orange parts with green-blueish spots.

Size: 11 cm

Biology: Inhabits protected rock and coral areas from lagoons and outreefs, 1–55 m.

Distribution: East Africa to SW Japan and French Polynesia.

Valentin's Sharpnose Puffer
Canthigaster valentini

Four saddle spots, the middle one extending right down the side. Similar to and mistaken for the Blacksaddle or Mimic Filefish (page 289).
Size: 10 cm
Biology: 1–55 m. Males have a territory with up to 7 females, each female lays eggs in an algae bush. These are protected from predators by a poison like that of the fish. Hatch after 3–5 days; 9–15 weeks as larvae.
Distribution: Red Sea, East Africa, Oman to SW Japan, Marshall Islands and French Polynesia.

Tyler's Toby
Canthigaster tyleri

Cream-coloured to orange-brownish. Snout and neck with blue lines. Rest of body covered with large reddish-brown spots.
Size: 8 cm
Biology: In outreefs, 3–40 m. Alone and usually near shelters such as crevices and caves.
Distribution: East Africa, Comoro Islands, Mauritius, Christmas Islands, to East Indonesia.

Shortfin Puffer
Torquigener brevipinnis

Ochre-brown with numerous whitish spots, those between snout and cheek merged into 4–5 short vertical stripes.
Size: 14 cm
Biology: Inhabits sand, rubble, mud and seagrass areas, 1–100 m. In small or somewhat larger groups. Not shy.
Distribution: Indonesia to S Japan and New Caledonia.

Milkspotted Puffer
Chelonodon patoca

Back with white patches and diffuse greenish-brown bands.
Size: 33 cm
Biology: Prefers estuaries, mangrove regions and protected coastal reefs with sandy or muddy grounds, 1–15 m. Rests close to the bottom.
Distribution: Arabian Gulf and Oman to SW Japan, PNG and Australia.

Porcupine Fish
Diodontidae

Like boxfish, their nearest relation, porcupine fish have a beak-like, very powerful set of teeth. The fish cracks hardshell food such as mussels, snails, sea urchins or hermit crabs. Porcupine fish have large eyes and are usually active at night. During the day the majority rest hidden in cavities. Some have fixed, others erectable barbs. Upon danger, it swallows water and blows up like a balloon and can get stuck in a predator's throat. Even large sharks or groupers can suffocate on a porcupine fish. For propagation, at dusk the fish rise up in open water towards the surface. The eggs drift away with the current. After a short time, four days for balloon porcupine fish, the larvae hatch.

Spotfin Burrfish
Chilomycterus reticulatus

Light brown with dispersed dark spots on body and fin. Short rigid barbs.
Size: 70 cm
Biology: Lives in shallow, protected zones at exposed outer reef slopes in coral and rock reefs, 1–141 m. During the day usually in a hiding place. Juveniles are pelagic.
Distribution: Circumglobal in tropics and subtropics, is however absent in the Red Sea, Central Pacific and Caribbean.

Orbicular Burrfish
Cyclichthys orbicularis

Brownish to rust-brown. Also pale cream-coloured above white sandy bottom. Often groups of dark patches. Fixed barbs.
Size: 15 cm
Biology: In protected reefs and bays above sand and rubble ground, 2–20 m. Rests during the day at protected places. At night also grazes the seabed in the open for crustaceans, molluscs and worms.
Distribution: Red Sea, Arabian Gulf, East Africa to S Japan and NE Australia.

Spotbase or Yellowspotted Burrfish
Cyclichthys spilostylus

Fixed, thorn-like barbs bordered in yellow or dark (usually in the lower half of the body).
Size: 34 cm
Biology: In lagoons and protected coastal and outreefs, 3–90 m. Often above seagrass and sand surfaces with isolated coral heads. Not shy. Feeds on hardshell invertebrates.
Distribution: Red Sea, Gulf of Oman and East Africa to S Japan, Australia and Galapagos.

Longspined Porcupinefish or Balloonfish
Diodon holocanthaus

Cream-coloured to light grey with isolated large dark patches. Juveniles also have numerous small black spots (not on fins), the number decreases with age.

Size: 29 cm

Biology: In lagoons and outreefs, frequently above open sand or rocky areas, 1–100 m. Juveniles pelagic up to a size of 7–9 cm.

Distribution: Circumglobal in tropical and warm-temperate seas.

Porcupinefish
Diodon hystrix

Body and fin with numerous small black spots. Long, mobile barbs.

Size: 80 cm

Biology: In coral and rock reefs, lagoons and outreefs, 2–50 m. During the day, usually rests below overhangs or in caves, less often suspended near the reef in open upper water. Goes predominantly at night in search of food, feeds on hermit crabs, sea urchins, crabs and shelled snails.

Distribution: Circumtropical.

Black-blotched Porcupinefish
Diodon liturosus

Brown to olive with several large bright-bordered black patches. Movable barbs.

Size: 50 cm

Biology: In lagoons and outreefs as well as offshore patch reefs, 3–90 m. Rests during the day in crevices or below overhangs. Feeds at night on hardshell invertebrates.

Distribution: Red Sea and East Africa to S Japan, Micronesia, Society Islands and SE Australia.

Fishes

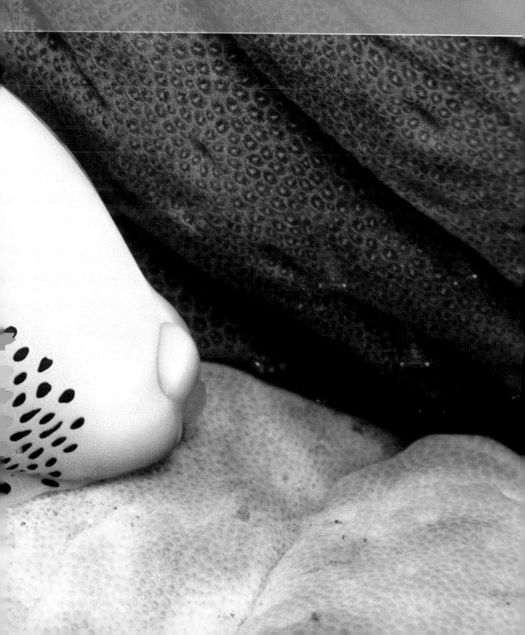

Invertebrates

Bristleworms and Flatworms
Polychaeta and Plathelminthes

There are about 10,000 known species of bristleworm (*Polychaeta*) almost all of which live in the sea. The free-moving species are usually predatory and are predominantly active at night. Sedentary species, the tube worms, live in chalk or in parchment-like burrows and catch plankton with their tentacle crown. Flatworms (*Plathelminthes*) are paper-thin and glide above the seabed. The majority feed on sessile invertebrates such as sponges, and are well protected from predators with their toxins.

Christmas Tree Worm
Spirobranchus giganteus

Two spiral tentacle wreaths, very variable in colour.
Size: Ø of a wreath 1.5 cm
Biology: Lives in chalk burrows. Catches plankton. Often in groups. Very shy, rapidly withdraws at suspicious shadows or pressure waves.
Distribution: Circumtropical.

Feather Duster Worm
Sabellastarte indica

Light to dark brown, one or two-coloured.
Size: Ø tentacle wreath 10 cm
Biology: Lives in parchment-like burrows. Feeds on plankton. The tentacle crown is the only way to observe tube worms.
Distribution: Circumtropical.

Beautiful or Golden Fireworm
Chloeia flava

Back with "eyespot" row. Bundle of long bristles.
Size: 10 cm
Biology: Along coastal regions on rubble and sand. Day-active, feeds on tiny animals and carrion. The bristles can just penetrate the skin and cause a burning pain.
Distribution: Red Sea and East Africa to West Pacific.

Marine Blue Flatworm
Cycloporus venetus

Blue to violet-blue with narrow white midline and yellow edge fringe.
Size: 2 cm
Biology: Feeds on sea squirts.
Distribution: Known from Indonesia to Australia and Japan.

Darkspotted Flatworm
Maritigrella fuscopunctata

Cream-coloured with orange to brown patches. Wavy edge fringe with dark lines or spots.
Size: 3–4 cm
Biology: On hard and rubble ground.
Distribution: Indo-West Pacific.

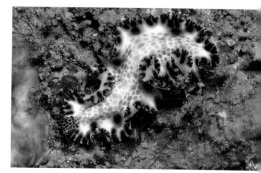

Gold-dotted Flatworm
Thysanozoon nigropapillosum

Black with white edge fringe. Numerous low papillae with yellow tips.
Size: 5 cm
Biology: Relatively common in some places. Occasionally swims a short distance above the seabed with undulating movements.
Distribution: Red Sea to Micronesia and Fiji. We are possibly dealing with more than one species in the distribution area.

Red Dwarf Flatworm
Pseudoceros rubronanus

Red, speckled with small, irregular white patches.
Size: 3 cm
Biology: On hard and sandy bottom in reefs, usually in shallow areas.
Distribution: Red Sea to West Pacific.

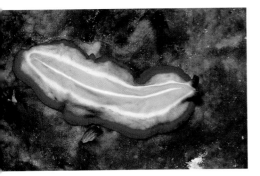

Susan's Flatworm
Pseudoceros susanae

Middle back orange with white horizontal stripe. Edge fringe usually purple-violet.
Size: 3 cm
Biology: Usually on hard ground, relatively common in some places.
Distribution: Known from central Indian Ocean (the Maldives, Seychelles) to Indonesia, the Philippines.

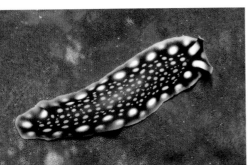

Linda's Flatworm
Pseudoceros lindae

Reddish brown with orange patches, towards the edge usually yellowish to white patches.
Size: 5 cm
Biology: On sand and hard ground.
Distribution: Indo-West Pacific.

Racing Stripe Flatworm
Pseudoceros bifurcus

Blue with a white middle stripe with a dark border line and with elongated orange-coloured spots at the front end.
Size: 6 cm
Biology: On hard ground, not rare.
Distribution: Indo-West Pacific.

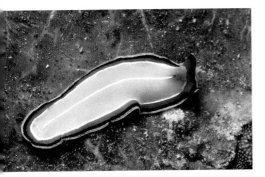

Two-band Flatworm
Pseudoceros bimarginatus

Pink-cream coloured with a white midline. Edge fringe from the outside to the inside: yellow, black, orange, white.
Size: 3 cm
Biology: On rubble and sandy bottom.
Distribution: Red Sea, Indo-West Pacific.

Tiger Flatworm
Pseudoceros cf. dimidiatus

Orange-coloured edge fringe. Distinctive black-yellow "tiger pattern".
Size: 8 cm
Biology: On overgrown hard ground. Its diet includes sea squirts. Still unknown whether or not it is a separate species.
Distribution: Red Sea to Japan and French Polynesia.

Script Flatworm
Pseudoceros scriptus

White with an orange edge fringe and variable patterns, black stripes and patches.
Size: 3 cm
Biology: On hard ground in coral reefs. Feeds on sea squirts, possibly also on sponges.
Distribution: Red Sea to Indonesia, the Philippines and Australia.

Laing Island Flatworm
Pseudoceros laingensis

Cream-coloured or yellow with numerous purplish patches.
Size: 6 cm
Biology: Usually on hard ground in shallow reef areas.
Distribution: Known in Indonesia and PNG.

Dotted or Thinspotted Flatworm
Pseudoceros leptostictus

Cream-coloured with numerous black, white and orange spots. Fringe edge with small black and yellow patches.
Size: 3 cm
Biology: Predominantly active at night. Feeds on colony sea squirts.
Distribution: Red Sea to Japan, Hawaii, New Guinea, Australia.

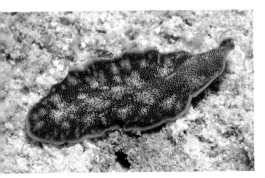

Fuchsia Flatworm
Pseudoceros cf. ferrugineus

Auburn to scarlet red with numerous white spots. Two-coloured edge fringe: Outside yellow, purple background.
Size: 6 cm
Biology: In rock and coral reefs, active day and night. Feeds on colony sea squirts.
Distribution: Red Sea to Hawaii and Polynesia.

Orsak's Flatworm
Maiazoon orsaki

Whitish-grey to light brown with a very fine white midline and very wavy edge and black edge fringe.
Size: 3.5 cm
Biology: Relatively common species.
Distribution: Known from Indonesia to Marshall Islands.

Bedford's or Persian Carpet Flatworm
Pseudobiceros bedfordi

Pattern with straight and curved, predominantly cross-wise coursing lines.
Size: 10 cm
Biology: Large, conspicuous species with variable intense colouration. Can glide quite quickly above the seabed and swim elegantly. Diet includes sea squirts.
Distribution: Red Sea to West Pacific.

Glorious Flatworm
Pseudobiceros gloriosus

Black with tricoloured edge fringe: outside ruby-red, middle pink, inside orange.
Size: 9 cm
Biology: Predominantly active at night, especially on encrusted overgrown hard ground. Can swim with undulating movements.
Distribution: Red Sea, Hawaii and Fiji.

Molluscs
Mollusca

Mussels, snails and *cephalopoda* belong to the largest classes of the phylum of molluscs which is very rich in species. The snails observed in the reef are the *Prosobranchia* with typical housings and the *Opisthobranchia,* of which some have a reduced or only rudimentary interior housing such as nudibranch snails, Aplysia, sap-sucking sea slugs and sidegill slugs. The majority, however, belong to the nudibranchs, or snails without a shell.

Triton's Trumpet
Charonia tritonis

Soft body is mottled cream. Feeler yellow-brown banded.
Size: 50 cm
Biology: On rock and soft ground. Nocturnal, hunts large starfishes, even feeds on crown-of-thorns starfishes.
Distribution: Red Sea and East Africa to Polynesia.

Hiby's Coriocella or Black Velutinid
Coriocella hibyae

Finger-shaped outgrowths. A few dark dots.
Size: 4 cm
Biology: Usually on rubble and dead stony coral, 2–15 m. Feeds on sea squirts. Often confused with nudibranchs, but has a concealed housing beneath the fleshy mantle.
Distribution: the Maldives, Indonesia.

Scorpion Conch
Lambis scorpius

Housing with seven knotty protrusions including the syphon canal. Underside with dark bars.
Size: 16 cm
Biology: On hard and sandy bottom, usually in low depths.
Distribution: West Indonesia to Marshall Islands and Fiji.

Bat Volute
Cymbiola vesperilio

Housing with reddish-brown markings and fine horizontal lines. Dark brown foot and syphon with pale yellow markings.
Size: 15 cm
Biology: On rubble, sand and muddy ground. Can dig in.
Distribution: Indo-West Pacific.

Umbilical Ovula or Black-spotted Egg Cowrie
Calpurnus verrucosus

White housing. Front and back always with one light yellow "navel". Mantle and foot white with dark to black spots.
Size: 4 cm
Biology: Feeds on *Lobophytum* and *Sarcophyton* soft coral, where it can usually be observed.
Distribution: Red Sea and East Africa to the Philippines, Japan, Australia and Fiji.

Common Egg Cowrie
Ovula ovum

Mantle black with yellow to white spots, shell white.
Size: 10 cm
Biology: In coral reefs from 0.3–20 m. Feeds on leather coral such as the *Sarcophyton* and *Sinularia* species. Juveniles with yellow-white finger and bubble-shaped appendages. Is often wrongly held to be a nudibranch.
Distribution: Red Sea to the Philippines, Micronesia and French Polynesia.

Tiger Cowrie
Cypraea tigris

Housing cream-coloured, irregular and variably speckled with black patches with blurred orange to red border. Mantle light grey with white and dark patches, fine lines and long appendages with white tips.
Size: 12 cm
Biology: Between coral and on sand surfaces. grazes on algae and eats small invertebrates.
Distribution: Indo-Pacific. In the Red Sea replaced by sister species *C. pantherina*.

Geographic Cone Snail or Geography Cone
Conus geographus

Cream with reddish-brown markings. Mantle with dark patches.
Size: 16 cm
Biology: Active at night, predominantly hunts fish. Most dangerous of all cone snails, responsible for the majority of human deaths.
Distribution: Red Sea to French Polynesia.

Textile Cone Shell
Conus textile

Pattern of light pyramid markings and dark, dashed patches. Syphon point black-and-white red banded.
Size: 15 cm
Biology: Nocturnal. Feeds on other cone snails, rarely also on fish and worms. Extremely dangerous. Sting can be fatal to humans.
Distribution: Red Sea to Hawaii and French Polynesia.

Striated Cone
Conus striatus

Orange-brown with dark brown fields of fine bars.
Size: 13 cm
Biology: On sand, rubble and hard ground, buried or below stones during the day. Predominantly nocturnal, feeds on fish. Very dangerous.
Distribution: Red Sea to Hawaii and French Polynesia.

Striped Paper Bubble
Hydatina physis

White shell with numerous dark lines. Very broad, waved crawl foot, brownish to purple with blue edge.
Size: 6 cm
Biology: Protected shallow sandy areas of shallow water. Feeds on bristleworms and molluscs.
Distribution: Red Sea to Hawaii.

Blue Velvet Headshield Slug
Chelidonura varians

Black with intense blue lines on the head, mantle edge and the two unequally long tail extensions.
Size: 5 cm
Biology: Occurs in larger numbers in some places. Can then be very regularly observed on sand, rubble and also hard ground. Can dig into the sand.
Distribution: Indonesia to Australia, Solomons and Fiji.

Forskal's Sidegill Slug
Pleurobranchus forskalii

Colouration variable. Surface with shallow papillae arranged in groups.
Size: 15 cm
Biology: In coastal areas on sand, mud, seagrass growth and coral. Buried or between seagrass during the day. Nocturnal, feeds on sea squirts and sponges. Mantle end often rolled tubular.
Distribution: Red Sea and East Africa to Japan, Guam and Polynesia.

Spanish Dancer
Hexabranchus sanguineus

Colouration variable, usually red. Also orange, yellow or brown.
Size: 60 cm
Biology: In coral reefs, 1–50 m. One of the largest nudibranchs. Can swim with elegant undulations. Lays its eggs as conspicuous, usually red veils on hard ground.
Distribution: Red Sea (where it is uniformly red with a white skirt) and East Africa to Hawaii and French Polynesia.

Pacific Thecacera
Thecacera pacifica

Orange to orange-brown with blue-black markings. Two long tube-shaped appendices.
Size: 5 cm
Biology: On coral debris, rubble and stony coral or on seagrass, from shallow area to about 20 m. Feeds on sea squirts.
Distribution: Red Sea and East Africa to the Philippines, Japan, Hawaii and Vanuatu.

Crested Nembrotha
Nembrotha cristata

Black with green round pustules. Green ring at base of rhinophores and gill bunches are green-edged.
Size: 12 cm
Biology: On hard ground in coral reefs, also on crushed stony coral, to 40 m. Feeds on sea squirts.
Distribution: the Maldives, Malaysia to Japan, Marshall Islands, Solomons and E Australia.

Gardiner's Banana Nudibranch
Aegiris gardineri

Very firm, stiff body. luminous yellow and black. The proportion of black and yellow is variable.
Size: 8 cm
Biology: On hard ground. Feeds on sponges.
Distribution: the Maldives to Australia, SW Japan, Indonesia, PNG.

Batangas Halgerda
Halgerda batangas

Body with very fine network of orange lines, tips of the hump likewise orange.
Size: 4 cm
Biology: On hard ground.
Distribution: Malaysia and Indonesia to the Philippines, Marshall Islands, Australia and Solomons.

Funeral Nudibranch
Jorunna funebris

White with annular black needle fields.
Size: 5.5 cm
Biology: Feeds on sponges such as blue *Haliclona* species.
Distribution: Red Sea and East Africa to SW Japan, Marshall Islands and Fiji.

Leopard Nudibranch
Chromodoris leopardus

Narrow, blue-violet mantle edge. Mantle with ochre brown-red parts and leopard-like marking.
Size: 6 cm
Biology: Feeds on sponges. The similar species *C. tritos*, *C. kuniei* and *Risbecia tryoni* have dots and no ringed "leopard patches".
Distribution: Indonesia and PNG to the Philippines, NW and East Australia.

Lumpy or Bus Stop Chromodoris
Chromodoris hintuanensis

Fine crimson mantle edge. Mantle with shallow, white tubercles. Some reddish-brown rings on the back.
Size: 3 cm
Biology: On hard and sandy bottom. Lifts and lowers the anterior mantle edge when moving.
Distribution: Andaman Sea and Indonesia to the Philippines, Japan and PNG.

Willan's Chromodoris
Chromodoris willani

Blueish-white with broken blue lines. Rhinophores and gills with numerous white opaque dots.
Size: 3.5 cm
Biology: At reef slopes and steep walls. Feeds on sponges.
Distribution: Malaysia and Indonesia to the Philippines, Guam and Vanuatu.

Coi Sea Snail
Goniobranchus coi (formerly Chromodoris coi)

Pale crimson mantle edge with fine violet outer edge.
Size: 5 cm
Biology: Makes undulating movements with the entire mantle edge when crawling. Usually at protected places, feeds on sponges.
Distribution: Indonesia to the Philippines, Japan, Marshall Islands, Fiji, Vanuatu, Australia.

Black-margined Nudibranch
Doriprismatica atromarginata

Very wavy, ruffled mantle fringe. Body cream to light brown. Mantle with black border line.
Size: 10 cm
Biology: Widespread and common species. Usually on hard ground. Feeds on sponges (e.g. *Hyatella*, *Spongia*). Previously attributed to the genus *Glossodoris*.
Distribution: Red Sea and East Africa to Japan, Hawaii, SE Australia and French Polynesia.

Purple Sea Slug
Hypselodoris apolegma

Mantle purplish with white edge fringe and yellow gill and tips of rhinophores.
Size: 10 cm
Biology: On hard ground, in some places not uncommon. It was only recognised a few years ago as an independent species.
Distribution: Malaysia and Indonesia to the Philippines and Japan.

Tryon's Nudibranch
Risbecia tryoni

Dark patches on cream-coloured surfaces in reddish-brown, often reticulated basic colouration.
Size: 7 cm
Biology: Frequently in pairs, where the rear animal touches the tail of its partner with its head flaps. Lifts and lowers its head when crawling.
Distribution: Malaysia, Indonesia to Japan, Marshall Islands, Australia and French Polynesia.

Many-lobed Ceratosoma
Ceratosoma tenue

Mantle fringe with broken purple blue border line. Two pairs of smaller side lobes, a very large horny lobe behind the gills.
Size: 10–12 cm
Biology: Feeds on sponges (*Dysidea*), whose poison it stores in its horny lobe. The concentrated poison serves as protection against predatory fish.
Distribution: East Africa to Japan, Hawaii and New Caledonia.

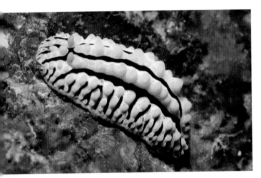

Varicose Nudibranch
Phyllidia varicosa

Blue with black horizontal furrows and with irregular, short bars at the foot edge.

Size: 11 cm

Biology: Widely distributed, common and probably the best known *Phyllidiidae*. Usually crawls over stony coral, also over rubble. Feeds on sponges.

Distribution: Red Sea and East Africa (to Madagascar and Réunion) to Japan, Palau and Society Islands.

Eyespot Nudibranch
Phyllidia ocellata

Very variable colour pattern. Usually yellow to orange with black and white markings.

Size: 7 cm

Biology: Relatively common, usually crawls conspicuously in the open. Feeds on sponges.

Distribution: Red Sea and East Africa to Japan, Marshall Islands Vanuatu and Fiji.

Serpent Pteraeolidia or Blue Dragon
Pteraeolidia ianthina

Colouration very variable, e.g. blue, green, beige, purple.

Size: 10 cm

Biology: In shallow coral reefs, usually on hard ground. Feeds on various *Assumesidae* and leather coral. Takes in their nettle cells and stores them in its back appendages.

Distribution: Indo-Pacific, including Red Sea.

Purple Band or Desirable Flabellina
Flabellina exoptata

Orange rhinophores. Cerata with long white point and, among them, a purple red ring.

Size: 3 cm

Biology: In shallow water, usually on hydrozoa of the genus *Eudendrium*, on which it feeds.

Distribution: East Africa to the Philippines, Japan, Guam, Hawaii and PNG.

Cephalopods
Class Cephalopoda

Bigfin Reef Squid
Sepioteuthis lessoniana

Colouration very variable, often several hues and iridescent. Arms shorter than the body.
Size: 36 cm
Biology: In middle open water of lagoons, bays and protected outer reefs, 0.5–100 m. During the day usually in small, sometimes also larger schools (photo above) near the surface. Pairing takes place during the day. Also particularly active at night (lower photo), hunts fish and crustaceans. Occasionally the white finger-shaped strands with the egg capsules laid on the seabed can be seen.
Distribution: Red Sea and East Africa to Japan, Hawaii and Polynesia.

Order Sepia

Broadclub Cuttlefish
Sepia latimanus

Can display very different colour patterns (for example, the two versions in the photos, of which the upper is more frequently seen).
Size: 50 cm
Biology: Large and most common species in the coral reefs of their distribution area, 2 to at least 30 m. Can adapt very well to their respective environment because of their extensive repertory of colour patterns and variable skin textures (from smooth to many outgrowths). Day-active, feeds on fish and crustaceans. Usually allows divers to get close if the approach is slow and cautious.
Distribution: Andaman Sea and Indonesia to Japan, Fiji and N Australia.

Pfeffer's Flamboyant Cuttlefish
Metasepia pfefferi

Mantle with large, pointy outgrowths. Can rapidly turn luminous yellow, red and white, often a pulsating pattern.
Size: 8 cm
Biology: On sandy muddy grounds of coasts and bays. Often "stalks" over the seabed using lower arms and a pair of mantle lobes, day-active, feeds on small fish and crustaceans. Its bite is extremely poisonous.
Distribution: Malaysia and Indonesia to the Philippines, North Australia and PNG.

Berry's Bobtail Squid
Euprymna berryi

Small rounded body, completely covered with dark patches. Colouration often iridescent blue-green.
Size: 5 cm
Biology: Inhabits sand and mud, also on dead stony coral. Can dig into the sand. Sand grains can adhere like a "breadcrumb coating" to the body, probably with the aid of adhesive glands and act as camouflage. Nocturnal, predominantly bottom-dweller.
Distribution: Indonesia and the Philippines to S Japan.

Day Octopus
Octopus cyanea

Various, mood-dependent colour patterns, as a definite determining characteristic, several have large oval spot at the mantle base on both sides. Often reddish-brown, towards the point, darker arms with rows of white dots (upper photo). Can also be very dark with a broad white stripe (lower photo).
Size: Arm length to 80 cm
Biology: The most common octopus In Indo-Pacific reefs sighted by divers. Also day-active. Uses small caves and rock crevices as shelter, and it often reduces the entrance with mussels and stones. Predominantly feeds on crustaceans, occasionally also molluscs and fish.
Distribution: Red Sea and East Africa to Hawaii and Polynesia.

Coconut Octopus
Amphioctopus marginatus

Body with dark, reticulated pattern. Often dark-reddish
brown, but can brighten colouration to light beige.
Conspicuously white to white-blue suction cups.
Size: Arm length to 15 cm
Biology: Inhabits shallow coarse sandy to muddy bays,
lagoons and protected coastal waters. Digs into the
sand. But also frequently uses empty mussels (see
lower photo) or shell pieces from coconuts as protective
hiding-places.
Distribution: Territorial waters the Indian Ocean and
West Pacific.

Starry Night Octopus
Callistoctopus luteus

Typically continuously red with numerous white spots.
Size: Arm length to 80 cm
Biology: Large species, however little is known about
its biology. Inhabits sand and rubble grounds and
is nocturnal. Shows little timidity, allows divers to
approach closely.
Distribution: Indonesia to the Philippines, Taiwan and
PNG.

Wonderpus Octopus
Wunderpus photogenicus

Long thin arms, more or less banded in high contrast.
In contrast to the similar *T. mimicus* without white line
along the suction cup bases.
Size: Arm length to 20 cm
Biology: Along sand and rubble grounds in shore proximity, about 3–20 m. Shy, withdraws into the seabed
upon approach of divers. Can rapidly take various
striking positions one after the other.
Distribution: Indonesia, the Philippines to Solomons
and Vanuatu.

Mimic Octopus
Thaumoctopus mimicus

Long, slender arms. Entire body with white and brown-black band markings. Continuous white line at the edge of the suction cups. This is absent in the very similar Wonderpus Octopus.

Size: Arm length to 30 cm

Biology: On sand and muddy grounds of protected coastal waters and bays. Usually shy. Often buried so that only the head protrudes vertically. This species is famous for its ability to imitate various animals in form and movement (e.g. flounder or sea snakes).

Distribution: Indonesia and the Philippines to PNG and New Caledonia.

Greater Blue-ringed Octopus
Hapalochlaena lunulata

Blue rings predominantly larger than the eye.

Size: Arm length to 7 cm

Biology: Inhabits protected and exposed coral reefs, from shallow areas to more than 10 m. During pairing, the male climbs on the back of the female, so that it completely covers her eyes. If it feels threatened, its rings, which are hardly visible in the normal state, light up an intensive blue. Hunts small crustaceans and fish on rubble ground and in the reef. Kills its prey with highly toxic saliva which is injected with the bite. The poison is also fatal for humans.

Distribution: Has the largest distribution area of the various blue-ringed octopuses: Sri Lanka and Indonesia to the Philippines, NE Australia and Vanuatu.

Crustaceans
Crustacea

About 50,000 species of crustaceans are known today. They have an external skeleton of chitin that is both hard and lightweight and completely encases the body. It does not grow with the animal and is therefore replaced at intervals: before moulting, a new, at first soft armour forms beneath the old one. When the crustacean extricates itself from the old casing, it makes a growth push before the new armour hardens. After each moulting, various species can achieve 30 per cent growth in length.

White-banded Cleaner Shrimp
Lysmata amboiensis

Red back with white stripe.
Size: 6 cm
Biology: In reef crevices, 1-30 m. In pairs or in small groups. Maintains cleaner stations. Uses typical movements of the antennae to draw attention to itself to attract cleaner clients.
Distribution: Indo-Pacific.

Squat Shrimp
Thor amboiensis

Keeps abdomen at steep upward angle.
Size: 2 cm
Biology: Usually in pairs or small groups. Often found in sea anemone. Female almost twice as large as male. Common species.
Distribution: Circumtropical.

Saron or Common Marbled Shrimp
Saron marmoratus

The *Saron marmoratus* group comprises more than 12 known colour variants. Species determination still incomplete.
Size: 6 cm
Biology: Shy and nocturnal. On hard ground with shelters and crevices and cavities.
Distribution: Red Sea, East Africa to West Pacific including Polynesia.

Banded Tozeuma Shrimp
Tozeuma armatum

Very slender with extremely long, tapered rostrum.
Always with cross-stripes.
Size: 5 cm
Biology: On gorgonian and black coral. Adapts to colouration of the host, e.g. yellow, grey-blue, red, orange.
Very well camouflaged.
Distribution: Indo-West Pacific, e.g. Indonesia (Bali) to
the Philippines, Japan and New Caledonia.

Banded Coral Shrimp
Stenopus hispidus

Head red-white. Body rear and the large pincers banded in red and white.
Size: 5 cm
Biology: In reefs from the tidal zone to more than 35 m.
In cavities and crevices, usually in pairs, males smaller
than females. Common species. Active as cleaner, entices fish customers by swinging its long antennae.
Distribution: Circumtropical.

Hingebeak Prawn or Dancing Shrimp
Rhynchocinetes durbanensis

Red with white lines and spots.
Size: 4 cm
Biology: In rock and coral reefs, on hard ground with
cavities and crevices as shelter. Often in groups, quite
common species.
Distribution: Red Sea to West Pacific.

Harlequin Shrimp
Hymenocera picta

Blueish-purple patches. Plate-like shears. Females
larger than males.
Size: 5 cm
Biology: On hard and rubble grounds, from shallow
water. Lives in pairs and territorial. Turns starfishes
upside down and feeds on their entrails and tube feet.
Pair bond by the pheromones of the female.
Distribution: Red Sea, East Africa, Indo-West Pacific.

Glass or Peacock-tail Anemone Shrimp
Periclimenes brevicarpalis

Transparent with large white patches. Five orange, dark-edged patches on the tail fan.
Size: 4 cm
Biology: Female about twice as large as the male. Inhabits anemone in pairs or groups, especially on the Adhesive Anemone *Cryptodendron adhaesivum*.
Distribution: Red Sea to Japan and French Polynesia.

Emperor Shrimp
Periclimenes imperator

Red to pale orange with white markings, adapted to the respective host.
Size: 2 cm
Biology: Lives as a commensal on larger nudibranchs, on sea cucumbers (especially *Bohadschia*, *Stichopus*, *Synapta* species) as well as starfish. Feeds on detritus and skin mucus.
Distribution: Red Sea and Indo-Pacific to Japan, Hawaii and French Polynesia.

Ambon Crinoid Shrimp
Laomenes amboiensis

Variable colouration, depending on its feather star host.
Size: 2 cm
Biology: Lives on feather stars, adapts its colouration and is therefore very well camouflaged and usually difficult to discover.
Distribution: Indo-Pacific.

Bubble Coral Shrimp
Vir philippinensis

Transparent body with fine violet-blue lines on legs and pincers.
Size: 1.5 cm
Biology: Exclusively inhabits the Bubble Coral *Plerogyra sinuosa*.
Distribution: Red Sea and Indo-West Pacific to Japan and NE Australia.

Painted Spiny Lobster
Panulirus versicolor

Antennae whitish, legs with a white horizontal stripe. Tail with black and white vertical stripes.
Size: 40 cm
Biology: Usually in crevices during the day, from which the long antennae often project. Gregarious, Often in small groups. Roams the reef at night, feeds on invertebrates and dead fish.
Distribution: Red Sea to Japan and French Polynesia

Stripe-leg Spiny Lobster
Panulirus femoristriga

A large, V-shaped lateral white marking on the head shield. Tail brown with numerous white spots.
Size: 30 cm
Biology: Usually below overhangs during the day, away from the shallow area. Goes in search of food at night (carrion and invertebrates).
Distribution: Indo-Pacific.

Blunt Slipper Lobster
Scyllarides squammosus

Two to three large reddish brown patches on the foremost abdomen segment. Rust to orange-red edge fringe on the broad, leaf-like antennae.
Size: 40 cm
Biology: Inhabits coral and rock reefs, usually from about 8 m depth. Nocturnal, usually sighted on hard ground.
Distribution: Indian Ocean to Japan, Hawaii and New Caledonia.

Red Reef Crab
Carpilius convexus

Smooth carapace. Variable colouration: uniformly orange-red to brown or mottled.
Size: 9 cm
Biology: On reef tops and slopes. Feeds at night on snails and sea urchins, opens shells with its powerful pincers.
Distribution: Red Sea to Japan, Hawaii and French Polynesia.

Anemone Hermit Crab
Dardanus pedunculatus

Green eyes, eyestalk ringed red-white. Large left claw.
Size: 10 cm
Biology: Nocturnal, omnivorous predator. Almost always in symbiosis with the anemone (*Calliactis*), which it takes along when changing to a larger snail housing.
Distribution: Indo-Pacific

Baba's Crinoid Squat Lobster
Allogalathea babai

Colouration adapted to the host feather star. Always with a light, broad middle stripe along the back.
Size: 2 cm
Biology: Exclusively inhabits feather stars. Picks trapped zooplankton from its arms. The species was only described in 2010, earlier often confused with *A. elegans* (with stripes on the arms).
Distribution: Indo-Pacific.

Spotted Porcelain Crab
Neopetrolisthes maculatus

Variable colouration, with large or numerous very small spots.
Size: 3 cm
Biology: Lives on sea anemones, almost always in pairs. Filter feeder by swinging a third appendage equipped with long, fine bristles through the water like a fan.
Distribution: Indo-Pacific to Japan.

Mosaic Boxer Crab
Lybia tesselata

White carapace with orange-brown fields arranged like a mosaic, with fine black border.
Size: carapace to 0.5 cm
Biology: On hard ground from shallow areas to more than 15 m depth. Bears a nettled sea anemone on its claws, which it employs for its defence.
Distribution: East Africa to Guam, Japan and Samoa.

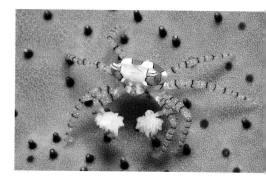

Zebra Urchin Crab
Zebrida adamsii

White with brown stripe. Two pointed "horns" between the eyes.
Size: Carapace 2 cm
Biology: Lives on short spiny sea urchins, among them also fire sea urchins and is therefore very well protected. Has hook-like foot for holding on to the barbs.
Distribution: West Pacific, to Japan and Hawaii.

Spider or Blunt Decorator Crab
Camposcia retusa

Formed like a tarantula. Body and legs completely overgrown with various crusty organic upgrowths, very often sponges.
Size: Carapace 3 cm
Biology: Can also be seen during the day, however predominantly nocturnal.
Distribution: Indo-Pacific.

Peacock Mantis Shrimp
Odontodactylus scyllarus

Usually green (males a darker green than the females), less frequently also red or light brownish. Typically has rounded eyes and club-shaped raptorial claws.
Size: 18 cm
Biology: In many reef zones from shallow coastal waters to outer reef slopes, 1–50 m. Also swims in the open during the day, however rapidly withdraws into its U-shaped burrow when disturbed.
Distribution: East Africa to Guam and Samoa.

Striped or Zebra Mantis Shrimp
Lysiosquillina maculata

Body with dark cross bands. It has the typical oval to peanut-shaped eyes and long thorns on its raptorial claws.
Size: 40 cm
Biology: On sand surfaces in coastal and semi-protected outreefs, 1–20 m. Inhabits burrow it digs itself (to 12 cm diameter, to 5 m length). Goes out at night in search of prey.
Distribution: Indo-Pacific, from East Africa.

Echinoderms
Echinodermata

The feather star, brittle starfish, starfish sea urchins and sea cucumbers belong to this marine phylum. Together they have a five-legged radial symmetric body design which is unique in the animal kingdom. This radial symmetry is immediately recognisable on sea and brittle starfish, but also apparent in the other members. The hydraulic channel system that provides their locomotion is also unique. The names are given by prickly skeleton elements below the skin which project especially high in the case of sea urchins.

Leopard Sea Cucumber
Bohadschia argus

Very variable in colour: e.g. cream-coloured, blueish-yellow, brown-orange, Always with "eye spots".
Size: 60 cm
Biology: On sand and rubble ground near the reef, from 1–40 m. When harassed, thrusts out white cuvieren sticky threads.
Distribution: Seychelles to SW Japan and French Polynesia.

Feathermouth or Lion's Paw Sea Cucumber
Euapta godeffroyi

Very variable in colour, always with "eye spots".
Size: 150 cm
Biology: When disturbed, can powerfully contract to a third of its length. Hidden during the day, in the open at night, usually on sandy bottom.
Distribution: Red Sea, Indo-Pacific, to Hawaii.

Leopard Sea Cucumber
Pearsonothuria graeffei

Numerous dark dots. Black, lobed mouth tentacle.
Size: 50 cm
Biology: On hard ground of rock and coral reefs, 3–30 m. Active day and night. Uses its broad tentacle ends to dab detritus and tiny animals from the bottom surface.
Distribution: Red Sea, Indo-Pacific to French Polynesia.

Blue Sea Star
Linckia laevigata

Small body plate, long arms. Rough surface. Usually blue, also peach-coloured, brown, scarlet or light aquamarine.
Size: 30 cm
Biology: On various hard grounds and seagrass fields, from 1 m depth. Often in light-flooded shallow water during the day.
Distribution: East Africa to West Pacific, also Hawaii.

Granular Sea Star
Chroriaster granulatus

High-backed body with short thick arms. Variable in colour from light cream to orange-brown. Arm tips usually bright or dark.
Size: 25 cm
Biology: On hard ground and coral on reef tops and slopes, less often also on coral debris, 2–40 m. During the day partly hidden in crevices.
Distribution: Red Sea, East Africa to Japan and Fiji.

Cushion Star
Culcita novaeguineae

Hemispherical pillow-shaped, very variable in colour.
Size: 25 cm
Biology: In coral reef on hard ground and rubble, from the shallow water. Feeds on mussels, snails, worms, sea urchins and other starfish, especially also polyps of stony corals such as *Acropora* and *Pocillopora* species.
Distribution: Eastern Indian Ocean and West Pacific.

Crown-of-thorns Starfish
Acanthaster planci

7–23 arms (usually 15 or 16). Poison barbs up to 5 cm long. Colouration variable: cream, light brown, olive to red and blue-violet.
Size: Usually to 30, max. more than 50 cm
Biology: In coral reefs, 0.5 to more than 30 m. Feeds on coral polyps. Normally nocturnal and hidden between corals during the day.
Distribution: Red Sea and East Africa to Japan, Mexico and Polynesia.

Globe Urchin
Mespilia globulus

5 or 10 bands with barbs, always a blue field in between.
Size: 6 cm
Biology: On hard ground and rubble from which it scrapes algae. "Camouflages" itself often with small pebbles.
Distribution: Indonesia to the Philippines, Australia and New Caledonia.

Fire Urchin
Asthenosoma varium

Cluster short barbs with partly blue poison bubbles. Body reddish.
Size: 25 cm
Biology: Usually on sand, mud and rubble grounds, 1–285 m. Usually hidden during the day, usually nocturnal and then in the open. Injuries from the barbs are very painful.
Distribution: Oman to SW Japan, Australia and New Caledonia.

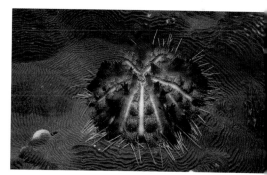

Slate Pencil Urchin
Heterocentrotus mammillatus

Large thick barbs, two or three edged to a blunt point. Luminous red to reddish brown.
Size: 30 cm
Biology: On the reef roof and upper reef slopes, from shallow water. Nocturnal, wedged by the barbs during the day in crevices and holes.
Distribution: Red Sea and East Africa to Polynesia.

Blue-spotted or Radiant Sea Urchin
Astropyga radiata

Groups of dark pink barbs. Barb-free radial zones with rows of luminous blue dots.
Size: 25 cm
Biology: On soft ground, often in groups on open sandy grounds, from 6 m. Barbs can cause painful injuries.
Distribution: East Africa to the Philippines, SW Japan and New Caledonia.

Reptiles and

Sea Mammals

Sea Turtles
Testudines

Sea turtles swim long distances through the oceans. The Hawksbill Turtle is known to migrate more than 11,000 kilometres. Their excellent magnetic sense orientation is very similar to migratory birds. The females even find their way back to their former birth places in order to lay their eggs. Pairing takes place at sea. Only the females crawl on land to lay their eggs and afterwards return to the sea straightaway. In many cases, the egg-laying cycle takes place every two years. The eggs are incubated by the warmth of the sun. Whether males or females hatch from the eggs depends on the clutch temperature. For the Loggerhead Sea Turtle, at more than 30°C it is female, below 28°C it is male – both sexes occur at temperatures in between. The young turtles hatch after about two months.

Hawksbill Turtle
Eretmochelys imbricata

Two pairs of brow shields. Upper beak half juts out ("hook beak"). Dorsal shields overlap, often with serrated edge.
Size: 114 cm, 77 kg
Biology: Common in all reef zones. The most common turtle in the majority of tropical reefs. Omnivorous, however predominantly feeds on invertebrates, especially sponges, soft coral, also sea anemone, jellyfish as well as highly toxic box jellyfish. It is threatened by worldwide persecution: drift nets, hunting, tortoise shell trade.
Distribution: All tropical and subtropical seas.

Green Turtle
Chelonia mydas

A pair of large brow shields.
Size: 150 cm, 150 kg
Biology: Inhabits all reef zones, especially coomon on seagrass fields. Adults predominantly feed on plants such as mangroves and seagrass, juveniles predominantly on soft invertebrates. Lays eggs every 2–3 years, with 100–150 eggs per nest at intervals of 10–15 days.
Distribution: All tropical and subtropical seas.

Green turtle during nest building: the female crawls out onto the beach almost always at night – so high that its nest cannot be flooded even by the highest tide. She digs a ditch about 40-50 cm deep into which she lays the eggs. She subsequently covers them carefully with sand, endeavours to leave behind as few indications of the nest as possible, and crawls back into the sea.

Hatching: The young hatch usually after about 50 to 80 days, burrow out of the sand and cross the beach as quickly as possible in order to reach the sea. This short stretch is already dangerous because of sea birds and crabs, and can match running the gauntlet. Once in the sea, the juveniles are threatened with many dangers so that only about one animal in 100 hatchings reaches sexual maturity.

Sea Snakes
Elapidae

As a former land animal which in the course of its evolution returned to the water, sea snakes have lungs, and must therefore come up to the surface for air. However, sea snakes are excellent divers and achieve immersion times of up to two hours. When diving, though, they usually remain less than thirty minutes under water. Often busily seeking small prey, primarily fish, in the crevices of the reef. Its bite rapidly leads to the paralysis or death of the prey, which subsequently is swallowed whole. Sea snakes possess a poison which is also deadly for humans, but are fortunately surprisingly unaggressive towards people in the water. Coral reef snakes (56 species) spend their whole life in water and are viviparous. *Laticaudina* (eight species) crawl on land to lay eggs and also to rest.

Black and White or Colubrine Sea Krait
Laticauda colubrina

Body with 20 to 65 black bands, snout and upper lip yellowish.
Size: 150 cm (larger in Fiji)
Biology: Species most commonly sighted by divers in its distribution area. Belongs to the *Hydrophiinae* sea snakes. Very strong poison available in large quantities. Feeds exclusively on moray eels, for large examples it can take about 15 minutes before they succumb to the poison. Is generally extremely unagressive to humans – however, do not touch, do not provoke.
Distribution: Sri Lanka and Indies to SW Japan and Tonga.

Dugong
Dugong dugong

Flattened fork tail.
Size: usually to 350 cm
Biology: Inhabits shallow, broad bays with seagrass fields. Reaches at least 400, a maximum of 900 kg weight and can live to about 70 years old. After 13 to 15 months gestation period, a single calf is born in shallow water. Mother and calf maintain very stable, intimate contact. The young are suckled up to 18 months.
Distribution: Red Sea to Vanuatu, but only sporadic presence today.

Seacows
Dugongidae

The family consists of only one species, the *Dugong*, which is related to the manatees (Antillean manatee, three species). Manatees inhabit coastal and inflowing rivers (two species in South-east USA, Caribbean and Amazonia, one species in West Africa). The Dugong however is a marine species and lives in coastal waters of the Indo-Pacific. It is the only herbivorous mammal which lives exclusively in the sea. Seagrass has very low nutritional value, a mature animal therefore requires about 60 kg per day. Pairing can take place during the entire year, depending however on seagrass availability. The newborn measures about 100 to 120 cm in length. A female only gives birth to young every three to seven years. In the past, gatherings of hundreds of animals have been reported, today usually small groups of about six animals is the norm. The Dugong is greatly threatened by humans because of hunting and destruction of seagrass fields and in many places is already extinct.

Dolphins
Delphinidae

Dolphins are highly developed, intelligent sea mammals and live gregariously in groups with a more or less strong bond. Dolphins show multi-faceted behavioural patterns, curiosity, playfulness and a complex social life. Their streamlined bodies make them powerful, skilful swimmers and good divers. They have a repertoire of clicking and whistle tones for communicating with each other. They have a round organ in the brow, the melon, for the production of sonar sounds which they focus and transmit in a directed manner. When the sonar sounds hit on an object, they are reflected and received back as an echo by the animal. This echo ranging gives them images of their environment, particularly in dark or turbid water.

Indo-Pacific Bottlenose Dolphin
Tursiops aduncus

Size: 260 cm

Biology: Predominantly inhabits territorial waters. It is relatively true to its range in regions up to 300 square km and therefore can regularly be observed at various reefs, lagoons and bays. It usually forms schools of 5 to 15 animals (photo below right, a mother with her young), rarely also large associations of up to a thousand. Makes diving excursions of usually only 3 to 4 minutes' duration and feeds on fish (usually less than 30 cm length) and cephalopods. It was long considered a subspecies of the Common Bottlenose Dolphin (*T. truncatus*), but in recent times has obtained the status of an independent species.

Distribution: Red Sea to Japan, Australia and Melanesia.

Index